MAKING DEMOCRACY WORK

Frontispiece. Italy: A Voyage of Inquiry

MAKING DEMOCRACY WORK

CIVIC TRADITIONS IN MODERN ITALY

Robert D. Putnam

with Robert Leonardi and Raffaella Y. Nanetti

PRINCETON UNIVERSITY PRESS   PRINCETON, NEW JERSEY

Library of Congress Cataloging-in-Publication Data

Putnam, Robert D.
Making democracy work : Civic traditions in
modern Italy / Robert D. Putnam with Robert Leonardi
and Rafaella Y. Nanetti
p.   cm.
Includes index.
ISBN 0-691-07889-0
ISBN 0-691-03738-8 (paperback)
1. Regionalism—Italy.   2. Decentralization in
government—Italy.   3. Democracy—Italy.
I. Leonardi, Robert, 1945– .   II. Nanetti, Raffaella Y.
III. Title.
JN5477.R35P866   1992
306.2'0954—dc20   92-18377

Fifth printing, and first Princeton paperback printing, 1994

This book has been composed in Linotron Times Roman

Princeton University Press books are
printed on acid-free paper and meet the guidelines
for permanence and durability of the Committee
on Production Guidelines for Book Longevity
of the Council on Library Resources

Printed in the United States of America

10

Per Alberto ed altri

Contents

List of Figures   ix

List of Tables   xi

Preface   xiii

Chapter 1
Introduction: Studying Institutional Performance   3

A Voyage of Inquiry   3
Charting the Voyage   7
Methods of Inquiry   12
Overview of the Book   15

Chapter 2
Changing the Rules: Two Decades of Institutional
Development   17

Creating Regional Government   18
*The Regional Political Elite: "A New Way of
   Doing Politics"*   26
The Deepening of Regional Autonomy   38
Putting Down Roots: The Region and its Constituents   47
Conclusions   60

Chapter 3
Measuring Institutional Performance   63

Twelve Indicators of Institutional Performance   65
*Coherence and Reliability of the Index of Institutional
   Performance*   73
Institutional Performance and Constituency Evaluations   76
Conclusions   81

Chapter 4
Explaining Institutional Performance   83

Socioeconomic Modernity   83
The Civic Community: Some Theoretical Speculations   86
The Civic Community: Testing the Theory   91
Social and Political Life in the Civic Community   99
Other Explanations for Institutional Success?   116

Chapter 5
Tracing the Roots of the Civic Community   121
  The Civic Legacies of Medieval Italy   121
  Civic Traditions After Unification   137
  Measuring the Durability of Civic Traditions   148
  Economic Development and Civic Traditions   152

Chapter 6
Social Capital and Institutional Success   163
  Dilemmas of Collective Action   163
  Social Capital, Trust, and Rotating Credit Associations   167
  Norms of Reciprocity and Networks of Civic Engagement   171
  *History and Institutional Performance: Two Social
    Equilibria*   177
  Lessons from the Italian Regional Experiment   181

Appendix A
Research Methods   187

Appendix B
Statistical Evidence on Attitude Change among Regional
Councilors   193

Appendix C
Institutional Performance (1978–1985)   198

Appendix D
Regional Abbreviations Used in Scattergrams   200

Appendix E
Local Government Performance (1982–1986) and Regional
Government Performance (1978–1985)   201

Appendix F
Traditions of Civic Involvement (1860–1920)   205

Notes   207

Index   249

Figures

Frontispiece. Italy: A Voyage of Inquiry

1.1. Italian Regional Study, 1970–1989   14

2.1. Left-Right Depolarization, 1970–1989   30

2.2. Sympathy toward Political Opponents among Regional Councilors, 1970–1989   32

2.3. Trends in Councilors' Views of Conflict, 1970–1989   35

2.4. Influence of Party Leaders in Three Arenas, 1970–1989   40

2.5. Declining Support for National Party Discipline, 1970–1989   42

2.6. Regional and Local Contacts of Regional Councilors, 1970–1989   43

2.7. Regional Councilors' Attitudes toward Central Government, 1970–1989   45

2.8. Public Satisfaction with Northern and Southern Regional Governments, 1977–1988   55

2.9. Northern and Southern Satisfaction with National, Regional, and Local Government (1988)   55

2.10. Optimism about Regional Government: Councilors, Community Leaders, and Voters, 1970–1989   56

2.11. Support for Subnational Government: Germany (1952–1978) and Italy (1976–1987)   59

3.1. Institutional Performance, 1970–1976 and 1978–1985   76

3.2. Institutional Performance (1978–1985) and Citizen Satisfaction (1977–1988)   77

3.3. Satisfaction with Regional Government, by Government Performance and Party Support   79

3.4. Institutional Performance (1978–1985) and Community Leaders' Satisfaction (1982)   81

4.1. Institutional Performance in the Italian Regions, 1978–1985   84

4.2. Economic Modernity and Institutional Performance   85

4.3. Referenda Turnout and Preference Voting   95

4.4. The Civic Community in the Italian Regions   97

4.5. The Civic Community and Institutional Performance   98

4.6. "Clientelism" and the Civic Community   100

4.7. "Particularized Contacting" and the Civic Community   100

4.8. Leaders' Support for Political Equality and the
Civic Community   103

4.9. The Civic Community and Republicanism, 1946   104

4.10. The Civic Community and Electoral Reformism, 1991   105

4.11. Leaders' Fear of Compromise and the Civic Community   106

4.12. Clericalism and the Civic Community   108

4.13. Citizens' Feelings of Powerlessness, Education,
and the Civic Community   110

4.14. Satisfaction with Life and the Civic Community   113

5.1. Republican and Autocratic Traditions: Italy, c. 1300   134

5.2 Civic Traditions in the Italian Regions, 1860–1920   150

5.3. Civic Traditions and the Civic Community Today   151

5.4. Traditions of Civic Involvement, 1860–1920, and
Institutional Performance, 1978–1985   151

5.5. Possible Effects among Civic Involvement, Socioeconomic
Development, and Institutional Performance: Italy, 1900s–1980s   155

5.6. Actual Effects among Civic Involvement, Socioeconomic
Development, and Institutional Performance: Italy, 1900s–1980s   157

E.1. Regional and Local Government Performance   202

E.2. Regional and Local Government Satisfaction   203

Tables

2.1. Italian Regional Spending (by Sector), 1989   25

2.2. Components of Left-Right Issues Index   31

2.3. Depolarization of Regional Councilors, 1970–1989   31

2.4. Trends in Elite Political Culture, 1970–1989   33

2.5. Community Leaders' Views of Regional Administration
(1982)   49

2.6. Democratic Attitudes among National and Regional
Administrators (1971–1976)   51

2.7. Attitudes of Italian Voters and Community Leaders
toward Regional Autonomy (1982)   53

2.8. Public Satisfaction with Regional Government, 1977–1988   54

2.9. Evaluations of the Regional Reform, 1960–1987/89   58

3.1. Assessing Legislative Innovation   69

3.2. Index of Institutional Performance, 1978–1985   75

3.3. Community Leaders' Evaluations of Regional
Government, 1982   80

4.1. Local Associations in Italy: Spheres of Activity   92

4.2. Index of Referenda Turnout, 1974–1987   94

4.3. Index of Preference Voting, 1953–1979   95

4.4. The Civic Community Index   96

4.5. Honesty, Trust, Law-Abidingness, and the Civic
Community   112

5.1. Traditions of Civic Involvement, 1860–1920   149

5.2. Civic Traditions and Socioeconomic Development   153

B.1. Declining Ideological Extremism, 1970–1975 and 1975–1980:
Replacement, National Politics, or Conversion?   195

B.2. Increasing Cross-Party Sympathy, 1970–1975 and 1975–1980:
Replacement, National Politics, or Conversion?   196

B.3. Declining Salience of Conflict, 1970–1975 and 1975–1980:
Replacement, National Politics, or Conversion?   197

C.1. Intercorrelations (*r*) among Components of Index of
Institutional Performance, 1978–1985   199

E.1. Components of Index of Local Government Performance
(1982–1986)   202

F.1. Intercorrelations (*r*) among Components of Index of
Traditions of Civic Involvement, 1860–1920   205

Preface

THIS BOOK explores some fundamental questions about civic life by studying the regions of Italy. It is written with two very different audiences in mind—those who share my fascination with the subtleties of Italian life, and those who do not, but who care about democratic theory and practice.

The research itself began in conversations with Peter Lange and Peter Weitz in the spring of 1970, while we were all three in Rome studying various aspects of Italian politics. Unexpectedly, the Italian government agreed to implement a long-neglected constitutional provision for regional governments. Since these new institutions were to be built from scratch in each of Italy's diverse regions, the experiment offered an unusual opportunity to begin a long-term, systematic study of how institutions develop and adapt to their social environment. Had I realized, however, that the subsequent inquiry would last nearly a quarter century, or that it would eventually lead me into the farther reaches of game theory and medieval history, I am not sure that I would have had the good sense to embark.

With encouragement from the late Professor Alberto Spreafico, and with financial support from the University of Michigan, in the fall of 1970 I directed an initial survey of newly-elected councilors in several regions scattered along the peninsula. Later, back in Ann Arbor, I began to analyze these interviews with help from two talented young colleagues, Robert Leonardi and Raffaella Nanetti. By 1975, when a new cohort of councilors had been elected, Bob and Raffi had become faculty members elsewhere, in political science and urban and regional planning, respectively. We agreed to join forces to conduct a second wave of interviews, thus formalizing a close, durable, and productive collaboration.

Over the ensuing decades, the three of us spent hundreds of hours together, planning and carrying out the research described in this book. In the later stages, Bob and Raffi had primary responsibility for the exhaustive field research. All three of us returned repeatedly to the six regions that formed the core of our research. In addition, as our study became better known in Italy, several other regional governments invited us to conduct parallel studies of their operations.

Some of the subsequent publications from the project were authored collaboratively,[1] while others (such as this book and several that Bob and Raffi have produced[2]) were written independently, though drawing on evidence and ideas that had been produced collaboratively. Although neither of the other two scholars bears responsibility for the arguments developed in this book, their names appear on the title page as a mark of recognition and gratitude for more than twenty years of collaboration, creativity, hard work, and friendship.

The conceptual evolution of this project has been at least as complex as the development of the regional governments themselves. Social science is conventionally reported as though hypotheses were straightforwardly deduced from theory, evidence gathered, and verdicts rendered. Though theory and evidence have been important in this project, too, its progress has seemed more like an engrossing detective story, in which various suspects emerge and are cleared, shoe leather is wasted on false leads, new subplots materialize, some hunches pay off, earlier suspicions are reinterpreted in light of later evidence, each puzzle solved poses yet another, and the sleuth is never quite sure where the trail will lead.

At the outset, our research focused on continuity and change, using the 1970 interviews as a benchmark against which to measure institutional development. Later, as evidence mounted of compelling differences in the success and failure of various regional governments, our attention was drawn to comparisons across space, rather than across time. Gradually, it became clear that these differences among the regions had astonishingly deep historical roots. (In retrospect, as in many a tale of detection, the answer seems so obvious that we should have spotted the clues much earlier.) These historical continuities raised theoretical issues of import well beyond the confines of Italy, touching fundamental questions about democracy, economic development, and civic life.

Reflecting this evolution of the research, the organization of this book begins with a tight, close focus on the regional governments themselves and gradually pans outward to encompass the broader meaning of our discoveries. Taken as a whole, the book embodies an argument about democracy and community that I believe is also relevant to the discontents of contemporary America, but spelling out those implications is a task that I have set aside for the future.

Dozens of researchers have collaborated on this project over more than two decades, but special mention should be made of Paolo Bellucci, Sheri Berman, Giovanni Cocchi, Bryan Ford, Nigel Gault, Celinda Lake, Franco Pavoncello, and Claudia Rader.

Among the numerous Italian scholars and officials who provided guidance and assistance, I would like especially to thank Carmelo Azzarà, Sergio Bartole, Gianfranco Bartolini, Sabino Cassese, Franco Cazzola, Gianfranco Ciaurro, Leonardo Cuoco, Alfonso Del Re, Francesco D'Onofrio, Marcello Fedele, Elio Gizzi, Luciano Guerzoni, Andrea Manzella, Nando Tasciotti, Lanfranco Turci, and the hundreds of local, regional, and national leaders who have spoken with us anonymously over the years.

In this project, as in dozens of other studies of contemporary Italy, a unique role was played by Alberto Spreafico. Alberto introduced me to Italy a quarter century ago, the Comitato per le Scienze Sociali that he founded hosted me on numerous occasions, and his gentle, wise encouragement was crucial in the initial stages of this project. The dedication of this volume reflects my profound debt to Alberto and to the scores of other generous, civic-minded Italians who have aided my efforts to understand the marvelous mysteries of their complex society.

Over the years, many colleagues have offered insightful and unsparing critiques of earlier drafts and outlines. In particular, I want to thank Alberto Alesina, James Alt, Robert Axelrod, Edward C. Banfield, Samuel H. Barnes, Michael Barzelay, Terry Nichols Clark, John Comaroff, Jeff Frieden, Paul Ginsborg, Richard Goldthwaite, Raymond Grew, Peter A. Hall, Jens Joachim Hesse, John Hollander, Steven Kelman, Robert O. Keohane, Robert Klitgaard, Jacek Kugler, Daniel Levine, Marc Lindenberg, Glenn C. Loury, Charles Maier, John D. Montgomery, Kenneth A. Shepsle, Judith N. Shklar, Malcolm Sparrow, Federico Varese, Jeff W. Weintraub, Vincent Wright, Richard Zeckhauser, and several anonymous reviewers. Aaron Wildavsky's gentle advice to "squeeze out of the stone of self one more ounce of creative thought" prodded me not to conclude the work prematurely, and Walter Lippincott's steady, thoughtful encouragement sustained my enthusiasm through moments when I was otherwise preoccupied.

Funds for various stages of the research were generously provided by the University of Michigan, the National Science Foundation (under grants GS-33810, SOC76-14690, and SES-7920004), the German Marshall Fund of the United States, Harvard University, the John Simon Guggenheim Memorial Foundation, l'Istituto Carlo Cattaneo, la Presidenza del Consiglio dei Ministri, the European University Institute, the Commission of the European Community, and an assortment of regional governments (Basilicata, Friuli-Venezia Giulia, Emilia-Romagna, Marche, Toscana, and Umbria).

The University of Michigan, Harvard University (especially its Center for International Affairs), the Center for Advanced Study in the Behavioral Sciences, the Woodrow Wilson International Center for Scholars, the Bellagio Conference Center of the Rockefeller Foundation, and the Centre for European Studies at Nuffield College, Oxford University, have each provided gracious hospitality at various stages of my work.

Rosemary, Jonathan, and Lara Putnam have collaborated in this project for as long as any of us can remember, traveling through the regions, helping with data-analysis, commenting on endless drafts, and sharing my enthusiasm for our discoveries. For all this and more I am deeply grateful.

MAKING DEMOCRACY WORK

CHAPTER 1

Introduction:
Studying Institutional Performance

WHY DO some democratic governments succeed and others fail? This question, though ancient, is timely. As our tumultuous century draws to a close, the great ideological debates between liberal democrats and their adversaries are waning. Ironically, the philosophical ascendancy of liberal democracy is accompanied by growing discontent with its practical operations. From Moscow to East St. Louis, from Mexico City to Cairo, despair about public institutions deepens. As American democratic institutions begin their third century, a sense is abroad in the land that our national experiment in self-government is faltering. Half a world away, the former communist nations of Eurasia find themselves having to build democratic systems of governance from scratch. Women and men everywhere seek solutions to their shared problems—cleaner air, more secure jobs, safer cities. Few believe that we can dispense with government, yet fewer still are confident that we know what makes governments work well.

This book aims to contribute to our understanding of the performance of democratic institutions. How do formal institutions influence the practice of politics and government? If we reform institutions, will practice follow? Does the performance of an institution depend on its social, economic, and cultural surround? If we transplant democratic institutions, will they grow in the new setting as they did in the old? Or does the quality of a democracy depend on the quality of its citizens, so that every people gets the government they deserve? Our intent is theoretical. Our method is empirical, drawing lessons from a unique experiment in institutional reform conducted in the regions of Italy over the last two decades. Our explorations will draw us deep into the character of civic life, into the austere logic of collective action, and into medieval history, but the journey begins in the diversity of today's Italy.

A VOYAGE OF INQUIRY

On the *autostrada* that soars along the Apennine spine of Italy, a hurried traveler can cover the 870 kilometers from Seveso in the north to Pietrapertosa in the south in one long day, looping first through the busy industrial suburbs of Milan, crossing rapidly the fertile Po Valley, plunging past the proud Renaissance capitals of Bologna and Florence, circling the grimy, joyless outskirts of Rome and then Naples, and climbing at last into the desolate mountains of Basilicata, isolated in the instep of the Italian boot.[1] To the thoughtful observer, however, this swift passage is less impressive for the distance spanned than for the historical contrasts between the point of departure and the destination.

In 1976 Seveso, a modest, modern town in the mixed industrial-and-farming belt ten miles north of Milan, became world-famous as the site of a major ecological disaster, when a local chemical plant exploded, spewing poisonous dioxin across its homes and workshops and fields and inhabitants. For many months thereafter, motorists on the superhighway that passes Seveso sped by with their windows rolled tightly shut, gawking at the boarded-up houses and the dreadful, white-hooded, goggle-masked figures laboring to decontaminate the town and its lands. Throughout the industrialized world, Seveso came to symbolize the growing risks of ecological disaster. For dazed local officials, the catastrophe at Seveso embodied the looming public policy challenges of the twenty-first century.[2]

From the perspective of public governance, to travel from Seveso to Pietrapertosa in the 1970s was to return centuries into the past. Many Pietrapertosesi lived still in one- and two-room stone hovels, clinging to the mountain face just below the rocky summit to which their Lucanian ancestors repaired many generations ago. Nearby, farmers still threshed grain by hand, aided only by the wind blowing through the tines of their rakes, as Mediterranean peasants had done for millennia. Many local men had sought temporary jobs in northern Europe, and the success of a few was marked by the German license plates on several automobiles parked just below the village. For less fortunate residents, however, transportation was provided by the donkeys that shared their rocky shelters, alongside a few scrawny chickens and cats. Lower on the hill, some returned emigrants had built stucco houses, complete with indoor plumbing, but for much of the village, the absence of running water and other public amenities remained the most pressing problem, as it had been throughout much of Europe three or four centuries earlier.

Like their compatriots in Seveso, the people of Pietrapertosa confronted grave problems of what economists call "public goods" and "public bads." The economic and social and administrative resources of the two towns differed dramatically, as did the details of their problems, but people in both needed help from government. In the early 1970s the primary responsibility for addressing these diverse problems of public health and safety, along with much else of concern to ordinary Italians, was suddenly transferred from the national administration to a newly created set of elected regional governments. For solutions to their shared concerns, the citizens of Seveso and Pietrapertosa were now directed to nearby Milan and Potenza rather than distant Rome. Studying how well those new institutions responded to their constituents and why will lead us to confront basic issues about civic life and collaboration for the common good.

The borders of the new governments largely corresponded to the territories of historic regions of the peninsula, including such celebrated principalities as Tuscany and Lombardy. Since the unification of Italy in 1870, however, its administrative structure had been highly centralized, modeled on Napoleonic France. For as long as anyone could remember, local officials had been closely controlled by prefects reporting directly to Rome. No level of government corresponding to the regions had ever existed. Thus the fact that the public problems of Seveso and Pietrapertosa and thousands of other Italian communities, large and small, would be addressed by the untried regional governments was, for their citizens, an experiment of considerable practical importance.

Beginning in 1970, we have closely followed the evolution of a number of these nascent regional institutions, representing the range of economic, social, cultural, and political environments along the Italian peninsula. Our repeated visits to the various regional capitals soon revealed dramatic differences in institutional performance.

Even finding officials of the Puglia regional government in the capital city of Bari proved a challenge for us, as it is for their constituents. Like visiting researchers, ordinary Pugliesi must first locate the nondescript regional headquarters beyond the railroad yards. In the dingy anteroom loll several indolent functionaries, though they are likely to be present only an hour or two each day and to be unresponsive even then. The persistent visitor might discover that in the offices beyond stand only ghostly rows of empty desks. One mayor, frustrated at his inability to get action from the region's bureaucrats, exploded to us, "They don't answer the mail, they don't answer the telephone, and when I go to Bari to finish paperwork, I have to take along my own typewriter and typist!" A rampant spoils system undermines administrative efficiency: as a clerk once responded to his nominal superior in our presence, "You can't give me orders! I am 'well-protected.'" Meanwhile, the region's leaders engage in Byzantine factional feuds over patronage and posts, and offer rhetorical promises of regional renewal that seem never to reach reality. If Puglia is to become "a new California," as local boosters sometimes say, it will be despite the performance of its new regional government, not because of it. The citizens of Puglia do not disguise their contempt for their regional government; indeed, they do not often think of it as "theirs."

The contrast with the efficiency of the government of Emilia-Romagna in Bologna is stark. Visiting the glass-walled regional headquarters is like entering a modern, high-tech firm. A brisk, courteous receptionist directs visitors to the appropriate office, where, likely as not, the relevant official will call up a computerized data base on regional problems and policies. Bologna's central piazza is famous for its nightly debates among constantly shifting groups of citizens and political activists, and those impassioned discussions about issues of the day are echoed in the chambers of the regional council. A legislative pioneer in many fields, the Emilian government has progressed from words to deeds, its effectiveness measured by dozens of day care centers and industrial parks, repertory theaters and vocational training sites scattered throughout the region. The citizen-debaters in the Bologna piazza are not uncritical of their regional government, but they are vastly more content than their counterparts in Puglia. Why has the new institution succeeded in Emilia-Romagna and not in Puglia?

The central question posed in our voyage of inquiry is this: *What are the conditions for creating strong, responsive, effective representative institutions?* The Italian regional experiment offers an unparalleled opportunity for addressing this question. It presents a rare opportunity to study systematically the birth and development of a new institution.

First, fifteen new regional governments were established simultaneously in 1970, endowed with essentially identical constitutional structures and mandates. In 1976–77, after an intense political struggle described in Chapter 2, all regions were granted authority over a wide range of public issues. In partial contrast with these fifteen "ordinary" regions, another five "special" regions had been created some years earlier, with somewhat greater, constitutionally guaranteed powers. These five regions were in border areas that had been threatened by separatist sentiment at the end of World War II. In some respects, the somewhat greater longevity and broader powers of the special regional governments make them distinctive. For most purposes, however, they may be safely considered alongside the fifteen ordinary regions. Generally speaking, in this book we draw evidence from all twenty regions.

By the beginning of the 1990s, the new governments, barely two decades old, were spending nearly a tenth of Italy's gross domestic product. All regional governments had gained responsibility for such fields as urban affairs, agriculture, housing, hospitals and health services, public works, vocational education, and economic development. Despite continuing complaints from regionalists about constraints imposed by the central authorities, all the new institutions had acquired enough authority to test their mettle. On paper, these twenty institutions are virtually identical and potentially powerful.

Second, however, the social, economic, political, and cultural contexts into which the new institutions were implanted differed dramatically. Socially and economically, some regions, such as Pietrapertosa's Basilicata, ranked with countries of the Third World, whereas others, such as Seveso's Lombardia, were already becoming postindustrial. Cutting across this developmental dimension were differences of political tradition. Neighboring Veneto and Emilia-Romagna, for example, had similar economic profiles in 1970, but Veneto was ardently Catholic, whereas Emilia-Romagna, the buckle of Central Italy's "Red Belt," had been controlled by Communists since 1945. Some regions had inherited patron-client politics more or less intact from the feudal past. Others had been transformed by massive waves of migration and social change that swept across Italy during *il boom* of the 1950s and 1960s.

The Italian regional experiment was tailor-made for a comparative study of the dynamics and ecology of institutional development. Just as a botanist might study plant development by measuring the growth of genetically identical seeds sown in different plots, so a student of government performance might examine the fate of these new organizations, formally identical, in their diverse social and economic and cultural and political settings. Would the new organizations actually develop identically in soils as different as those around Seveso and Pietrapertosa? If not, what elements could account for the differences? The answers to these questions are of importance well beyond the borders of Italy, as scholars and policymakers and ordinary citizens in countries around the world—industrial, postindustrial, and preindustrial—seek to discover how representative institutions can work effectively.

CHARTING THE VOYAGE

Institutions have been an enduring concern of political science since ancient times, but recently theorists have attacked institutional questions with renewed vigor and creativity in the name of "the new institutionalism." The tools of game theory and rational choice modeling have been put to use, casting institutions as "games in extensive form," in which actors' behavior is structured by the rules of the game.[3] Organization theorists have emphasized institutional roles and routines, symbols, and duties.[4] Historical institutionalists have traced continuities in government and politics and emphasized timing and sequences in institutional development.[5]

The new institutionalists differ among themselves on many points, both theoretical and methodological. On two fundamental points, however, they are agreed:

1. *Institutions shape politics.* The rules and standard operating procedures that make up institutions leave their imprint on political outcomes by struc-

turing political behavior. Outcomes are not simply reducible to the billiard-ball interaction of individuals nor to the intersection of broad social forces. Institutions influence outcomes because they shape actors' identities, power, and strategies.

2. *Institutions are shaped by history.* Whatever other factors may affect their form, institutions have inertia and "robustness." They therefore embody historical trajectories and turning points. History matters because it is "path dependent": what comes first (even if it was in some sense "accidental") conditions what comes later. Individuals may "choose" their institutions, but they do not choose them under circumstances of their own making, and their choices in turn influence the rules within which their successors choose.

Our study of the Italian regional experiment is intended to contribute empirical evidence to both these themes. Taking institutions as an independent variable, we explore empirically how institutional change affects the identities, power, and strategies of political actors. Later, taking institutions as a dependent variable, we explore how institutional performance is conditioned by history.

Between these two steps, however, we add a third that has been neglected in recent work on institutions. The practical performance of institutions, we conjecture, is shaped by the social context within which they operate.

Just as the same individual may define and pursue his or her interests differently in different institutional contexts, so the same formal institution may operate differently in different contexts. Though not stressed in recent theories, this point is familiar to most observers of institutions and institutional reform. The Westminster-style constitutions left behind by the British as they retreated from empire had very different fates in different parts of the world. We move beyond this generalization that "context matters" to ask which features of social context most powerfully affect institutional performance.

What do we mean by "institutional performance?" Some theorists see political institutions primarily as "the rules of the game," as procedures that govern collective decision-making, as arenas within which conflicts are expressed and (sometimes) resolved.[6] (Theories of this sort often use the U.S. Congress as a model.) "Success" for this kind of institution means enabling actors to resolve their differences as efficiently as possible, given their divergent preferences. Such a conception of political institutions is pertinent, but it does not exhaust the role of institutions in public life.

Institutions are devices for achieving *purposes*, not just for achieving *agreement*. We want government to *do* things, not just *decide* things—to educate children, pay pensioners, stop crime, create jobs, hold down prices, encourage family values, and so on. We do not agree on which of these things is most urgent, nor how they should be accomplished, nor even whether they are all worthwhile. All but the anarchists among us, however, agree that at least some of the time on at least some issues, *action* is required of government institutions. This fact must inform the way we think about institutional success and failure.

The conception of institutional performance in this study rests on a very simple model of governance: societal demands → political interaction → government → policy choice → implementation. Government institutions receive inputs from their social environment and produce outputs to respond to that environment. Working parents seek affordable day care, or merchants worry about shoplifting, or veterans decry the death of patriotism. Political parties and other groups articulate these concerns, and officials consider what, if anything, to do. Eventually, a policy (which may only be symbolic) is adopted. Unless that policy is "Do nothing," it must then be implemented—creating new nurseries (or encouraging private agencies to do so), putting more cops on the beat, flying flags more often. A high-performance democratic institution must be both responsive and effective: sensitive to the demands of its constituents and effective in using limited resources to address those demands.

Complexities abound in this domain. To be effective, for example, government must often be foresighted enough to anticipate demands that have not yet been articulated. Debates and deadlocks may stall the process at any point. The effects of government action, even when well designed and effectively implemented, may not be what proponents had hoped. Nevertheless, institutional performance is important because in the end the quality of government matters to people's lives: scholarships are awarded, roads paved, children inoculated—or (if government fails) they are not.[7]

Understanding the dynamics of institutional performance has long been of interest to comparative social science. Three broad modes of explaining performance can be discerned in the existing literature. The first school of thought emphasizes *institutional design*. This tradition has its roots in formal legal studies, a mode of political analysis that grew out of the ferment of constitution building in the nineteenth century.[8] John Stuart Mill's "Considerations on Representative Government" reflects the faith this school of thought has in "structural and procedural contrivance."[9] Mill's famous treatise is largely concerned with constitutional engineering, with discovering the institutional forms most favorable to effective representative government.[10] This school of thought continued to dominate the analysis of democratic performance well into the first half of the twentieth century. "It was widely assumed [by such analyses] that viable representative government . . . depended . . . only on the proper arrangement of its formal parts and reasonable good luck in economic life and institutional affairs; and that good structure would serve even in the absence of good luck."[11]

The collapse of the interwar Italian and German democratic experiments and the immobilism of the French Third and Fourth Republics, along with increasing sensitivity to the social and economic bases of politics, led to a more sober view of institutional manipulation. Painstaking design did not ensure good performance. Nevertheless, in the contemporary era attention to the organizational determinants of institutional performance has re-emerged among advocates of the "new institutionalism," as well as among practical reformers. Constitution drafters, management consultants, and development advisers devote much attention to institutional design in their prescriptions for improved performance. Arturo Israel, a specialist in Third World development, observes that it is easier to build a road than to build an organization to maintain that road. In his recent work on institutional development, he draws our attention to managerial and organizational constraints on implementation and recommends improvements in institutional design to increase the prospects for success.[12] Elinor Ostrom is a thoughtful observer of institutions intended to overcome "the tragedy of the commons"—the dilemma of collective action that threatens "common pool resources" such as water supplies, fishing grounds, and the like. From a comparison of many such efforts, failures as well as successes, Ostrom extracts lessons about how to design institutions that work.[13]

Our research speaks only indirectly to these questions of institutional design. In fact, in our study, institutional design was held constant: regional governments with similar organizational structure were all introduced at the same time. What varied in our research design were environmental factors, such as economic context and political tradition. Such factors are harder for would-be reformers to manipulate, at least in the short run, so our research is not likely to suggest shortcuts to institutional success. On the other hand, the fact that institutional design is a constant in the Italian regional experiment means that we can detect more reliably the influence of other factors on institutional success.

While we do not explore directly the effects of institutional *design* on performance, our research does address the consequences of institutional *change*. Our examination of how the regional governments evolved over their first two decades includes a "before-after" comparison that helps us to assess the impact of institutional reform. How the institution and its leaders learned and adapted over time—the "developmental biology," so to speak, of institutional growth—is encompassed by our research. Did the creation of the new regional institutions lead to changes in the practice of politics and governance in Italy? What difference did institutional change make for the way in which leaders and citizens collaborate and contend over public policy? In practice, how do institutional reforms change behavior and by how much? We return to these issues in Chapter 2.

A second school of thought about the performance of democratic institutions emphasizes *socioeconomic factors*. Political sociologists since Aristotle have argued that the prospects for effective democracy depend on social development and economic well-being. Contemporary democratic theorists, too, like Robert A. Dahl and Seymour Martin Lipset, have stressed various aspects of modernization (wealth, education, and so on) in their discussions of the conditions underlying stable and effective democratic government.[14] Nothing is more obvious even to the casual observer than the fact that effective democracy is closely associated with socioeconomic modernity, both across time and across space. Social scientists concerned with explaining institutional development in the Third World have also emphasized socioeconomic factors. Arturo Israel, for example, asserts that "improved institutional performance is part and parcel of the process of modernization. Unless a country becomes 'modern,' it cannot raise its performance to the level now prevailing in the developed world."[15] The sharp differences in levels of socioeconomic development among the Italian regions allow us to assess directly the complex linkage between modernity and institutional performance.

A third school of thought emphasizes *sociocultural factors* in explaining the performance of democratic institutions. This tradition, too, claims a distinguished lineage. In the *Republic* Plato argued that governments vary in accordance with the dispositions of their citizenry. More recently, social scientists have looked to political culture in their explanations of cross-national variations in political systems. The modern classic of this genre, Almond and Verba's study of the *Civic Culture*, seeks to explain differences in democratic governance in the United States, Great Britain, Italy, Mexico, and Germany through an examination of political attitudes and orientations grouped under the rubric of "civic culture."[16] Probably the most illustrious example of the sociocultural tradition of political analysis (and one that is especially germane to our study) remains Alexis de Tocqueville's *Democracy in America*.[17] Tocqueville highlights the connection between the "mores" of a society and its political practices. Civic associations, for example, reinforce the "habits of the heart" that are essential to stable and effective democratic institutions. This and related propositions will play a central role in our analysis.

As we sought to extract lessons of general import from the details of the Italian experiment, we came to appreciate the admonitions of an earlier student of local institutional development. In his classic study of *TVA and the Grass Roots*, Philip Selznick observed that "theoretical inquiry, when it is centered upon a particular historical structure or event, is always hazardous. This is due to the continuous tension between concern for a full grasp and interpretation of the materials under investigation as history, and special concern for the induction of abstract and general relations."[18] While striving not to do violence to the rich particularities of the Italian experience, we must also try to do justice to its broader implications for our understanding of democratic governance.

METHODS OF INQUIRY

Truth, Karl Deutsch observed, lies at the confluence of independent streams of evidence. The prudent social scientist, like the wise investor, must rely on diversification to magnify the strengths, and to offset the weaknesses, of any single instrument. That is the methodological maxim that we have followed in this study. To understand how an institution works—and still more, how different institutions work differently—we must deploy a variety of techniques.

From the anthropologist and the skilled journalist, we borrow the technique of disciplined field observation and case study. "Soaking and poking," as Richard Fenno describes it, requires the researcher to marinate herself in the minutiae of an institution—to experience its customs and practices, its successes and its failings, as those who live it every day do. This immersion sharpens our intuitions and provides innumerable clues about how the institution fits together and how it adapts to its environment. At many points our story draws on illustrations and insights gleaned from two decades of poking around the regions of Italy and soaking up the local ambience.

Social science reminds us, however, of the difference between insight and evidence. Our contrasting impressions of governance in Bari and Bologna, no matter how keen, must be confirmed, and our theoretical speculations disciplined, by careful counting. Quantitative techniques can warn when our impressions, rooted in a single striking case or two, are misleading or unrepresentative. Equally important, statistical analysis, by enabling us to compare many different cases at once, often reveals more subtle, but important patterns, much as a pointillist painting by Seurat can best be appreciated by stepping back from the canvas.

The logic of our inquiry requires the simultaneous comparison of fifteen or twenty regions along multiple dimensions, and such techniques as multiple regression and factor analysis drastically simplify this task. Nevertheless, we have sought to minimize the intrusiveness of complicated statistical procedures into our story, usually relying on such devices as percentages and scattergrams. The results that we present here satisfy the conventional tests of statistical significance, but more important, they also satisfy John Tukey's famed "interocular traumatic test."[19]

As with many a detective tale, solving the mystery of institutional performance requires us to explore the past—or more precisely, the contrasting pasts of the various regions. For some epochs, historians of Italy have provided marvelously rich accounts that are remarkably relevant to our task, and our story draws heavily on their work. In addition, for the last hundred years or so, we unearthed a wide range of statistical material that allowed us to quantify, and thus to test more rigorously, some of our most striking conclusions. We are not historians by trade, and our efforts in this direction are rudimentary, but in any rounded institutional analysis the tools of the historian are a necessary complement to anthropological and behavioral methods.

In short, the diversity of our goals demanded methods that would provide both breadth—the ability to cover different problems and their transformation over a period of time—and deeper analysis of particular issues, regions, and periods of the reform. We wished to gather systematic evidence across both time and space to allow both longitudinal and cross-sectional analysis.

To provide this type of information we conducted a number of separate studies that began with a focus on six regions selected to represent the vast diversities along the Italian peninsula. Our studies were then extended to all twenty regional governments. (Figure 1.1 provides an overview of our research sites.) Our studies, described in more detail in Appendix A, included the following:

- Four waves of personal interviews with regional councilors in the six selected regions between 1970 and 1989. More than seven hundred interviews over nearly two decades provided us with an unparalleled "moving picture" of the regional institutions from the point of view of their chief protagonists.
- Three waves of personal interviews of community leaders in the six selected regions between 1976 and 1989, as well as a nationwide mail survey of community leaders in 1983. Bankers and farm leaders, mayors and journalists, labor leaders and business representatives—these respondents knew their regional government well and could give us the perspective of informed outsiders.
- Six specially commissioned nationwide surveys, as well as several dozen other surveys of voters between 1968 and 1988. These interviews enabled us to chart differences in political outlook and social engagement across the regions and to probe the views of the constituents of the new institutions.

FIGURE 1.1
Italian Regional Study, 1970–1989

- Close examination of a multitude of statistical measures of institutional performance in all twenty regions, as described in Chapter 3.
- A unique experiment in 1983, described in more detail in Chapter 3, that tested government responsiveness to "street-level" citizen inquiries in all twenty regions.
- Case studies of institutional politics and of regional planning in the six selected regions between 1976 and 1989, as well as a detailed analysis of the legislation produced by all twenty regions from 1970 to 1984. These projects provided raw material for our assessment of the day-to-day business of politics and government in the regions and helped us interpret more antiseptic statistical data. (Our regular visits to each of the six selected regions incidentally allowed us to experience firsthand the devastating earthquake that struck southern Italy in 1980 and its aftermath.) In short, we came to know these regions and their protagonists well.

OVERVIEW OF THE BOOK

In the 1970s a tumultuous period of reform broke with Italy's century-long pattern of centralized government and delegated unprecedented power and resources to the new regional governments. In Chapter 2 we ask how the process of reform transpired, and what difference it made for the practice of politics and the quality of government at the grassroots. How was reform accomplished, given the inertia of older institutions? Did the new institution actually affect the character of political leadership and the way politicians ply their trade? Did it reshape the distribution of political power and influence? Did it lead to changes that were perceptible to the constituents of the new governments, and if so, what was their assessment? What evidence is there of the leverage that institutional change is said to exert on political behavior?

A primary concern of this study is to explore the origins of effective government. To lay the basis for that inquiry, Chapter 3 presents a comprehensive, comparative evaluation of policy processes, policy pronouncements, and policy implementation in each of the twenty regions. Whereas Chapter 2 examines change through time, Chapter 3 (and those that follow) make comparisons across space. How stable and efficient are the governments of the various regions? How innovative are their laws? How effectively do they implement policies in such fields as health, housing, agriculture, and industrial development? How promptly and effectively do they satisfy the expectations of their citizens? Which institutions, in short, have succeeded and which have not?

Explaining these differences in institutional performance is the objective of Chapter 4, in some respects the core of our study. Here we explore the connection between economic modernity and institutional performance. Even more important, we examine the link between performance and the character of civic life—what we term "the civic community." As depicted in Tocqueville's classic interpretation of American democracy and other accounts of civic virtue, the civic community is marked by an active, public-spirited citizenry, by egalitarian political relations, by a social fabric of trust and cooperation. Some regions of Italy, we discover, are blessed with vibrant networks and norms of civic engagement, while others are cursed with vertically structured politics, a social life of fragmentation and isolation, and a culture of distrust. These differences in civic life turn out to play a key role in explaining institutional success.

The powerful link between institutional performance and the civic community leads us inevitably to ask why some regions are more civic than others. This is the subject of Chapter 5. Pursuing the answer leads us back to a momentous period nearly a millennium ago, when two contrasting and innovative regimes were established in different parts of Italy—a powerful monarchy in the south and a remarkable set of communal republics in the center and north. From this early medieval epoch through the unification of Italy in the nineteenth century, we trace systematic regional differences in patterns of civic involvement and social solidarity. These traditions have decisive consequences for the quality of life, public and private, in Italy's regions today.

Finally, Chapter 6 explores why norms and networks of civic engagement so powerfully affect the prospects for effective, responsive government and why civic traditions are so stable over long periods. The theoretical approach we develop, drawing on the logic of collective action and the concept of "social capital," is intended not merely to account for the Italian case, but to conjoin historical and rational choice perspectives in a way that can improve our understanding of institutional performance and public life in many other cases. Our conclusions reflect on the power of institutional change to remold political life, and the powerful constraints that history and social context impose on institutional success. This book does not promise to be a practical handbook for democratic reformers, but it does frame the broader challenges we all face.

CHAPTER 2

Changing the Rules:
Two Decades of Institutional Development

THE ITALIAN regional experiment inaugurated in 1970 remains, as Sidney Tarrow observed, "one of the few recent attempts to create new representative institutions in the nation-states of the West."[1] In an era of heightened hopes for democratization in other parts of the globe, lessons from the Italian experience are especially relevant, for at issue is how changes in formal institutions induce changes in political behavior.[2] One conundrum facing would-be reformers in former authoritarian states is whether rewriting the rules of the game will produce the intended effects—or any effects at all—in how it is actually played. The Italian regional experience can help us come to grips with this important issue.

The new institutionalism argues that politics is structured by institutions. James March and Johan Olsen summarize this theory about the effects of institutions:

> The organization of political life makes a difference, and institutions affect the flow of history. . . . Actions taken within and by political institutions change the distribution of political interests, resources, and rules by creating new actors and identities, by providing actors with criteria of success and failure, by constructing rules for appropriate behavior, and by endowing some individuals, rather than others, with authority and other types of resources. Institutions affect the ways in which individuals and groups become activated within and outside established institutions, the level of trust among citizens and leaders, the common aspirations of political community, the shared language, understanding, and norms of the community, and the meaning of concepts like democracy, justice, liberty, and equality.[3]

If institutional reforms can have such profound effects, that is good news for reformers.

Two centuries of constitution-writing around the world warn us, however, that designers of new institutions are often writing on water. Institutional reform does not always alter fundamental patterns of politics. As Deschanel characterized politics and government in the French Fourth Republic: "The republic on top and the empire underneath."[4] "Old wine in new bottles" was a common expectation when the Italian regions were established, for Italians had had much experience with institutional change that changed nothing.[5] That institutional reforms alter behavior is an hypothesis, not an axiom. Theorists of institutions have lacked controlled settings in which to assess empirically the effects of changing the rules.

Against this backdrop, the Italian regional experiment takes on special interest. This chapter begins our assessment of this experiment and its implications for institutionalism by asking how the new institutions were created and how they evolved during their first two decades. Did this institutional reform actually reshape the identities of political actors, redistribute political resources, and inculcate new norms, as institutionalists predict? How were the customary practices of Italian governance shifted by these new institutions? Indeed, *were* they altered in any noticeable way?

CREATING REGIONAL GOVERNMENT

Strong regional and local identities are part of history's bequest to Italy. Regional entities—geographically defined, politically independent, economically differentiated, and generally dominated by a strong city—have been prominent threads in the tapestry of Italian history for more than a millennium.[6] Indeed, when the Italian state was proclaimed in 1860, linguistic variegation was so pronounced that no more than 10 percent of all "Italians" (and perhaps as few as 2.5 percent) spoke the national language.[7] For the Piedmontese monarchists who unified Italy, regional differentiation was the principal obstacle to national development. *Fatta l'Italia, dobbiamo fare gli italiani* was their slogan: "Having made Italy, we must now make Italians." The highly centralized Franco-Napoleonic model was the latest word in administrative science. Strong central authority was, they concluded, the necessary remedy for the weak integration of the new nation state.[8]

A few voices called for the establishment of autonomous regional governments within the new state. Fearing the reactionary tendencies of the Church and the peasants, as well as the backwardness of the South, however, the majority of the makers of modern Italy (like most of their counterparts in the emerging states of today's Third World) insisted that decentralization was incompatible with prosperity and political progress. The centralizers quickly won the debate. Top local officials were appointed by the national government in Rome. Local political deadlock (or even local dissent from national policy) could lead to years of rule by a commissioner appointed by the national government.[9] Strong prefects, modeled on the French system, controlled the personnel and policies of local governments, approving all local ordinances, budgets, and contracts, often in the minutest detail.[10] Most areas of public policy, from agriculture to education to urban planning, were administered by field offices of the Roman bureaucracy.

In practice, the rigor of this extreme administrative centralization was somewhat moderated by characteristic Italian political accommodations. To maintain their fragile political support in the nascent parliament, Italy's leaders developed the practice of *trasformismo*, in which patronage deals were struck with local notables. Support for the national governing coalition was bought by adjustments in national policy to suit local conditions (or at least to suit the locally powerful). The prefects, though responsible for controlling local government, were also responsible for conciliating traditional local elites, especially in the South. Vertical networks of patron-client ties became a means of allocating public works and softening administrative centralization. *Trasformismo* allowed local elites and national deputies to bargain for local interests against national directives in return for electoral and parliamentary support.[11] Political channels to the center were more important than administrative channels, but in either case the link to the center remained crucial.[12]

This negotiated, differentiated system of central controls survived *de facto* throughout the Fascist interlude. Elections, parties, and political liberties were abolished, but the traditional organs of executive power and much of the older ruling class remained in power.[13] Despite the highly centralized formal institutions, the reality of Italian governance embodied a certain implicit responsiveness to local elites. Nevertheless, for local policymakers under the monarchy, under Fascism, and for more than two decades under the post-Fascist Republic, all roads led to Rome.

Only after World War II, with the advent of democratic politics and growing grassroots revulsion against extreme centralization, did regionalist sentiment begin to re-emerge. Newly powerful political parties, both the Christian Democrats on the center-right and the Socialists and Communists on the left, had historically opposed the national government and thus generally had argued for greater decentralization. Under their aegis, the new Constitution of 1948 provided for directly elected regional governments.[14]

This constitutional mandate was carried out almost immediately in five "special" regions, located along the national borders and on the islands of Sicily and Sardinia, areas threatened by separatism and ethnic problems.[15] Creation of the remaining, "ordinary" regions, containing 85 percent of Italy's population, required enabling legislation, however, and was delayed by intense political resistance. The central administration was naturally reluctant to divest itself of any significant authority. More important, the Christian Democrats, now dominant at the national level, feared with good reason that several of the regions in the Red Belt of north-central Italy would be controlled by the Communists. For more than twenty years, the constitutional provision for regional governments remained a dead letter, and central control remained the rule.

By the middle of the 1960s, however, much had begun to change. In the background was the astounding pace of social and economic transformation in postwar Italy. During the two decades from 1950 to 1970, the economy grew faster than ever before in Italian history and faster than virtually every other Western economy. Millions of Italians migrated from the impoverished South to the industrial North.[16] Agriculture's share of the workforce plummeted from 42 percent to 17 percent in half the time that similar changes had taken elsewhere in Western economic history. Diets improved; illiteracy and infant mortality were cut by two thirds; bicycles were replaced by Vespas, and then Vespas by Fiats. Millions of Italians changed jobs, homes, and life styles. Italy, and most of her regions and citizens, experienced one of the most concentrated periods of social change ever recorded.

Politics and government lagged far behind these social and economic changes. Nevertheless, the increasingly frustrating sclerosis of Italian central administration, an emergent interest in regional planning, and a leftward drift in national politics combined to raise once again the issue of regional governments. In February 1968, after a record-breaking filibuster by hostile conservatives, parliament passed a law providing electoral machinery for the ordinary regions. Two years later a bill ordering regional finances was approved, allowing the first regional councils (numbering thirty to eighty members, depending on the region's population) to be elected in June 1970. In the ensuing months each council, following the conventions of the Italian party-dominated parliamentary system, elected a regional president and cabinet (*giunta*) and wrote a regional "statute," spelling out organization, procedures, and areas of regional jurisdiction, subject to the provisions of the Constitution and national enabling legislation.

A wide variety of objectives had been enunciated by proponents of the new institutions. Populists claimed that regional government would raise levels of *democracy*, by fostering citizen participation and responsiveness to local needs. Moderates argued that decentralization would increase *administrative efficiency*. Southerners believed that regional government could speed *social and economic development*, reducing regional inequalities. *Regional autonomy* appealed to whichever group happened to be the "outs" in national politics—Communists at midcentury, like Catholics several decades earlier. Progressive technocrats argued that the regions were necessary for rational *socioeconomic planning* and could lead to a *"new way of doing politics,"* more pragmatic than the traditional, ideological Italian political style.

Proponents of regionalism believed in the power of institutional change to reshape politics. They interpreted the destiny of the new governments in almost messianic terms, believing that "the creation of politically autonomous regional governments would be responsible for a radical social and political renewal of the country."[17] Our first wave of interviews with the newly elected councilors in 1970 found them full of hope and enthusiasm. Optimistic about the reform's future, they saw the regions as posing a potent challenge to the central authorities. These were years of idealism and euphoria among Italian regionalists.

But the struggle to assure adequate funding and authority for the new regions was only beginning. Two more years were required for the central government to issue decrees transferring powers, funds, and personnel to the regions, so that the new governments effectively did not open for business until April 1, 1972. Worse yet, at the regional level, the 1972 decrees were widely condemned as wholly inadequate by representatives of almost all parties and by the attentive public, as well as by regional officials themselves. During these early years, an alliance of conservative national politicians, an entrenched national bureaucracy, and a tradition-minded judiciary combined to impose numerous legal, administrative, and fiscal restraints on the regions. The central authorities retained general powers of "direction and coordination" over regional affairs, and they did not hesitate to use those powers. For example, roughly one-quarter of all the laws passed by the regions during the first legislature were vetoed by the central administration. Moreover, the central government kept a tight grip on the purse strings of the new governments. Spending projections published in 1972 foresaw virtually stationary allocations to the regions over the next three years, while expenditures by the central bureaucracy were to grow by 20 percent. Euphoria turned to dismay and anger, as the regionalists realized that real devolution would require a political struggle with the center.

Led by the independent-minded regional governments of Lombardia (controlled by progressive Christian Democrats) and Emilia-Romagna (controlled by the Communists) and encouraged by a leftward tide in national politics in 1974–75, the regionalist forces renewed their attack. A sympathetic press helped rally grassroots support from regional interest groups and public opinion. Regional governments of various stripes— North and South, red and white—joined forces in the so-called "regionalist front." This coalition was strengthened by support from new national organs that had been established as part of the original reform—the Ministry for the Regions and the Interparliamentary Committee for the Regions. Institutional change was creating its own momentum.

In July 1975, just after a powerful swing to the left in the second round of regional elections, the regionalists succeeded in pushing through parliament Law 382, authorizing the decentralization of important new functions to the regions. To shift the arena for decision making and forestall further obstruction by the central bureaucracy, Law 382 required the government to obtain parliamentary approval of the implementing decrees. Preparation of those decrees occupied two more years of intense and often acrimonious negotiation among the national government, the regional authorities, and the parliamentary committee for the regions, as well as all the major political parties. Our 1976 wave of interviews found our respondents much less confident about the ability of the regions to assert their autonomy. They reported more conflict between center and periphery, and more central control, than they had foreseen six years earlier. Their previous optimism about the new institution's capacity to address urgent social and economic problems was now more restrained, and they were quick to point the finger of blame at foot dragging in Rome. Naturally, demands for autonomy stood much higher on their agendas now.

As is true of intergovernmental relations everywhere, this center-periphery game was played simultaneously in two distinct, but related forms, which we term "one-on-one" and "all-on-one." In the one-on-one version, the individual region tried to escape or mitigate central controls over specific decisions. In the all-on-one version, the regional governments as a group struggled to shift the rules of the one-on-one games, in order to increase their bargaining resources. In these early years, the one-on-one battles were mostly lopsided victories for the central authorities. All sides agreed that relations between center and periphery during these years were formalistic, antagonistic, and unproductive.

But while the one-on-one battles favored the center, the all-on-one battle reached a climax more favorable for the regions. In a lengthy series of summit meetings among representatives of the major parties in June and July of 1977, agreement was reached on a packet of regulations (the so-called 616 decrees) that dismantled and transferred to the regions 20,000 offices from the national bureaucracy, including substantial portions of several ministries, such as the Ministry of Agriculture, as well as hundreds of semipublic social agencies. Comprehensive legislative authority in several important fields, including social services and territorial planning, was delegated to the regions. Fiscal provisions of the 616 decrees gave the regions responsibility for approximately one-quarter of the entire national budget, with some estimates running as high as one-third, including independent reforms that transferred to the regions virtually full responsibility for the national hospital and health care systems. By 1989, this sector alone accounted for more than half of total regional spending (and like health policy everywhere, well more than half the administrative headaches).

This regionalist victory came partly for national political reasons. The Christian Democratic party (DC) was under siege from the Communists (PCI), whose star was rising rapidly in the mid-1970s. Supported by the Socialists and by left-wing Christian Democrats, the PCI pressed hard for further decentralization to the regions. The 616 decrees represented a concession by the DC Prime Minister Giulio Andreotti to maintain Communist support for his government. Equally important, however, the existence of directly elected regional governments had created strong pressures and political incentives for more effective decentralization. The winning regionalist front drew on forces that had been unleashed by the initial reform and, in some cases, had actually been created by that reform.

Devolution is inevitably a bargaining process, not simply a juridical act. The legal and constitutional framework, the administrative framework (controls, delegated powers, personnel patterns, and so on), and finances are both key resources in today's game and outcomes of earlier games. As seen by regional leaders, the central authorities' main bargaining chips were control of funds and control over the delegation of formal authority—the pocketbook and the rulebook. Leaders of the richer, more ambitious regions of the North were more concerned about the rulebook, while the South was more conscious of the pocketbook.

In the face of central recalcitrance fortified by central control over laws, rules, and money, the regions turned to less formal political resources. They relied heavily on interregional solidarity and on grass-roots support from regional and local interest groups, the press, and public opinion. Southerners depended more on "vertical" strategies, such as private petitions to sympathetic national patrons, while northerners were readier to resort to "horizontal" collective action by a broad, regionalist front. (This distinction between vertical politics in the South and horizontal politics in the North will recur repeatedly in various guises throughout this book.) The climactic confrontation with the central authorities was led primarily by the northerners. As we shall see later in this chapter, by the mid-1970s voters and community leaders, in both North and South, had become strong supporters of the principle of regional reform, even when they were critical of the actual operations of their own regional government. The political momentum for devolution had become self-sustaining.

The 616 decrees reflected the regions' victory in the crucial struggle to establish their formal authority. The less dramatic, but more demanding, struggle to deploy the new powers and spend the new money still lay ahead. The regions' all-on-one victory was sufficiently sweeping that they could no longer so plausibly blame the central authorities for their own shortcomings. With the benefit of hindsight, one regional leader told us in 1981, "They threw us into the water, hoping that we could swim."

A senior figure in the Roman bureaucracy used a more cynical, but perhaps more accurate image: "With the 1977 decrees we finally gave the regions enough rope to hang themselves."

The changing of the guard at the top of several leading regions during the second legislature (1975–1980) symbolized the changing challenges facing the regions. Charismatic crusaders, such as Piero Bassetti, DC President of Lombardia, Guido Fanti, PCI President of Emilia-Romagna, and Lelio Lagorio, Socialist (PSI) President of Toscana, moved up and out of regional politics and were replaced by more prosaic managerial types.

The new division of authority between the center and the regions was still far from federal. Most regional funds came from the center, and the central authorities retained a veto over regional legislation. But the regions were more powerful than local government had ever been in unified Italy. The legislative authority of the regions now encompassed such areas as health, housing, urban planning, agriculture, public works, and some aspects of education. In addition, the regional statutes successfully claimed jurisdiction over territorial, economic, and structural planning. The far-flung activities of the *Cassa per il Mezzogiorno* [Fund for the South], responsible for massive public investments in the South, were subjected to increased control by representatives of the regional governments.

> Henceforth the regions, or the municipalities under regional supervision, could found and staff their own specialist agencies for welfare, run their own subsidy schemes for farmers and artisans, and organize their own co-operatives and nursery schools. They could draw up regional development and land use plans; they could take over the Chambers of Commerce. . . . Perhaps most startling of all was the handing over of the vital task of 'safeguarding public morals'—i.e. the power to issue licenses to restaurant-owners, shopkeepers, taxi-drivers, gun-owners and the like. These were real powers of patronage and policing. Here, at last, was a revolution in government.[18]

Responsibility for many aspects of government that touch the lives of ordinary Italians—many of the essential functions that successive national governments had failed to perform—passed into the hands of the regions.

A practical measure of the importance of the regional governments was the resources they now controlled. Tens of thousands of administrative posts were created to serve the new governments and, during the waves of decentralization in the early 1970s, thousands of employees were transferred from the central bureaucracy to the regions. By April 1981, the fifteen ordinary regions accounted for 46,274 administrative personnel, a

TABLE 2.1
Italian Regional Spending (by Sector), 1989

	Current Account[a]	Capital Account[a]	Total[a]	Total[b]	%
Health	48779.2	2269.7	51048.9	37,208	56.3%
Agriculture	2004.3	4895.7	6900.0	5,029	7.6%
Transportation	4561.7	1646.9	6208.6	4,525	6.8%
General administration	4874.6	1059.0	5933.6	4,325	6.5%
Housing/public works	121.7	5149.4	5271.1	3,842	5.8%
Education	2232.4	385.4	2617.8	1,908	2.9%
Environment	340.6	1863.7	2204.3	1,607	2.4%
Social assistance	1364.4	539.0	1903.4	1,387	2.1%
Industry/artisanry	282.6	1513.9	1796.5	1,309	2.0%
Commerce/tourism	447.5	896.4	1343.9	980	1.5%
Culture	429.4	386.0	815.4	594	0.9%
Debt service	0.0	622.7	622.7	454	0.7%
Other	1711.2	2262.9	3974.1	2,897	4.4%
Total spending	67149.6	23490.7	90640.3	66,064	100.0%

[a] Total in billions of lire.
[b] Total in millions of U.S. dollars.

figure that had grown by 76 percent in the preceding five years. (The five special regions employed another 29,383 persons.)[19]

Total funds available to the regions grew exponentially during the 1970s and 1980s, rising from roughly $1 billion in 1973 to roughly $9 billion in 1976, roughly $22 billion in 1979, and more than $65 billion in 1989, the lion's share of this coming from the central government in the form of general-purpose and special-purpose transfers.[20] (The profile of regional spending in 1989 is summarized in Table 2.1.) By the beginning of the 1990s, nearly one-tenth of Italy's gross domestic product was being spent by the regional governments, only slightly below the figure for American states. For organizations that existed only on paper barely fifteen years earlier, the regions had come to control extremely large sums of money. Indeed, during most of the 1970s and 1980s, unspent appropriations carried over from one fiscal year to the next ballooned nearly everywhere, as the resources flowing to the regions exceeded their unfledged administrative capacity.

Apart from establishing the organization and procedures of the new institution, the major focus of regional legislation during the early years was distributing funds—loans for agricultural cooperatives, scholarships for needy students, aid for the handicapped, subsidies for interurban buses, subventions for La Scala, and so on. Seeking public support, but lacking the necessary administrative infrastructure and often even the legal authority for carrying out substantial social reforms, most regions occupied themselves with distributive politics—often in the highly disaggregated form that Italians call *leggine* [little laws] and *interventi a pioggia* [projects "showered" indiscriminately over the region].

On the other hand, some regions did introduce substantive reforms in such areas as urban planning, environmental protection, and Italy's chaotic health and social services. The basic organizational structure for the subsequent national reform of health and social assistance—the "local unit for health and social services"—was pioneered by several of the regions. Most experts agreed that urban planning improved significantly once responsibility for that function was shifted from the center to the regions. In certain "new" areas of public policy, such as energy and the environment, a number of regions moved into the void left by the ponderous Roman ministries, which had been slow to adapt to changing public demands and social needs. Whether the regions' legislative reach exceeded their administrative grasp is an important issue to which we shall return in the following chapters. But for better or for worse, much of Italian domestic policy was now regionalized. Regional government had become, in Max Weber's evocative phrase, "a strong and slow boring of hard boards."[21]

THE REGIONAL POLITICAL ELITE:
"A NEW WAY OF DOING POLITICS"

The rules of the game of government in Italy were altered in the two decades after 1970. What effect, we must now ask, did these institutional changes have on the way politics was actually played and Italians were actually governed?

Montesquieu observed that, at the birth of new polities, leaders mold institutions, whereas afterwards institutions mold leaders. Interaction between institutional change and the political elite is an important part of the story of the Italian regional experiment.

During the debate before the regions were established, some critics had prophesied that the councils would be packed by the parties with "falling stars," that is, superannuated party hacks. A few utopian regionalists, on the other hand, had predicted the emergence from the regional grass-roots of a new group of novice citizen-politicians. In the event, neither expectation was justified. From the very beginning, the new councils have been composed of well-trained, upwardly mobile, ambitious, and highly professional politicians.[22]

About 45 years old at the time of his election, the average councilor has had nearly a quarter century of prior involvement in party affairs. Councilors are on average a few years younger and less experienced than members of the national parliament, although in other respects the councilors' profile is closer to that of a national deputy than to that of a city councilor. In fact, at least 20 percent of all regional councilors between 1970 and 1985 (and more than a third of all those who had held a regional leadership post) left for seats in the national parliament.[23] On the Italian political ladder, the job of regional councilor has become an important step, marking broadly the passage from the domain of the part-time amateur to the domain of the professional politician.

The new regional political elite is mostly comprised of self-made men. (Fewer than 5 percent of the regional councilors are women; whatever its accessibility along other important dimensions, the regional council, like Italian politics more generally, remains a male-dominated world.) The councilors' social origins are more modest than those of national deputies, but much higher than the levels found among city councilors. With one exception, the regional legislators have firm roots in the towns and villages of their respective regions.[24] Roughly 35–40 percent of the regional councilors are sons of workers, artisans, or farmers, but only 15–20 percent of the councilors themselves have ever engaged in these professions. More than half of the fathers of the councilors did not go beyond elementary school, and only about 10–15 percent of the fathers attended university. Among the councilors themselves, however, the overwhelming majority (77 percent in 1989) attended university, a figure that is close to the average for the national parliament and roughly double the average for Italian city councilors.

The regional councilors are seasoned politicians with long experience in local government and party affairs. Over three-quarters have held prior elective office, and more than four-fifths have held a major leadership post in their political party. The city council remains an important springboard toward the regional council, for two-thirds of all regional councilors have served previously in city government. Over the first two decades of the regional government, the region itself gradually replaced the province (the administrative unit between the region and the local government) as a crucial step in the Italian political hierarchy. Between 1970 and 1989 the number of former provincial office holders among regional councilors declined from 45 percent to 20 percent, and the number of past or present provincial party leaders fell from 82 percent to 65 percent. By contrast, the number of councilors who have held (or now hold) a major post in their regional party organization rose from 26 percent in 1970 to 59 percent in 1989. This trend in career paths reflects the steady (though still incomplete) "regionalization" of the Italian party organizations, and offers initial evidence for the emergence of a distinctive regional political *cursus honorem.*

The regional councilor has gradually come to see his role as a full-time job, one indicator of increased institutionalization.[25] The number of councilors who continue to pursue some other occupation in addition to their post in regional government fell from 69 percent in 1970 to 45 percent in 1989. The regional council has become a recognized arena for professional politicians.[26] The first test for any new political institution is that it must engage the aspirations and harness the ambitions of serious politicos. The Italian regional governments have passed this important hurdle.

Even more important, the regional government has transformed elite political culture. The most striking metamorphosis in regional politics to appear in our repeated talks with both councilors and community leaders between 1970 and 1989 is a remarkable ideological depolarization, coupled with a strong trend toward a more pragmatic approach to public affairs.

The ideological depolarization is attributable primarily to a rightward convergence of views on a whole series of controversial issues, sparked by a powerful trend toward moderation among Communist and other leftist politicians. The proportion of leftists (PCI, PSI, and other minor left-wing groups) who agreed, for example, that "capitalism represents a threat to Italy" fell sharply and steadily from 97 percent in 1970 to 76 percent in 1976, 54 percent in 1981–82, and finally 28 percent in 1989.[27] On this and a wide range of similar questions, on the other hand, Christian Democrats and politicians from other center-right parties displayed a much more modest and uneven conservative trend. The proportion of centrists and rightists who concur, for instance, that "unions have too much power in Italy" fluctuated from 67 percent in 1970 to 74 percent in 1976, 86 percent in 1981–82, and back to 65 percent in 1989. As a result, the gap between the parties of the left and right narrowed substantially between 1970 and 1989.

The net effect of these changes is summarized in Figure 2.1, which pictures the distribution of our politicians on a composite *Left-Right Issues Index*, based on questions about capitalism, union power, the distribution of income, divorce, and public sector strikes. (The components of the *Left-Right Issues Index* are listed in Table 2.2.) In 1970 the views of these politicians were distributed in a classic polarized bimodal fashion, skewed to the far left. Six years later the distribution remained bimodal, but the distance between the modes had narrowed. By 1981–82 the center of gravity had moved further to the right, so that the distribution, though no longer so polarized, was still quite wide. By 1989, the pendulum had swung back toward the center, so that the distribution was archetypically "normal," with the mode at the center of the distribution, and the left-right spread much narrower than two decades earlier.[28]

Table 2.3 presents the same evidence in a slightly different format, showing a sharp decline in the proportion of councilors who espoused extreme positions on either the far left or the far right of the *Left-Right Issues Index*; the share of extremists in this sense plummeted from fully 42 percent in 1970 to barely 14 percent in 1989. The first two decades of the new institution witnessed a steady, powerful centripetal tendency in regional politics.

As ideological distances narrowed, tolerance across party lines blossomed. In each survey we asked each politician to indicate his sympathy or antipathy toward the various political parties by rating them on a "feeling thermometer" from 0 (complete antipathy) to 100 (complete sympathy). Figure 2.2 charts the changing sympathy scores assigned to each party by opposing politicians. The results show a steady trend toward greater mutual acceptance among virtually all parties. The average sympathy expressed for the Italian Communist party by non-Communists rose from 26 in 1970 to 44 in 1989, for example, while the average sympathy toward Christian Democrats among councilors of all other parties rose from 28 in 1970 to 39 in 1989. Only the neo-Fascist Italian Social Movement (and to a lesser extent, the far left Proletarian Democracy) remained ostracized by the rest of the political elite, and even this repulsion was less wholehearted by the end of the 1980s than earlier in the 1970s.

Virtually all of these scores remain in the lower half of the sympathy-antipathy scale, for politicians in a competitive system could hardly be expected to express deep affection for their opponents. Sympathy toward opposing parties (even toward the relatively well-received Italian Socialist Party) seems bounded by a ceiling of 50–50 neutrality. Nevertheless, during the first two decades of the regional experiment the high-voltage tensions that had traditionally characterized Italian party politics gradually dissipated, to be replaced by budding mutual respect.

The mellowing of partisanship within the regional political elite did not merely mirror broader changes in Italian society. Our parallel surveys of the mass public show that during the late 1970s, while interparty relations within the regional political elite were warming, partisan hostility was actually on the increase among ordinary Italian voters. In the 1980s partisanship at the mass level began to recede. That timing is consistent with an interpretation that depolarization in Italian politics has been "elite-led," although further research would be necessary to confirm that hypothesis in detail. Be that as it may, at the founding of the regional governments, newly elected councilors from different parties were more hostile to one another than were their respective constituents. Two

FIGURE 2.1
Left-Right Depolarization, 1970–1989

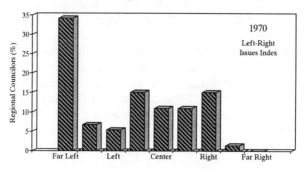

1970

Left-Right
Issues Index

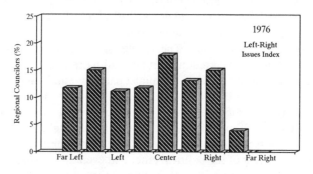

1976

Left-Right
Issues Index

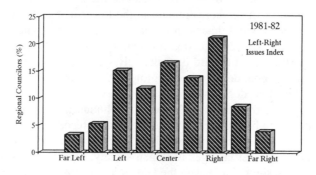

1981-82

Left-Right
Issues Index

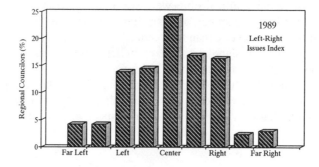

1989

Left-Right
Issues Index

TABLE 2.2
Components of Left-Right Issues Index

1. In the distribution of income the workers are really in an unfavorable position. (agree)
2. The unions have too much power in Italy. (disagree)
3. The institution of divorce in Italy is a sign of progress. (agree)
4. In the public services (for example, gas, transport) the right to strike should be limited. (disagree)
5. Capitalism represents a threat to Italy. (agree)

Note: Respondents "agreed completely," "more or less agreed," "more or less disagreed," or "disagreed completely" with each item. The *Index* is additive across all five items. Scoring is reversed for items 2 and 4 to ensure left-right alignment.

TABLE 2.3
Depolarization of Regional Councilors,
1970–1989

	Percentage			
	1970	*1976*	*1981–82*	*1989*
Extremist	42	31	21	14
Moderate	58	69	79	86
	100	100	100	100
(Number)	(72)	(154)	(151)	(166)

Note: Extremism and moderation are measured by scores on the *Left-Right Issues Index*. Scores in the four "outer" categories of Figure 2.1 (two at the far left and two at the far right) are coded "extremist," while scores in the five middle categories are coded "moderate." The *Index* and cutting points are constant across all four waves of interviews.

FIGURE 2.2

Sympathy toward Political Opponents among Regional Councilors,
1970–1989

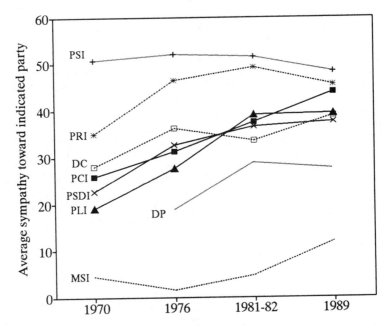

PSI: Italian Socialist Party

PRI: Italian Republican Party

DC: Christian Democracy

PCI: Italian Communist Party

PSDI: Italian Social Democratic Party

PLI: Italian Liberal Party

DP: Proletarian Democracy

MSI: Italian Social Movement

decades later, this pattern had been completely reversed, so that interparty relations were significantly more open and tolerant among regional politicians than among partisan voters.[29]

One important consequence of these trends for regional policymaking is that the process of reaching accommodation on practical issues is no longer so inhibited by partisan hostility. This conclusion is fortified by evidence that the ideological style of politics has steadily faded over these

TABLE 2.4
Trends in Elite Political Culture, 1970–1989

Statement with which Councilors Agreed	Percentage Agreeing			
	1970	1976	1981–82	1989
In contemporary social and economic affairs it is essential that technical considerations should have more weight than political ones.	28	43	64	63
To compromise with one's political opponents is dangerous because it usually leads to the betrayal of one's own side.	50	35	34	29
Generally in political controversies one should avoid extreme positions because the proper solution usually lies in the middle.	57	72	70	70
In the final analysis loyalty to one's fellow citizens is more important than loyalty to one's party.	68	72	84	94
(Approximate Number)	(77)	(158)	(154)	(171)

two decades. Regional politicians no longer see their world in stark blacks and whites, but in more nuanced (and more negotiable) shades of gray.

Table 2.4 summarizes how the political culture of the regional councilors was recast between 1970 and 1989. The proportion of councilors who agreed that "in contemporary social and economic affairs, it is essential that technical considerations should have more weight than political ones" surged up from 28 percent in 1970 to 63 percent in 1989. The proportion suspecting that "to compromise with one's political opponents is dangerous because it usually leads to the betrayal of one's own side" plummeted from 50 percent in 1970 to 29 percent in 1989. Those who counseled moderation, concurring that "generally in political controversies one should avoid extreme positions because the proper solution usually lies in the middle" rose from 57 percent in 1970 to 70 percent in 1989. The proportion endorsing the view that "in the final analysis loyalty to one's fellow citizens is more important than loyalty to one's party" soared from 68 percent in 1970 to 94 percent in 1989. The idea of putting civic loyalty ahead of party loyalty was transformed over these years from a debatable proposition into a platitude. Closer examination of the year-by-year changes in Table 2.4 suggests that most of this metamorphosis in elite political culture had been accomplished by the beginning of the 1980s.

After little more than a decade of the chastening and mellowing effects of involvement in regional government, ideological intransigence was being supplanted by an appreciation of the virtues of compromise and technical expertise. Asked to rate their own region on a five-point scale from "ideological" to "pragmatic," the proportion of councilors who described their region as distinctively ideological fell from 26 percent in 1970 to 21 percent in 1976, 14 percent in 1981–82, and a mere 10 percent in 1989. Pragmatism was no longer an epithet, but a way of doing business.

Comparison of the open-ended interviews with councilors in 1970, 1976, and 1981–82 reveals some interesting changes in the way these policymakers analyze specific regional issues, such as social services or economic development.[30] By comparison with our opening round of conversations, councilors in the later periods framed their analyses less in terms of ultimate goals and more in terms of practical means. Councilors came to interpret their role less as being "responsive to" and more as being "responsible for," less as eloquent tribunes for popular causes and more as competent trustees of the public interest. After a decade of regional government, regional leaders had become less theoretical and utopian and less concerned with defending the interests of particular regional groups at the expense of others. Practical questions of administration, legislation, and financing became more salient. Councilors now spoke more of efficient service delivery and of investment in roads and vocational education, and less of "capitalism" or "socialism," "liberty" or "exploitation."

These trends were doubtless related to the leaders' sense of institutional priorities. In talking about the most important issues facing the regional government and about their hopes for the future, councilors in the 1980s gave less attention to justice, equality, and social reform than they had in 1970. They now focused more on administrative, political, and procedural reforms. Legislative autonomy and administrative efficiency (or, more often, administrative inefficiency) bulked much larger in their discussions of regional government, whereas concern for the "radical social renewal" of the messianic early years had faded.

When they entered the council chambers for the first time, the new legislators had brought with them a conception of politics and social relations as essentially zero-sum, revolving about conflicts that were ultimately irreconcilable. This outlook, rooted in the social and ideological struggles of the Italian past, predisposed the councilors to stridency and hobbled practical collaboration. These perspectives on social and political conflict were singularly transformed during the first decade of the regional experiment. Figure 2.3 shows that during this period the councilors' emphasis on irreconcilable conflict ebbed, while their emphasis on consensus steadily heightened.

FIGURE 2.3
Trends in Councilors' Views of Conflict, 1970–1989

Councilors' Views of Social Conflict and Shared Interests, 1979–1981/82

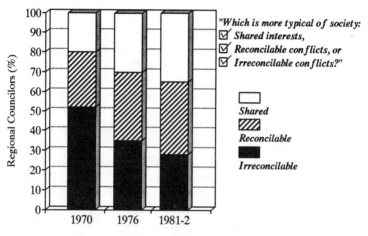

Councilors' Views of Own Region 1970–1989

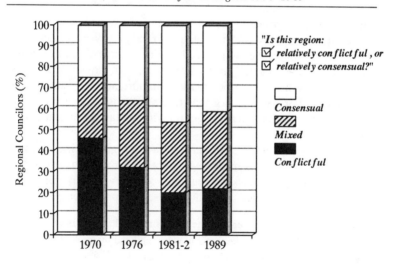

Politics in the regional arena is generally temperate. Most councilors throughout these twenty years have said that they can trust their colleagues, even their political adversaries. Roughly two-thirds insist that ideological opponents can reach agreement on practical problems of the region. Three-quarters say that council activities are marked more by collaboration than by conflict, a judgment shared by the overwhelming majority of community leaders with whom we have spoken.

These reports certainly do not mean that everyone agrees on all issues. Disagreement over specific policy matters actually increased after 1977, when the transfer of authority and resources from the central government gave regional leaders for the first time real choices, and thus real issues to disagree about. Controversy has not disappeared from regional politics, nor (as we shall see in Chapter 4) is conflict itself incompatible with good government. Nevertheless, contrary to the traditions of Italian politics, the regional councils are increasingly characterized by "open" rather than "closed" partisanship. The pluralism of party politics in the regions is not the "polarized pluralism" long ascribed to Italian national politics.[31] Regional leaders have learned to disagree without being disagreeable, and they have learned to respect their opponents.

The accumulation of evidence is overwhelming: The first two decades of the regional experiment witnessed a dramatic change in political climate and culture, a trend away from ideological conflict toward collaboration, from extremism toward moderation, from dogmatism toward tolerance, from abstract doctrine toward practical management, from interest articulation toward interest aggregation, from radical social reform toward "good government."

Some regionalists mourn "the relaxation of idealistic tensions," and we have a certain sympathy for their plaint. Trends away from idealism and toward mere "competence" might lead in time to an arid, uninspiring, and unresponsive technocracy.[32] In the Italian context, however, we believe that the trends we have described mark an important stage in transforming Italian politics. For better or for worst, the "idealistic tensions" were relaxed, as the new regional leaders got on with the task of building the new institution.

How did it happen that the political culture of regional elites changed so strikingly over these two decades? Accounting for these trends in the aggregate outlook of successive regional councils is far from simple. Among several alternatives, three hypotheses are prominent:[33]

· *Electoral replacement.* Perhaps the more firebrand members of the initial councils failed to win re-election and were replaced by moderates, more to the liking of voters or of party nominators outside the regional government itself. If so, minds were not changing, although the composition of the councils was. We can test this hypothesis by comparing councilors newly elected in 1975 and 1980 with those who departed in those years.

· *National politics.* Perhaps the changes we detected among regional councilors reflected a depolarization in national politics. Perhaps Italian politicians generally—not merely those directly involved in regional government—became more centrist and pragmatic during the 1970s and 1980s. As we have already noted, this interpretation is called into question by evidence that party polarization among ordinary Italians persisted and even intensified throughout much of this period. We lack directly comparable evidence on the changing outlooks of national politicians, but we can shed further light on this hypothesis by comparing the views of councilors newly elected in 1975 and 1980 with the initial views of their counterparts five years earlier. Were successive waves of entrants more moderate, suggesting that the nationwide pool of candidates from which they were drawn was becoming more moderate?

· *Institutional socialization.* Perhaps involvement in regional government itself converted its protagonists from ideological dogmatism to a more consensual pragmatism. Alone among these three alternative interpretations, this one implies that the institutional reform itself was consequential for regional politics, providing a venue within which political leaders could come to terms with one another and with the practical problems of their region. The most relevant evidence for this hypothesis comes from a direct comparison of the views of holdover councilors in 1975 and 1980 with *their own* views five years earlier.

Our panel surveys, in which we interviewed many of the same individuals in 1970 and 1976, and again in 1981–82, cast light on these alternative interpretations, although we cannot resolve the issue definitively.[34] Our study, however elaborate, was not a fully controlled scientific experiment. Although we can make a "before-after" comparison of councilors once elected, we have no straightforward control group of politicos outside the regional institution. Nevertheless, our evidence supports the following conclusions:[35]

· Electoral replacement made virtually no contribution to the growing moderation of the regional councils. Newly elected councilors were generally no more moderate than the outgoing councilors whom they replaced; indeed, the newcomers were sometimes *less* moderate than their predecessors. Replacement tended more often to brake than to accelerate trends toward moderation. Moderation was not imposed on the institution by voters or nominators outside.

· Nationwide trends, though sometimes difficult to distinguish from institution-specific trends, appear to have made a modest contribution to the story. Successive waves of newcomers to the council were more centrist than their predecessors *had initially been*, but less centrist than those predecessors *had by now become*. Although national effects were not important between 1970 and 1976, our evidence suggests that nationwide depolarization accelerated in the following five years and became a more significant influence on regional politics.

Institutional socialization, that is, conversion of individual incumbents, was powerful and explains much of the trend toward moderation. These institutional effects were strongest during the early years of the reform, as the new regional leaders first got to know one another and their shared problems. The same councilors who espoused ideological extremism and intense partisanship when first elected exhibited more moderate views five or ten years later. The growing moderation from one council to the next was concentrated precisely among the holdover incumbents. Members of the founding generation who ultimately survived into the third legislative period (roughly one-third of the original cohort) had been among the most extremist and dogmatic when they first entered the council, but by the time of our third wave of interviews, they had become among the most temperate and tolerant. The most obdurate partisans initially were also those who stayed on the council longest and, as they became more deeply engaged in the life of the institution, they succumbed to its moderating effects.

The most reasonable conclusion from these sometimes fragile data is that the new regional institution fostered a tolerant, collaborative pragmatism among its members. In Italy in the 1970s and 1980s, political change occurred both inside and outside the regional council chambers, but change was more rapid and far-reaching inside than outside, particularly during the early years. Italian politics had traditionally been characterized by ideological dogmatism and closed partisanship.[36] The hands-on, face-to-face political realities of the regional governments, warts and all, helped change that. Years spent grappling together with the difficult challenges of forging a new organization taught the regional councilors the virtues of patience and practicality and reasonableness. Just as its advocates had hoped, the regional reform nurtured "a new way of doing politics."

THE DEEPENING OF REGIONAL AUTONOMY

"The autonomy of political institutions is measured by the extent to which they have their own interests and values distinguishable from those of other social forces."[37] Are the Italian regional governments becoming institutionalized in this sense? Is there a trend toward an authentically *regional* political system, with an identity distinct from local and national social and political forces? Did the changed rules shift the real balances of power and interest in Italian politics and government?

The question is apt because the regions were born trapped between powerful national and local forces. As we have seen, the regions were in part a by-product of national party politics, and regional politics continues to be influenced by the national political climate. On the other flank, the first generation of regional councilors was firmly rooted in local politics. In those early years nominations for the regional council were mostly controlled by local party organizations, and the councilors' most important political connections were local. In the beginning the regions were essentially a national creation led by local politicians. If the regional government was to become an inspirited and powerful institution, rather than merely another formalistic addition to Italy's catalog of moribund public agencies, it would have to outgrow its origins. Its new leaders would have to gain greater independence from their erstwhile local and national patrons.

Our investigation suggests that regional institutional autonomy and identity have flowered, particularly after 1976. For example, in each survey we invited councilors and community leaders to rate the influence of a long list of actors, from local notables to national ministers, from agricultural organizations to labor unions, from business to the Church, and from the president of the region to local bureaucrats. One trend is unmistakable: The ascendancy of regional executives. The president of the region, members of the regional cabinet, regional party leaders, and regional administrators all moved up in the rankings between 1970 and 1989. By contrast, virtually all outside groups lost clout, whatever their political stripe: agriculture, unions, business, the press, the Church, national parliamentarians, and local party officials. These successive soundings chart a major shift toward the predominance of regional officials, increasingly autonomous from (though not unaffected by) outside forces, in precisely Huntington's sense. Within the limits of representative democracy, the leaders of the new institution came to be more and more in charge of their own destiny.[38]

Changes in patterns of power within the political parties confirm the institutionalization of regional politics. We regularly asked councilors about the influence of national, regional, and local party leaders in three specific arenas: nominations for the council, negotiations for the formation of the regional cabinet, and decisions about legislation before the council. In every arena and virtually every region, the power of regional leaders rose steadily from 1970 to 1989, while the power of national and local leaders declined. (See Figure 2.4.)

The once unchallenged monopoly of local party bosses over nominations to the council skidded, while the power of regional party officials to name candidates rose, although even in 1989 local officials retained a significant voice. Although national leaders were rarely involved in nominations, they often sought to influence coalition-making. In Sardinia, for example, the national DC held up the formation of a regional cabinet for many months, fearing that an alliance with the PCI (favored by the re-

FIGURE 2.4

Influence of Party Leaders in Three Arenas, 1970–1989

Influences on Nominations for Regional Council

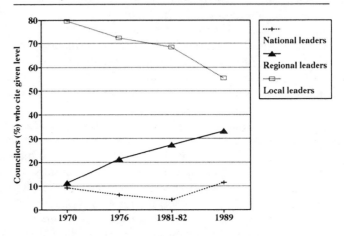

Influences on Formation of Regional Cabinet

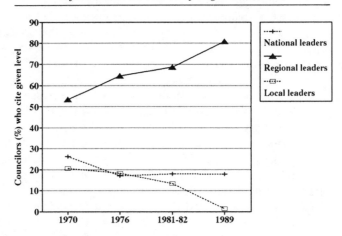

"Who has the most influence on [each of the three arenas]: national party leaders, regional party leaders, local party leaders, or [in the case of regional legislation] regional councilors themselves?"

gion's Christian Democrats) would undercut the national party's strategy. However, as Figure 2.4 reveals, regional autonomy in this domain, too, has surged upward over the last two decades. Finally, regional authority over legislative programs has become unquestioned. In this sector the most notable change in recent years has been a growing independence of

FIGURE 2.4 (*cont.*)

Influences on Regional Legislation

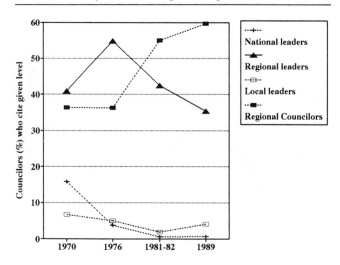

the councilors themselves from regional party leaders outside the council. This trend reinforces our theme of growing authenticity of the regional institution.

As a concomitant of this growing regional power and autonomy, regional politicians have become more reluctant to toe the national party line when that line conflicts with regional needs. Our *Index of Support for National Party Discipline*, summarized in Figure 2.5, shows how, particularly after 1976, the balance of opinion swung sharply toward support for more independence from national party dictates. In the early 1970s supporters of national party discipline outnumbered critics by more than two to one, whereas by 1989 critics outnumbered supporters by more than four to one. These changing attitudes appear to be reflected in behavior, as well. Marcello Fedele reports that the fraction of all *regional* government coalitions that shifted in the aftermath of *national* cabinet crises steadily declined between 1970 and 1990. One consequence is that the average durability of regional governments rose from 525 days in 1970–75 to more than 700 days in 1985–90, as compared with an average of only 250 days for national cabinets during this period.[39] In this domain, too, regional autonomy has grown.

The emergence of an autonomous regional political system is reflected in the workaday contacts of regional councilors. Once a primarily local figure who happened to hold a regional post, the councilor has become a genuinely regional figure though, like any elective politician, he retains a local political base. As Figure 2.6 shows, in 1970 the average councilor

FIGURE 2.5
Declining Support for National Party Discipline, 1970–1989

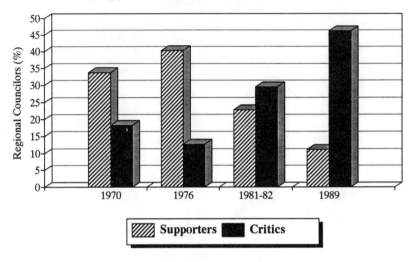

Index of Support for National Party Discipline

1. The regional political struggle ought to be seen above all as part of the national political struggle. (agree)

2. It is not necessary that a party's strategy be the same in every region. (disagree)

3. When one joins a political party, one must give up a certain measure of one's independence. (agree)

4. In the final analysis loyalty to one's fellow citizens is more important than faithfulness to one's party. (disagree)

Respondents were asked whether they "agree completely," "more or less agree," "more or less disagree," or "disagree completely" with each item. The Index is additive across all four items.

met more often with representatives of local groups than with representatives of regional groups and more often with local administrators than with regional administrators. By the 1980s those patterns were reversed, sharply so in the case of contacts with administrative officials.[40] Implicit in these charts is the emergence of an autonomous regional political system, with real decisions at stake (as represented in the contacts between councilors and regional administrators) and with real efforts to influence

FIGURE 2.6

Regional and Local Contacts of Regional Councilors, 1970–1989

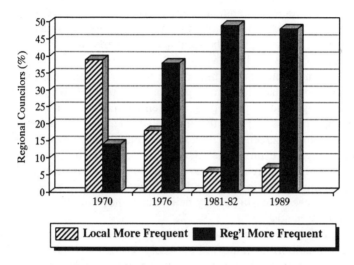

Frequency of Councilors' Contacts with Local and Regional Administrators

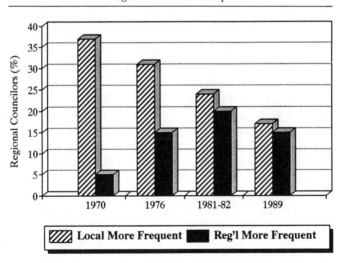

Frequency of Councilors' Contacts with Local and Regional Interest Groups

those decisions (as represented in the contacts between councilors and regional interest groups).

Consistent with this growing autonomy are councilors' reports about the changing influences on electoral behavior. In 1970 traditional party ties and national party programs were said to determine regional elections, while regional candidates themselves were deemed strictly secondary. In the ensuing years, however, individual candidates rose in perceived importance, and the significance of party identification and national platforms waned. Between 1970 and 1989 the proportion of councilors who attributed major importance to party identification as a factor in voters' decisions fell from 72 percent to 48 percent, while the proportion stressing national party programs fell from 55 percent to 24 percent. The proportion who rated the individual candidate as a major factor jumped from 38 percent to 57 percent, taking over the top slot.[41] We have no direct evidence on voters' motives, to be sure, but in the world of practical politics, perceptions have an importance of their own. Councilors see regional elections less and less as mere midterm referenda on national politics. Increasingly they believe that they hold their political fate in their own hands.

In strictly intergovernmental politics, relations between the regions and the central authorities improved markedly during the 1980s. The 616 decrees enacted in 1977 represented, as we saw earlier in this chapter, a watershed in the relationship between the state and the regions. Thereafter the climactic battles of the crisis of regional empowerment receded into the past. The great crusade of the 1970s to define the proper boundary between central and regional authority was followed in the 1980s by less rancorous border skirmishes. As battle lines stabilized between the centralist and regionalist fronts, the need to insist on regional autonomy was no longer so pressing. Both councilors and community leaders in the 1980s reported smoother relations with the central authorities than their predecessors had described in the mid-1970s. Conversely, the practical deficiencies of the regions became more apparent to their protagonists, as we shall see in detail later. In the aftermath of the 616 decrees, regional officials could no longer plausibly blame all their failings on excessive central control.

One consequence of these changes was that animosity toward the central authorities declined both among councilors and among community leaders. Between 1976 and 1989 the proportion of councilors, for example, who agreed that "the central government must rigorously exercise its rights of control over the activities of the regions" rose from 39 percent to 58 percent, while the proportion of community leaders who argued emphatically that "the institution of the prefect can and must be abolished" slipped from 60 percent to 32 percent. Combined in a single "Anti-Central

FIGURE 2.7
Regional Councilors' Attitudes toward Central Government, 1970–1989

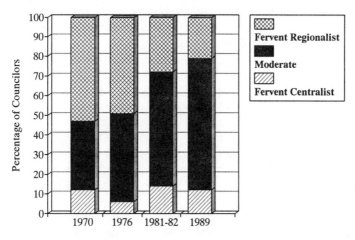

Index of Opposition to Central Government Controls

1. The institution of the prefect can and must be abolished. (agree)
2. The central government must rigorously exercise its rights of control over the activities of the regions. (disagree)

Respondents were asked whether they "agree completely," "more or less agree," "more or less disagree," or "disagree completely" with each item. The Index is additive across both items.

Government" Scale, these two questions trace a striking trend in councilor attitudes, as illustrated in Figure 2.7. While fervent centralists remained a tiny minority over these two decades (concentrated on the far right), the number of fervent opponents of the central government declined by more than half, and the proportion of moderate regionalists in the middle doubled. The tensions associated with the birth of the regional governments have progressively dissipated, and the regional elite are less fearful for regional autonomy now than they were two decades ago.

Both at the center and in the periphery, to be sure, one still hears frequent complaints about infringements on the respective turfs of the national and regional governments. Such charges mark the normal controversies endemic to any genuinely decentralized system of government. National officials, concerned about mounting budget deficits that they attribute to the regions' irresponsible inefficiency—"representation without taxation"—call for substantial cuts in regional funding. Regional officials retort that the lion's share of the funds they receive from the national government is too closely tied to particular programs, even to the point of identifying the species of agricultural products whose production can be subsidized. The national ministries, they say, see the regions too often as mere field offices of central administration.[42]

To Americans accustomed to governors' complaints about federal grants-in-aid and federal controls, these laments of Italian regional officials have a familiar ring. Similarly, members of the Italian parliament reportedly see regional officials as rivals for control of the patronage that is such an important political resource in much of Italy. Even deputies of the Left, ideologically committed to political decentralization, work behind the scenes in parliament, it is said, to restrict the discretion of regional government. Such rivalry between federal legislators and state and local officials is, of course, familiar in intergovernmental politics from Chicago to Bavaria.

Meanwhile, as the regions began to exercise their newfound powers of supervision over local governments, tussles between regional and local government began to take the place of the older simplicities of center-periphery conflict. In the intergovernmental triangle among central, regional, and local officials, new alignments and complicated three-cornered strategies began to evolve.[43] To the consternation of some Italian jurists, the Italian system moved in the direction of the marble cake model of intergovernmental relations, rather than the neater layer cake model.[44]

Instead of a simple contest over central and regional jurisdiction, most issues now evoke a multi-cornered struggle, including local governments, party officials at various levels, and even private agencies.[45] Rather than a clear division of responsibilities allocated to one and only one level, many programs in such fields as agriculture, housing, and health services are in effect shared among the national, regional, and local levels. Politicians and administrators from all three levels consult informally and negotiate with one another, often rancorously, even when one level has primary legal authority for decision-making. By the early 1980s nearly one hundred joint committees had been established to coordinate regional and national policies in particular sectors.

Conversely, the regions sought to increase their leverage in Rome on issues which are not formally within their jurisdiction, such as national economic policy and even international trade. Each region opened an office in Rome to represent its interests and to lobby the national government. In 1981 the chief executives of all the regions formed a permanent Conference of Presidents to provide a forum for expressing their views to the central government. By 1983 this group had established institutional ties with the national Council of Ministers, with the aim of improving top-level coordination between the central and regional authorities. As the

European Community moved toward greater integration in 1992, the regions also sought direct influence on decisions in Brussels.

It would be premature at best to proclaim an "era of good feelings" between the regional and national governments, for as James Madison pointed out to his countrymen at the birth of the American federal system, shared powers mean permanent controversy. Nor has the Italian system of government become fully federal, for the constitutional and political status of the Italian regions is less autonomous than, for example, the American states or the German *Länder*. The distinction between centralized and federal systems is a continuum, however, not a dichotomy.[46] Over the last two decades Italy has moved significantly toward the decentralized end of that dimension, not only in formal terms, but also in terms of practical politics and policymaking.

Regional leaders exercised more independent influence at the end of this period than their predecessors had at the beginning. Although the new structures did not determine informal power relations in any simple sense, changes in the formal structures gradually remolded informal relations. The logic of decentralization has become self-sustaining. Over the last two decades the region has become an authentic, autonomous, and increasingly distinctive arena in Italian politics.

PUTTING DOWN ROOTS:
THE REGION AND ITS CONSTITUENTS

"The protest marches now all go to the regional headquarters instead of the prefecture," lamented one southern prefect privately. In Basilicata, one of the most backward regions of Italy, in a single day in November 1980—as it happened, only two days before the regional government would be forced to confront the devastation of a major earthquake—the press carried reports about a regional tourist development on the Ionian sea, a protest by handicapped citizens against regional inaction, claims for regional aid to the investors in a bankrupt industrial development, demands for regional assistance to laid-off workers in a steel plant and a local supermarket, a report on a newly opened regionally funded home for the aged, and criticism about the role of the region in a proposed petrochemical project. The protest marchers' changing destination subtly symbolizes the growing significance of the regional government in Italian governance.

As early as 1976, community leaders across Italy, such as mayors, labor leaders, bankers, industrialists, merchants, agricultural representatives, and journalists were actively engaged with the new governments. Nearly half the community leaders with whom we spoke met regularly with regional cabinet members, councilors, and administrators. These community and organizational leaders had more frequent contact with regional officials than with the equivalent figures either in local government or in the field offices of central government. (One impact of the regionalization of Italian government is that many national organizations, including the trade union federations and business and agricultural organizations, as well as political parties, have also been reorganized along regional lines in recent years.) By the 1980s, most community leaders in our surveys (roughly 60 percent) reckoned that the regional government had a "very" or "rather" significant impact in their field, while fewer than one in ten claimed that the region had had no impact at all. Although (as we shall shortly see in detail) these community leaders were often critical of the new institution, roughly two-thirds judged that its impact in their own field was fundamentally positive. Within less than a decade, the new governments had begun to put down roots.

Up to this point our description of the Italian regional experiment has emphasized trends consistent with the hopes of the proponents of the experiment. However, nearly all sides in the regionalist debate agree that the actual administrative performance of most of the new governments has been problematical. Public management in many regions has been a Kafkaesque combination of lethargy and chaos.

Throughout the late 1970s and the 1980s, a sense of frustrated hopes, fruitless plans, missed opportunities, and wasted hours pervaded many regional offices, especially in the South but not only there. Gloom about the gap between the regionalists' high aspirations and their limited practical achievements began to spread. By 1976, 42 percent of the councilors and 67 percent of the community leaders approved the region's official policies in the areas of most concern to them, but only 24 percent of the councilors and 35 percent of the community leaders approved the implementation of those policies. Although regional planning had been a high priority of most regional governments, two-thirds of the councilors themselves in 1976 rated their region's efforts as unsuccessful, fully one-half as "very" unsuccessful. The most common criticism was a lack of administrative follow-through on the regional governments' promising ideals.

Community leaders amplified these criticisms, focusing on the administrative failings of regional government. Throughout the 1980s, more than half of the community leaders we interviewed (55 percent in 1982 and 60 percent in 1989) agreed that "the administration in this region is decidedly inefficient."[47] Regionalization of the national health system, the largest sector transferred to regional jurisdiction in the reforms of the mid-1970s, was regarded by many as an administrative fiasco. In interviews with both community leaders and ordinary citizens, only a third

TABLE 2.5
Community Leaders' Views of Regional Administration (1982)

Aspects of Regional Government Activities[a]	Percentage of Leaders "Rather" or "Very" Satisfied
Openness to consultation with your organization	55
Programmatic choices	41
Qualifications and diligence of personnel	32
Coordination with local government	28
Feasibility of regional projects	23
Time required to process a case	15
(Approximate Number)	(302)

[a] Survey participants were asked, "How satisfied are you with these six aspects of the activities of the regional government in this region?"

agreed that "the regionalization of the health services has produced positive results," and barely 5–10 percent accepted this upbeat assessment without qualification.

Table 2.5 spells out the community leaders' complaints.[48] Bureaucratic procedures (patterned too often on practices of the central administration) are maddeningly slow and inefficient, cramped by controls designed to assure procedural regularity, not real effectiveness. Regional administrators are often unmotivated, unprofessional, inefficient, and unqualified. Agencies of the regional government act in mutual ignorance, without coordination with one another or with other levels of government. Projects proposed by regional officials too often seem impractical and unfeasible. Business and labor leaders are united in the view that no one at the regional government is able to discuss regional development plans intelligently. Worst of all, it takes forever to get an answer—any answer—from the region. Regional officials, the community leaders acknowledge, are eager to get their input, and the basic policy directions are often admirable. But implementing those shared objectives has proved beyond the capacity of too many regional agencies.[49] All in all, these community leaders say, the regional governments *sanno ascoltare, ma non sanno fare*—"they know how to *listen*, but they do not know how to *act*."

Many of the regions' administrative difficulties derive from personnel problems. Throughout the 1980s, nearly two-thirds of the community leaders we spoke with rejected the proposition that "the civil servants of this region are well trained and conscientious." Fearing bureaucratic elephantiasis (and perhaps ambivalent about strengthening the regions), the national parliament had stipulated that the regional governments be staffed primarily by bureaucrats transferred from the national ministries

and semipublic agencies, thus restricting the ability of the regional governments to select their own employees. Worse yet, the transfer system
gave no incentive to the national agencies to provide the regions with the
best qualified staff, committed to the success of the regional reform. The
system was virtually guaranteed to provide personnel ill suited to admin-
ister the "radical social and political renewal" of which the regionalists
had dreamed.

It is far from clear that the regions would have exercised any more
discretion wisely. Clientelism and party affiliation, rather than expertise
and experience, were the main criteria for recruitment where the decisions
were left to the regional authorities. Regional politicians were ready to
demand autonomy, but less ready to manage that autonomy when it was
granted. In many regions parties saw the new governments as a lucra-
tive new source of money and jobs. Particularly in the impoverished
South, efficient administration is less productive in electoral terms than
old-fashioned patronage. Too much money has been spent on door-
keepers, chauffeurs, and phantom jobs of various sorts. Neither the national transfer system nor the regional recruitment system has produced a
cadre of officials eager and able to implement innovative regional policy.

Top regional executives often acknowledge the justice of these criticisms. Indeed, 88 percent of the senior regional administrators we interviewed in 1981–82 judged the quality and training of regional personnel
to be an important obstacle to efficient administration in their region, and
81 percent expressed a similar view about coordination among the regional departments. Said one, "In too many respects we have reproduced
the defects of the Roman mentality."

Against this background of severe criticism, it is interesting that (as
shown in Table 2.5) the community leaders are generally pleased with the
accessibility of the regional administration, an important factor that
sharply differentiates the regions from the national administration. Regional and local organizations have been able to get regional government
officials to listen to their complaints and suggestions. In our four waves of
interviews with community leaders, three out of four leaders consistently
have agreed that "contacts with the national administration are more frustrating than those with the regional administration." Despite their complaints about the region, Rome is much worse.[50]

One important reason for the greater accessibility of the regional administrators, of course, is propinquity: the regional capital is simply
easier to get to than Rome. But administrative culture may be as important
as geography, for regional bureaucrats appear to be more democratic in
outlook than their national counterparts. Research in 1971 on the national
bureaucratic elite found that "the typical member of the Italian administrative elite [is] the very essence of a classical bureaucrat—legalist, illiberal,

TABLE 2.6
Democratic Attitudes among National and Regional Administrators
(1971–1976)

Statement with which Administrators Agreed	Percentage Agreeing	
	National Administrators	Regional Administrators
Few people know what is in their real interest in the long run.	75	39
In a world as complicated as the modern one, it doesn't make sense to speak of increased control by ordinary citizens over governmental affairs.	63	23
The freedom of political propaganda is not an absolute freedom, and the state should carefully regulate its use.	57	14

elitist, hostile to the usages and practices of pluralist politics, fundamentally undemocratic."[51] Among the regional administrators we interviewed just five years later, however, we found much more openness to democratic politics. As Table 2.6 shows, top regional administrators seem more comfortable with democratic government than was the norm in the national bureaucracy from which many of them have come.

In sum, on the "input" side of government the regions represent a substantial improvement over the central authorities, but on the "output" side regional administration leaves a great deal to be desired. Regional leaders may have learned a "new way of doing politics," but most of them have yet to discover an efficacious "new way of managing." Interestingly, regional officials themselves are at least as critical of regional shortcomings as are community leaders outside the government.

The verdict rendered on the regional reform by the Italian electorate is muffled by ignorance. Public awareness of the new regional institution spread slowly in the first years. In 1972, when the regions still existed mainly on paper, a nationwide survey found that two-thirds of the electorate had heard little or nothing about their own regional government, including 43 percent who had heard nothing at all. The salience of the new institution rose during the mid-1970s, as the great debates about the new regional government rose on the national agenda, and information about it filtered into the less politically conscious strata of the population. Thereafter, a certain plateau in public awareness was reached, although attention to the regional governments faded somewhat in the South, where (as we shall see) the new institutions were slower to make their mark.[52] By the end of the 1980s, two-thirds of southern voters and three-quarters of northern voters had heard at least something about their regional government. Regional governments lack the immediacy of contact with the daily lives of citizens that characterizes local government, and they lack the kind of media attention that is devoted to national affairs. Like American states, the regions are probably fated to remain less visible to the public than the levels of government above and below them.[53]

In absolute terms Italians are far from satisfied with the performance of their regional governments. By the beginning of the 1980s, only one-third of Italians were reasonably enthusiastic supporters of the region, saying they were "very" or "rather" satisfied with the activities of the regional government; one-half were disgruntled, declaring themselves "little" satisfied; and one in six was outraged, that is, "not at all" satisfied. These figures were virtually identical for both community leaders and ordinary voters. Most agreed with the mayor who told us in 1976, "The general lines of the region are fine, but the operative reality is not."

Both voters and leaders are less critical of the regional governments when they consider the alternative of centralized government. For many years Italians have had very little confidence in their public institutions. This alienation deepened just as the new institutions were being founded at the beginning of the 1970s. Indeed, the very disenchantment of Italians with the central administration may have inflated expectations of the new regional governments. In any event, despite their unhappiness with the results of the regional reform, both voters and community leaders have been consistently less critical of the performance of the new regional governments than of the national government. In 1981–82, for example, 34 percent of all Italians were at least "rather" satisfied with their regional government, as compared to only 15 percent for the national government; the comparable figures for community leaders were 29 percent for the regional government and 8 percent for the national government. In a head-to-head comparison, supporters of the regional governments outnumbered those who had more faith in the national government by eight to one. Community leaders who preferred to work with regional officials outnumbered those who favored national administrators by three or four to one. In a climate of general repudiation of public institutions, the regional government, though barely a decade old, was already more respected than the national government.

However vigorously Italians criticize the failures of their regional governments, they favor broader regional jurisdiction and autonomy instead of central authority. Table 2.7 presents illustrative evidence from our 1982 surveys.[54] Most Italians want to keep law and order in the hands of the central government, but roughly half would transfer greater powers to the regions in sectors now dominated by the state, such as education and industrial development, and roughly two-thirds favor regional pre-

TABLE 2.7

Attitudes of Italian Voters and Community Leaders toward
Regional Autonomy (1982)

Policy Sector	*Percentage Who Want to Give More Power to the Region*[a]	
	Voters	*Community Leaders*
Environment	72	85
Agriculture	70	84
Health	63	70
Industrial development	50	69
Education	47	46
Police	24	13
(Approximate Number)	(1585)	(295)

Policy Sector	*Percentage Who Agree That the Regions Should Have More Financial Autonomy from the State*	
	Voters	*Community Leaders*
Finance	78	81
(Number)	(1376)	(305)

[a] Survey participants were asked, "Here is a list of things with which the State and the Region can be concerned. In each of these sectors is it preferable that the State or the Region have more power?"

eminence in such fields as health, agriculture, and the environment. Four out of five Italians support the demands of regional officials for greater financial autonomy from the state. Among community leaders, the pro-regional majorities on these questions are even more lopsided. Despite Italians' criticisms of the regional governments, they want the regions to be stronger, not weaker.[55]

Voter satisfaction with the performance of the regional government rose slowly but steadily throughout the 1980s, as Table 2.8 shows. Between 1977 and the end of 1988, the proportion of Italians at least "rather" satisfied increased from 33 percent to 45 percent. These national averages conceal important disparities across the regions. By the end of 1988, as Figure 2.8 demonstrates, 57 percent of the northern electorate was reasonably satisfied with their regional government, as contrasted with only 29 percent of southern voters.[56] By the end of the 1980s, *nearly all* the

TABLE 2.8
Public Satisfaction with Regional Government, 1977–1988

Degree of Satisfaction[a]	Percentage				
	1977	1981	1982	1987	1988
Very satisfied	3	2	2	2	3
Rather satisfied	30	33	32	38	42
Little satisfied	43	44	42	42	39
Not at all satisfied	24	22	23	17	17
	100	100	100	100	100
(Number)	(1497)	(1936)	(1845)	(1923)	(1899)

[a] Survey participants were asked, "How satisfied are you with the activities of the regional government here?"

northern regional governments (9 of 10) were satisfying most of their citizens, but *none* of the southern regions approached that goal.[57]

Figure 2.9—which compares voter satisfaction with national, regional, and local government—makes plain that, from the point of view of most Italians, the three major levels of government form a ladder of increasing efficacy as one moves from the most distant and most distrusted level (national government) to the closest and most trusted (local government). In the North, however, voters see a stark difference between the central government, on the one hand, with which most of them are heartily dissatisfied, and regional and local government, on the other hand, with which most of them are reasonably content. By contrast, southerners are dissatisfied with all levels of government, and regional and local government are barely less censured than the central authorities.[58]

Queries about administrative inefficiency and legislative ineffectiveness highlight North-South differences. Throughout the 1980s, roughly 60 percent of southern voters agreed that "in this region the administration is definitely inefficient," as contrasted to roughly 35 percent of northern voters. On the other hand, roughly 60 percent of northerners agreed that "all in all, the council in this region has functioned so far in a satisfactory manner," as compared to only 35 percent of southerners.

Whatever the shortcomings of the new regional administration, northern Italians prefer to be governed from closer to home. For many southerners, by contrast, being ruled from Bari or Reggio Calabria is not much better than being ruled from Rome, and for many the region has the additional disadvantage of unfamiliarity. "Better a known evil than a new one" is a view still occasionally heard in the South, but not in the North.

FIGURE 2.8
Public Satisfaction with Northern and Southern Regional Governments,
1977–1988

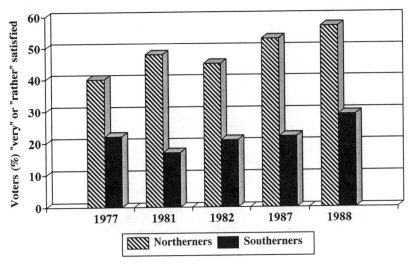

FIGURE 2.9
Northern and Southern Satisfaction with National, Regional, and
Local Government (1988)

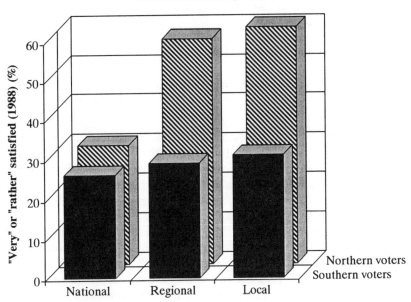

FIGURE 2.10

Optimism about Regional Government: Councilors, Community Leaders, and Voters, 1970–1989

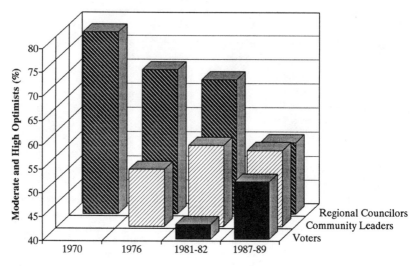

Index of Optimism about Regional Government

1. All in all, the council in this region has functioned satisfactorily so far. (agree)
2. Realistically speaking, in this region it is difficult to foresee great concrete accomplishments of the regional government. (disagree)

Respondents were asked whether they "agree completely," "more or less agree," "more or less disagree," or "disagree completely" with each item. The Index is additive across both items.

This strong North-South discrepancy in public satisfaction is consistent with other measures of the performance of the various regional governments, and we shall return to this topic repeatedly in subsequent chapters. On the other hand, Figure 2.8 also shows that by the end of 1988, in the South as in the North, the standing of regional governments in the eyes of their constituents was higher than ever before.

We can summarize much of the dynamics in regional government over the last two decades by directly comparing the changing views of regional councilors with those of their constituents, both community leaders and ordinary voters. (See Figure 2.10.) In the earliest years of the reform, the councilors, as the main protagonists of the new institution, were upbeat and ebullient. Between 1970 and 1989, however, this buoyant euphoria about their venture in institution-building was steadily replaced by a grimly realistic assessment of the practical challenges of making the new government work. Community leaders and voters, on the other hand, were initially much more skeptical, but their doubts have gradually been replaced by modest optimism.[59] By the end of the 1980s, as this chart shows, all strata in regional political life were converging toward moderate, but still hopeful realism.

After two decades of experience, the average Italian seems, in effect, to distinguish two different issues:

1. Is his or her own regional government performing satisfactorily?
2. Is the principle of the regional reform desirable?

Many Italians, particularly in the South, respond negatively to the first question, but affirmatively to the second. In that sense, we may term them "sympathetic critics." This distinction is politically significant, because while their criticism calls attention to the need for major improvements in the regional governments, their strong sympathy for the principle of regionalism underlines the need to reinforce the authority of those governments. Discontent with the practical performance of the regional government has not undermined popular support for a strong and autonomous regional institution. This paradoxical combination of sharp practical criticism and strong fundamental support is even more characteristic of the younger generation of voters, as well as of community leaders.[60] The vast majority (especially among the younger generation) wish to improve the regional institution, not to diminish or replace it.

What Italians want is not more limited regional government, but more effective regional government. No doubt an important part of the explanation is that most Italians are even more skeptical about the performance of the central authorities than they are about the regions. However, another part of the explanation may be that many citizens are still willing to give the benefit of the doubt to the new regional institution. The Italians' gradually increasing satisfaction with the regional governments, and their greater approval of regional than of national government, correspond to real differences in performance. Recall that regional governments are, for example, more than twice as stable as national governments and that the stability of regional governments has steadily increased.[61]

Table 2.9 presents some additional evidence that synthesizes this conclusion. The basic question summarized here has been asked of Italians for nearly thirty years, beginning well before the advent of the ordinary regions.[62] Not surprisingly, in the earliest years a substantial portion of the public simply had no idea what to expect, and many others feared the worst. In the ensuing years, the ratio of favorable to unfavorable judgments rose steadily, so that by 1987 (the latest year for which comparable

TABLE 2.9
Evaluations of the Regional Reform, 1960–1987/89

	Percentage						
Mass Public[a]	1960	1963	1976	1979	1981	1982	1987
More good than harm	19	31	38	31	31	31	41
Neither good nor harm	6	11	16	29	30	28	30
As much good as harm	4	6	7	8	13	11	7
More harm than good	20	22	21	14	18	21	17
Don't know	51	30	18	18	8	9	5
	100	100	100	100	100	100	100
Support-criticism Index[b]	−1	9	17	17	13	10	24

	Percentage		
Community Leaders[a]	1981	1982	1989
More good than harm	65	59	62
Neither good nor harm	22	6	13
As much good as harm	6	18	17
More harm than good	7	17	8
	100	100	100
Support-criticism Index[b]	58	42	54

[a] Survey participants were asked, "Do you think that from the creation of the regions has come [in 1960 and 1963: "would come"] more good than harm or more harm than good?"

[b] Support-criticism Index = (More good than harm – more harm than good).

results are available), nearly two-and-a-half times as many Italian voters approve (41 percent) as disapprove (17 percent) of the regional reform. Among community leaders, the balance of opinion is even more favorable to the regional reform, despite their severe criticism of the practical operations of the regional government. During the 1980s supporters of regionalism among community leaders outnumbered the critics by roughly six to one.[63] In light of southern grievance over the practical operations of the regional government, it is important to emphasize that southerners on balance endorse the regional reform.[64]

Creating a new political institution is neither quick nor easy. Ultimately, success must be measured not in years, but in decades. It is instructive to pause for a brief comparison with the history of German attitudes toward the state governments (Länder) created in 1949. Asked whether it would be a good idea or a bad idea for the Länder to be dissolved, critics outnumbered supporters in the German public in 1952, 49 percent to 21 percent. A 1960 poll found, for the first time, a slim majority (42 percent to 24 percent) opposing the abolition of the new institu-

FIGURE 2.11

Support for Subnational Government: Germany (1952–1978) and Italy (1976–1987)

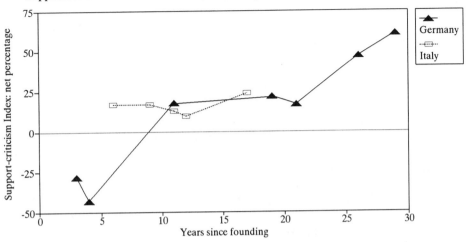

Germany: "What would you say if the state governments were dissolved and there were only the federal government in Bonn? How do you feel about that suggestion?"
Support-criticism Index: Net percentage favorable to the states

Italy: "Do you think that from the creation of the regions has come more good than bad, or more bad than good?"
Support-criticism Index: Net percentage favorable to the regions

tions, and support remained at this lukewarm level for more than a decade. During the third decade after their creation, however, support for the *Länder* rose steadily, and by 1978 supporters had become vastly more numerous than critics (71 percent, compared to 10 percent).[65]

Figure 2.11 charts the gradual growth of support for strong subnational government in Germany, in comparison with similar trends during the early years of the Italian regions. This figure shows that the regions had won the support of a plurality of their constituents even earlier than the German *Länder* and that, thereafter, public support for the regions drifted upwards relatively slowly. There is no assurance, of course, that public support for the Italian regions will accelerate in the years ahead, following the path blazed by the German *Länder*, nor that the Italian regions will prove as durable and effective as their more powerful German counterparts. But evidence from the German experiment in building subnational institutions reminds us that the popular legitimacy of new institutions, even successful ones, grows only gradually. This standard provides a realistic and sobering benchmark for evaluating changes in public attitudes to the Italian regional governments, as well as the new democratic institutions now being established elsewhere in the world.

CONCLUSIONS

Examined week by week, or month by month, or sometimes even year by year, development in any human institution is hard to chart. The rhythms of institutional change are slow. Often several generations must pass through a new institution before its distinctive effects on culture and behavior become clear. Evanescent fads and the vagaries of individual participants obscure deeper trends. Occasionally in the early years of our regional research we thought we had discerned signs of some important development, only to have our expectations disrupted by new evidence from our next visit. Those who build new institutions and those who would evaluate them need patience—this is one of the most important lessons of the Italian regional experiment.

The trends discussed in this chapter, however, have been sustained through several decades of Italian political tumult. Our research methods allow us directly to compare today's attitudes and behavior with those of a decade or two ago, without relying on vague and fallible reminiscence. We can compare a leader's views on party discipline or capitalism or regional efficiency today with what he (or his predecessors) actually told us years ago, not merely with what people now recall about prevailing views then.

By these demanding evidential standards, the regional reform has significantly affected grassroots politics in Italy. As a result of this institutional change, Italian political leaders pursue different career paths, espouse different ideals, address social ills in different terms, struggle with different rivals, and collaborate with different partners. Italian citizens and community leaders depend on different agencies for government action. Often they receive improved service, though certainly not always, and when they don't, they address their complaints to different officials. Important things have changed because of the regional reform.

Twenty years into the regional experiment, subnational government is clearly more important on major issues of public policy in the early 1990s than in 1970. The new institutions have taken root, gained autonomy, and (slowly) won constituent support. They have attracted an up-and-coming cadre of professional politicians. This institutional reform has had powerful consequences for the way Italian politics and government work. But what is the balance sheet for these new institutions in terms of the *quality* of politics and government?

On the positive side, the new institutions are closer to the people, as proponents had claimed they would be. The regional governments are more familiar with regional realities and more accessible to regional demands than the remote Roman ministries they replaced. They provide multiple laboratories for policy innovation (as we shall see in more detail in Chapter 3). They help to nurture a moderate, pragmatic, tolerant style of policy making and conflict management—"a new way of doing politics." They engage the interests of regional social groups and community leaders, and they are gradually earning cautious approval from their constituents.

Against these gains must be laid two important entries on the negative side of the ledger. First, the administrative efficiency that some regionalist reformers anticipated has not materialized. On the contrary, any fairminded jury would convict many of the regions of maladministration. Second, and perhaps even more important for the future of Italian politics, the regional reform appears to be exacerbating, rather than mitigating, the historical disparities between North and South. The reform freed the more advanced regions from the stultifying grasp of Rome, while allowing the problems of the more backward regions to fester.

In assessing these two indictments, however, we must ask about actual alternatives, not unattainable ideals. After an hour of passionate and detailed criticism of his region by a southern mayor, we asked whether things were better under the centralized regime. Looking stunned at the naïveté of our question, he exclaimed, "For the love of God, no!"

By the beginning of the regions' third decade, a new season of revived regionalism seemed to be opening. Despite widespread disappointment that the regional governments had not lived up to the original hopes, renewed concern about the ineffectiveness of the central government led to widespread talk of further "regionalization" of the Italian state. In the wealthy northern regions, upstart regionalist "leagues," such as the *Lega Lombarda* and the *Lega Veneta*, made major gains in regional and local elections in 1990 and 1991 and in national elections in 1992. The rise of the leagues was fueled by regional pride, anger against the inefficiences of Rome, backlash against "handouts" to corrupt southerners, and veiled racism. The *Lega Lombarda*, which called for "liberation of the Lombard nation," won more than 20 percent of votes in the richest, most populous region in the country. A dozen regional governments petitioned for a national referendum to transfer major additional powers to the regional level.

In 1991 the Constitutional Affairs Committee of the Chamber of Deputies approved virtually unanimously a constitutional amendment that would completely eliminate several major national ministries (including Education, Health, Agriculture, Social Affairs, and Urban Affairs, among others), transferring their responsibilities to the regions, and more than doubling the regions' share of the entire national budget to almost 70 percent.[66] In some respects, the ambitions were reminiscent of the mood at the birth of the regions in the 1970s, although the mood in the North was darker and more resentful than in the earlier, more optimistic period. The history of governmental reform in Italy suggests caution in interpreting these developments, since the central authorities strongly resisted any further devolution of their powers, but regionalist pressures continued to mount, especially in the North. Another page was about to be turned in the story of Italian regional government.

Whatever the new chapter may bring, we have already seen signs that any uniform verdict on the regional experiment so far is misleading, given the heterogeneity of the regions and their performance. It is time to appraise institutional performance itself and to explore these differences.

Measuring Institutional Performance

"WHO GOVERNS?" and "How well?" are the two most basic questions of political science. The former raises issues of distribution and redistribution: "Who Gets What, When, and How?" Such issues have been at the forefront of the discipline's debates in recent decades. By contrast, rigorous appraisals of institutional performance are rare, even though "good government" was once at the top of our agenda. The undeniable admixture of normative judgments in any inquiry about performance and effectiveness has made most scholars over the last forty years reluctant to pursue such questions: *de gustibus non disputandum est*, at least in a value-free, "objective" social science. Even though political scientists, as ordinary citizens, are often quite willing to judge a government's performance, the discipline has too readily relinquished this important patrimony of political science—this "ancient obligation of our craft"[1]—to political philosophers and publicists.

We aspire to a multifaceted evaluation of each of the twenty Italian regional governments, as a prelude to our investigation of the causes of institutional success and failure. But how should we begin? What criteria must be met by a rigorous, impartial, persuasive evaluation of institutional success? Indeed, how can we be sure that some governments actually are *systematically* more effective than others, so that it makes sense to speak generically of "institutional success"?

The institution we want to evaluate is a representative government. Therefore, we need to evaluate both its responsiveness to its constituents and its efficiency in conducting the public's business.[2] Democratic theorists from John Stuart Mill to Robert Dahl have asserted that "the key characteristic of a democracy is the continuing responsiveness of the government to the preferences of its citizens."[3] Democracy grants citizens the right to petition their government in the hope of achieving some individual or social goal, and it requires fair competition among different versions of the public interest. Good government is, however, more than a forum for competing viewpoints or a sounding board for complaints; it actually gets things done. A good democratic government not only considers the demands of its citizenry (that is, is responsive), but also acts efficaciously upon these demands (that is, is effective).

In order to study institutional performance, we must measure it carefully and convincingly. Before we can explore in a rigorous way *why* the new regional government succeeded in Emilia-Romagna but failed in Puglia, we must first show that these assessments are not merely whimsical or impressionistic. Any serious measurement of government performance must meet four severe tests:

1. It must be *comprehensive*. Governments do many things—pass laws, spend money, deliver services, and manage their internal operations. Occasionally, governments move beyond such routines to aim at innovative reforms, whether of the left like Lyndon Johnson's or of the right like Margaret Thatcher's. Our assessment must encompass all these activities, both conventional and novel. Moreover, governments have responsibilities in many different policy areas—health, agriculture, public works, education, social services, economic development, and so on. Our appraisal must assay all these fields, if it is to be comprehensive. We cannot hope to measure every single thing that twenty regional governments have done over two decades, but we must cast our net as widely as possible in sampling their effectiveness.

2. It must be *internally consistent*. Precisely because governments do so many different things, they have no single "bottom line," like profit in a capitalist firm. This fact opens the possibility that different governments might simply be good at different things—some the leaders in health care, others in road-building, some creative legislatively, others more effective managers, and so on. We must thus look closely at the concordance among our various operational measures of institutional performance and be alert for signs of "multidimensionality." *If and only if* our varied indicators turn out empirically to rank the regions in roughly the same way will we be justified in speaking summarily of institutional success and failure.

3. It must be *reliable*. To be worth explaining in general terms, institutional performance must be reasonably durable, not volatile. Some variation over time is to be expected, particularly in the early years of a new institution. One government may stumble while another gains momentum. If the rank ordering of the regions were to change kaleidoscopically from one year to the next, however, our basic conception of institutional performance would require revision. But if the same regions are well governed year after year, that suggests that performance turns on something more than a momentary constellation of political forces or the skill (or luck) of a particular incumbent.

4. It must *correspond to the objectives and evaluations of the institution's protagonists and constituents*. These are, after all, *democratic* governments, responsible to the citizens of the various regions. We must beware of imposing alien standards that are uncongenial to those constituents. We need carefully to compare our "objective" measures of performance with the views of voters and community leaders in each of the regions. We already know from

the previous chapter that satisfaction varied considerably from region to region. Before rendering verdicts on the quality of governance in the various regions, we need to check our measurements against the judgments of people in Bologna and Bari, Seveso and Pietrapertosa.

This chapter is organized to accomplish these four tasks.[4] We begin by looking at each of a dozen diverse probes of government effectiveness in the twenty regions. Next we explore the correlations among those twelve measures, and we ask how stable our summary assessment of performance is over time. Finally, we compare our evaluations, region by region, with the views of Italian voters and community leaders. This rigorous process is an essential first step toward our goal of understanding institutional success and failure.

TWELVE INDICATORS OF INSTITUTIONAL PERFORMANCE

For each regional government, we seek to evaluate (1) policy processes; (2) policy pronouncements; and (3) policy implementation.

An institution's effectiveness depends, first of all, on how well it manages its essential internal affairs. Thus, we may measure the stability of an institution's decision-making apparatus, for example, or the efficacy of its budgetary process, or the effectiveness of its management information systems.[5] (See indicators 1–3, pp. 67–68.) Essentially this family of measures asks: Whatever else this institution is doing, is it conducting its crucial internal operations smoothly and with dispatch?

But studying the performance of governments means studying policies and programs as well. Are the governments prompt to identify social needs and propose innovative solutions? Does legislation enacted by the governments reflect a capacity to react comprehensively, coherently, and creatively to the issues at hand? (See indicators 4–5, pp. 68–70.)

Finally, our appraisal must move beyond words to deeds. We must evaluate the success of these governments in their roles as problem-solvers and service-providers. Are the regional governments successful in using the available resources to address the needs of a rapidly changing society? Have they succeeded in implementing their avowed policy objectives—establishing health clinics, building day care centers, and so on? How efficient are they in responding to the demands of individual citizens? (See indicators 6–12, pp. 70–73.)

While our evaluation of government must measure actions, not just words, we must be careful not to give governments credit (or blame) for matters beyond their control.[6] In the language of policy analysis, we want to measure "outputs" rather than "outcomes"—health care rather than mortality rates; environmental policy rather than air quality; economic development programs rather than business profits. Health, air quality, and profits are surely important, but the reason for excluding them from our evaluation of government performance is simple: social outcomes are influenced by many things besides government. Health depends on factors like diet and life-style that are beyond the direct control of any democratic government. Air quality is influenced by meteorology, demography, and industry, as well as government policy. Profits represent entrepreneurial skill, worker diligence, world economic conditions, and so on. To include social outcomes in an assessment of government performance is to commit the "Massachusetts Miracle Fallacy": only a modest part of the praise for the affluence of New England in the 1980s (and a similarly modest portion of the blame for the subsequent recession) was realistically attributable to state government, despite 1988 presidential campaign rhetoric to the contrary.

Assessing outputs comparatively and quantitatively is, of course, a complex, value-laden task. To be persuasive, any measure of policy performance should be reasonably unaffected by differences in substantive priorities. It is not easy to compare the innovativeness, effectiveness, and social importance of, say, a scholarship program and an irrigation program. In the context of our study, however, these difficulties are reduced to manageable proportions. Broadly speaking, the same themes were stressed in our interviews with policymakers and community leaders all across Italy. Although the urgency of certain problems varied from region to region, in their early years all regional governments grappled with similar issues, such as public health, vocational education, and public works. But they did not address these issues equally promptly or comprehensively or effectively or creatively, and the results did not equally satisfy the policymakers and their constituents. As Eckstein has noted, "It is ludicrous to expect polities to attain goals they do not want to attain, but surely reasonable to expect them efficaciously to pursue those that are in fact strong preferences."[7]

Our detailed assessment of institutional success is founded on twelve diverse indicators, covering internal processes, policy pronouncements, and policy implementation in many different policy sectors. For the most part, these measures are drawn from the period 1978 to 1985, that is, after the reform law 382 of 1976 and the 616 decrees of 1977 had delegated substantial authority and significant funding to all the regions. This period encompasses most of the second and all of the third legislatures of the new institutions. Some of our indicators are quantitatively precise, although their connection to substantive outcomes is indirect. The relevance of others to institutional performance is clear-cut, although their quantification is less exact. No single metric, taken in isolation, would suffice to rate the regions fairly. Collectively, however, these indicators can undergird a broad-based assessment of institutional success and failure.

We begin with three measures of policy processes and internal operations: cabinet stability, budget promptness, and statistical and information services.

1. Cabinet Stability

Like the national Italian government, each regional government is led by a cabinet that must retain majority support in the legislature. Some regions had highly stable cabinets and thus were able, in principle, to pursue a coherent line of policy. Others, by contrast, found it hard to patch a coalition together and harder to keep it together. Our metric here is the number of different cabinets installed in each region during the 1975–1980 and 1980–1985 legislative periods. Ratings on this metric varied from two cabinets in ten years in Trentino-Alto Adige and Umbria to nine cabinets in ten years in Sicily, Sardinia, and Campania.[8] Although the simplest of all our indicators of performance, this measure turns out to be one of the more powerful.

2. Budget Promptness

Beginning in 1972, all regions were supposed to complete action on their annual budgets by January 1, the start of the fiscal year. Virtually none met this target, and in the early 1980s all regions were hampered by delays beyond their control in the national budget cycle. However, the average delay varied considerably from region to region. Our metric here was simply this: On average, during the period 1979–1985, when was the budget actually approved by the regional council? Ratings varied from an average of January 27 (several weeks late) in Friuli-Venezia Giulia to August 7 (when the fiscal year was already nearly two-thirds over) in Calabria.[9]

3. Statistical and Information Services

Other things being equal, a government with better information about its constituents and their problems can respond more effectively. Thus all twenty regions were rated according to the breadth of their statistical and information facilities. At the bottom were six regions that had no such facilities at all—Abruzzi, Calabria, Campania, Marche, Molise, Puglia, and Sicily. At the top were five regions—Emilia-Romagna, Friuli-Venezia Giulia, Lazio, Lombardia, and Toscana—with well-equipped information services, including field stations and facilities for original data collection, statistical processing, and computer-based analysis.[10]

Next, our investigation carried us beyond "process" measures and explored the content of policy decisions. The following pair of measures are based on a comprehensive examination of regional legislation.

4. Reform Legislation

In three diverse policy areas—economic development, territorial and environmental planning, and social services—we examined the entire legislative output of each region during the period 1978 to 1984. The topics of this extensive body of law ranged from urban zoning and kidney dialysis to in-service training for social workers and regional centers for industrial research and marketing. Our analysis used three broad criteria of evaluation:

- The *comprehensiveness* of the legislation, that is, the degree to which the corpus of regional law produced during this period addressed a broad or narrow range of social needs.
- The *coherence* of the legislation, that is, the degree to which the various legislative initiatives were coordinated and internally consistent; for example, a program of aid for small business that was coordinated with job-training and infrastructural projects ranked higher than one that (as Italians say) "showered" grants indiscriminately across the region.
- The *creativeness* of the legislation, that is, the degree to which it identified new needs, experimented with new services, or created incentives for new forms of private initiative.

Each region was graded from 1 to 5 in each of the three policy sectors. The summed scores ranged from 15 for Emilia-Romagna, representing excellent performance in all three sectors, to 3 for Calabria and Molise, corresponding to poor performance in all three. Although these legislative assessments are somewhat more impressionistic and less precise than the previous measures, they reflect a careful assessment of the content of regional policy, and (as we shall see later) they turn out to mirror closely the evaluations offered by the citizens of each region. Our criteria for evaluating reform legislation do not seem very different in practice from the criteria used by Italian voters.[11]

5. Legislative Innovation

In Italy, as in the United States, many legislative ideas tend to diffuse across subnational governments, as an attractive innovation introduced by a relatively advanced council is picked up and passed in less advanced regions.[12] We examined twelve diverse topics on which similar laws appeared in many of the regions: air and water pollution, promotion of fisheries, consumer protection, preventive medical clinics, strip mining regulation, hotel classification, wildlife protection, and so on. Despite differing local needs and priorities, certain regions were consistent leaders or consistent laggards on nearly all these topics, with only three or four exceptions. (The leaders and laggards on mental health care, regional "ombudsmen," and promotion of voluntarism did not match the overall pattern. The entire set of model laws is shown in Table 3.1.)[13] Our metric here is as follows: On average, across these twelve domains, how soon after the first appearance of a model law was it picked up by a given region? The region that pioneered a particular law was given a score of 100, and a region that had not adopted it at all was given a score of 0.[14] Average scores ranged from 74 for Emilia-Romagna to 4 for Calabria. In fact, only one of these twelve model laws was ever enacted by Calabria, whereas Emilia-Romagna had passed all twelve and had been the pioneering region for five of the twelve.

TABLE 3.1
Assessing Legislative Innovation

Content of Model Law	Factor Loading
Strip mining regulation	0.812
Promotion of fisheries	0.806
Air/water pollution control	0.776
Hotel classification	0.756
Preventive medical clinics	0.718
Wildlife protection	0.638
Rationalization of commerce	0.624
Consumer protection	0.501
Labor market monitoring	0.432
Promotion of voluntary service	0.392
Regional ombudsmen	0.222
Mental health care	−0.026

Next, we turned from policy pronouncements to policy implementation. The following six indicators measure a region's capacity to carry out policy in virtually all of the major sectors of regional government activity, including public health, social welfare, industrial and agricultural development, and housing and urban policy. The first two of these indicators represent direct service delivery; the next one reflects the repertoire of policy tools deployed by each region; and finally three focus on how effective the regional governments were at using funds offered to them by the central government ("spending capacity").

Spending capacity might not be an appropriate indicator of institutional performance in all circumstances. However, in these three cases (agriculture, health, and housing), the need for additional investments was widely accepted, and full-cost funding was readily available to each region from the central authorities. Nevertheless, some regional governments accumulated enormous unexpended appropriations [*residui passivi*], because they lacked the organizational capacity and managerial infrastructure necessary to translate their expanding resources into action. On the other hand, more efficient regions were able to spend what they hoped to spend when they planned to spend it.

6. Day Care Centers

One of the earliest and most successful policy initiatives undertaken by the new regional governments was the provision of publicly supported day care centers. In 1977 the central government made substantial special funding for this purpose available to each region, so that the "opportunity cost" to the region itself for the program was negligible. By 1983, six years later, a number of regions had established wide networks of day care centers, but others had made virtually no progress. Our metric here is the number of regionally supported day care centers in operation by December 1983, standardized by the population of children aged zero to four.[15] This measure provides an unusually crisp indicator of a region's ability to implement policy at the grass-roots, given assured external funding. Scores ranged from one center per 400 children in Emilia-Romagna to one center per 12,560 children in Campania.

7. Family Clinics

In the health sector one important experiment, originally authorized by national legislation in 1974, was the family clinic (*consultorio familiare*).

One useful measure of a region's ability to implement policy reforms is the number of family clinics, standardized for regional population, in operation by May 1978. On that date, Umbria (at the top of this ranking) had one family clinic for every 15,000 residents; Puglia had exactly one clinic to serve its 3,850,000 inhabitants; and the regions of Trentino-Alto Adige, Molise, and Valle d'Aosta had established no family clinics at all.[16]

8. Industrial Policy Instruments

In 1970, as we noted in Chapter 2, the widespread hope that the new regional governments could foster more rapid economic development was an important motivation for the institutional reform. When funds subsequently became available, some regions simply wrote checks to subsidize individual firms, often as a form of patronage. Other, more advanced regions, however, provided infrastructural support, improved public services, and encouraged public-private partnerships.[17] One crude measure of the sophistication of each region in the area of industrial policy can be computed by noting which of an array of potential tools of industrial policy the region actually deployed:

- regional economic development plan
- regional land use plan
- industrial parks
- regional development finance agencies
- industrial development and marketing consortia
- job-training programs

A few regions, such as Friuli-Venezia Giulia, had used all six of these techniques as of 1984. Calabria, at the other extreme, had tried only two.[18]

9. Agricultural Spending Capacity

In 1977 the central government allocated substantial funds to each region (totaling roughly $400 million) for investments in agriculture, including irrigation, reforestation, livestock production, horticulture, and viticulture. Lazio, for example, used its share of the national funds to upgrade the production of Frascati wines. On the other hand, political gridlock and administrative inefficiency kept several regions from spending any of the available funds at all, even though these happened to be regions in which agriculture is economically crucial. A region's ability to carry out policy initiatives in this important economic sector can be measured by the fraction of the funds allocated to the region that the region actually disbursed as planned during the next three years (1978–1980). Spending ranged from 97 percent in Valle d'Aosta to 0 percent in Calabria and Molise.[19]

10. Local Health Unit Expenditures

Financially speaking, the most substantial responsibility decentralized to the regions after 1977 was the national health service, including hospitals, clinics, and health insurance. The primary organizational innovation for implementing these new responsibilities, according to the national legislation of 1978, was to be the "Local Health Unit" (*Unità Sanitaria Locale* or USL). One measure of the readiness of each region to fulfill its responsibilities in this area is per capita USL expenditures, as of 1983, five years after the enactment of the national statute. (Once again, full funding for the health services was provided by the central authorities. Since USL expenditures are *negatively* correlated with measures of morbidity and infant mortality, the results are not vulnerable to the interpretation that the low-spending regions had less need for public health services.) Scores on this measure ranged from Toscana, which spent 34 percent more than the national average, to Sicily and Basilicata, each of which spent 25 percent below the national average.[20]

11. Housing and Urban Development

Our surveys showed that housing was a high and increasing priority for regional officials throughout Italy, especially in the 1980s. Beginning in 1971, and especially after 1978, the central government offered plentiful funding to each region to support subsidized housing (both public and privately owned), housing rehabilitation, and land acquisition for urban development. Regions were required to formulate four-year housing programs and to set criteria for the allocation of funds. We gathered data in 1979, 1981, 1985, and 1987 on the ability of the regions to use these funds, as measured by the fraction of the funds authorized by the central authorities that the region actually disbursed. (Spending capacity in this sense is *positively* correlated with earlier measures of housing quality, thus ruling out the possible interpretation that slow spending merely reflected low needs.) A composite measure covering all four years ranges, on average, from 67 percent in Emilia-Romagna to 32 percent in Sicily and Campania.[21]

All our measures of performance so far have taken the perspective of a policymaker: How efficient is the budget process? How innovative is the legislation? How many day care centers or family clinics or agricultural loans have been provided? What is missing from our analysis so far is an evaluation of the regional government from the point of view of a citizen with a problem.

12. Bureaucratic Responsiveness

To assess the governments' "street-level" responsiveness, we devised a slightly deceptive, but innocuous and highly informative experiment.[22] In January 1983 Italian colleagues approached the bureaucracies in each region, requesting information about three specific (but fictitious) problems:

- The health department was asked about reimbursement procedures for a medical bill incurred while the inquirer was on vacation abroad.
- The vocational education department was asked about job training facilities for "a brother" just finishing junior high school.
- The agriculture department was asked, on behalf of "a farmer friend," for information about loans and subsidies for experimental crops.

The initial requests were made by mail, and the replies were evaluated for promptness, clarity, and comprehensiveness. If no timely reply was received, follow-up telephone calls and (when necessary) personal visits were made. In either case, the quality and alacrity of the response was evaluated. This experiment enabled us to construct a composite index of the responsiveness of three important agencies, comparable across all twenty regions.[23] In the most efficient regions (Emilia-Romagna and Valle d'Aosta), two of the three inquiries received thorough replies within a week of our initial letter, and the third required a single telephone call. In the least efficient regions (Calabria, Campania, and Sardinia), none of the mailed inquiries received any reply at all, and two of the three requests required many weeks, several phone calls, and a personal visit to satisfy.

COHERENCE AND RELIABILITY OF THE INDEX OF INSTITUTIONAL PERFORMANCE

Our list of twelve indicators is intended to reflect the diversity of things that modern governments do to and for their citizens. The differences in performance levels suggested by these indicators are, in absolute terms, quite remarkable: cabinets five times more durable in one region than another; budgets delayed by three weeks in one region, seven months in another; day care centers and family clinics and agricultural loans and subsidized housing many times more common in one region than another (despite equal access to funding); citizen inquiries answered promptly in some regions and not at all in others.

Even so, we began this research skeptical that such independent indicators of institutional performance would closely cohere, given measurement frailties, differences in regional priorities, and the multiple influences on any single institutional activity. For example, although the collapse of a regional cabinet may typically represent institutional instability, it might also be caused by the untimely death of a key figure. Legislative creativity might be completely unconnected with administrative follow-through, we reasoned. Or perhaps some regions give special emphasis to housing, while others devote their energies to agriculture. Perhaps a region's failure to build day care centers or family clinics reflects ideological choice, not administrative inefficiency. No single indicator can capture all differences in institutional success with perfect fidelity, and perhaps success along one dimension would be quite uncorrelated with success along others.

Against this background, we were gratified to discover (as shown in Appendix C) a surprisingly high consistency among our twelve diverse indicators of institutional performance.[24] Regions that have stable cabinets, adopt their budgets on time, spend their appropriations as planned, and pioneer new legislation are, for the most part, the same regions that provide day care centers and family clinics, develop comprehensive urban planning, make loans to farmers, and answer their mail promptly. On the basis of these twelve indicators, we have constructed a summary Index of Institutional Performance. Table 3.2 displays the full list of indicators and shows how each is correlated with this summary index.

The intercorrelations among these measures of institutional performance are far from perfect. Most regions *are* better at some things than they are at others. Institutional success, examined microscopically, must be measured along more than one dimension. By and large, however, our technique for combining these diverse indicators into a single index reduces the idiosyncratic impact of any single measure. More important, as these data also confirm, some regions are high-ranked by virtually every yardstick, whereas other regions are unsuccessful by almost every measure. Our composite measure is both comprehensive and internally consistent.

How stable and reliable is this assessment over time? Is institutional performance as we have measured it a durable feature of the regional governments, or do regions move randomly up and down the standings from year to year?

TABLE 3.2
Index of Institutional Performance,
1978–1985

Performance Indicator	Factor Loading
Reform legislation, 1978–1984	0.874
Day care centers, 1983	0.851
Housing and urban development, 1979–1987	0.807
Statistical and information services, 1981	0.797
Legislative innovation, 1978–1984	0.779
Cabinet stability, 1975–1985[a]	0.681
Family clinics, 1978	0.640
Bureaucratic responsiveness, 1983	0.625
Industrial policy instruments, 1984	0.580
Budget promptness, 1979–1985[a]	0.577
Local health unit spending, 1983	0.545
Agricultural spending capacity, 1978–1980	0.468

[a] Scoring for cabinet stability and budget promptness has been reversed from that described in the text, so that a high absolute score corresponds to high performance.

In the earliest years of the Italian regional experiment, just after the completion of the first full legislature, we carried out a preliminary evaluation of the success of each of the fifteen "ordinary" regions.[25] This preliminary assessment was based on performance indicators broadly comparable to those described in this chapter, but the underlying data were drawn from the 1970–1976 period and thus did not overlap with the data we have been assessing here. The earlier assessment was also not as broad-gauged as that outlined in this chapter; in particular, since the regions had just opened for business, measures of policy implementation were unavailable.

Figure 3.1, which compares the results from these two analyses, shows a remarkable stability in relative success. For the most part, regions that had scored well in the earlier evaluation rank at the top of the later, fuller Index of Institutional Performance, and laggards on the former were laggards on the latter as well. A few exceptions to this pattern stand out: Lombardia, earlier ranked near the very top, fell back a bit in the later ratings, whereas Piedmont made notable gains. Nevertheless, the overall stability is striking. While this immobility might be disheartening to lower-ranked governments, it is theoretically important and methodologically reassuring. Differences in institutional performance, as measured here, are reasonably stable and thus worth explaining.

FIGURE 3.1
Institutional Performance, 1970–1976 and 1978–1985
*For a list of the abbreviations of regional names used in all
scattergrams in this book, see Appendix D.*

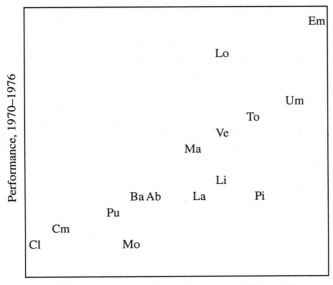

Index of Institutional Performance, 1978–1985
Correlation: $r = .78$

INSTITUTIONAL PERFORMANCE AND
CONSTITUENCY EVALUATIONS

This summary index reflects important, coherent differences in institutional performance. But are they consistent with the evaluations offered by the institutions' protagonists and constituents? Do "objective" measures of institutional performance correspond to the views of Italians about their own regional governments? Or are standards for judging government so thoroughly idiosyncratic and pervaded by cultural relativism that our judgments and the judgments of Italian voters and community leaders are unrelated?[26]

This test is not easy, for observers within any single region are not well placed to make fine-grained comparisons with other regional governments, nor is there assurance that inhabitants of the various regions have similar standards or thresholds of satisfaction.[27] On the other hand, our interviews revealed that businessmen, mayors, union leaders, journalists, and other community leaders, and even a fair number of ordinary citizens, know much about the strengths and weaknesses of their own regional

FIGURE 3.2
Institutional Performance (1978–1985) and
Citizen Satisfaction (1977–1988)

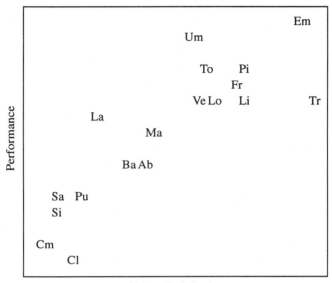

Citizen Satisfaction
Correlation: $r = .84$

government. Moreover, since these governments are meant to be representative institutions, their constituents' views have a special standing in
assessment of their performance.

In fact, the Index of Institutional Performance is remarkably consistent
with the appraisals offered by the regional attentive public and by the
electorate as a whole. Let us begin by asking how ordinary Italians evaluate their regional governments.

Six times between January 1977 and December 1988, or roughly once
every two years, we asked Italians, "How satisfied or unsatisfied are you
with the way in which this region is governed?" Although the sample
sizes in the smaller regions were too small in any single survey for wholly
reliable estimates of opinion, regional rankings were generally stable
from year to year, so the six surveys can be combined to obtain a single,
much more reliable estimate of citizen satisfaction, region by region.[28]

Thus we are in a position to compare our "objective" assessment of the
performance of the regional governments with the views of their own
constituents. Figure 3.2 shows the remarkably strong concordance between the two measures. With only one minor anomaly, involving the
"special" region of Trentino-Alto Adige, the citizens of Italy's regions
completely concur with our evaluation of those governments.[29] Effective-

ness and responsiveness—the two fundamental criteria for democratic government—turn out (at least in this case) to be closely associated with one another. Regional governments that enact innovative legislation, implement their budgets as planned, build day care centers, answer their mail, and so on, are more popular with their constituents than those that do not.[30]

Institutional performance as we have measured it is, in fact, the only consistent predictor of who is satisfied with regional government and who is dissatisfied. Across our six national surveys, approval of the activities of the regional government is uncorrelated with *any* of the standard sociological categories. The well educated do not differ from the uneducated, nor the wealthy from the poor, nor city-dwellers from rural folk, nor farmers or housewives from businessmen or blue collar workers, nor men from women, nor young from old.[31] In other words, in the regions that are relatively successful by our "objective" measures, people from all walks of life are relatively satisfied, while in the low-performance regions most people are dissatisfied. These governments apparently differ less in terms of which particular interests they serve than in terms of how well they serve the common interest.

Supporters of the party in control of the regional government, not surprisingly, express more satisfaction with its performance than do supporters of the opposition. Party loyalty is a less powerful determinant of satisfaction, however, than is the "objective" performance of the government. Throughout our six surveys between 1977 and 1988, *supporters* of the ruling party in *low*-performance regions were less satisfied with the performance of regional government than were *opposition* party supporters in *high*-performance regions. As Figure 3.3 shows, an average of 42 percent of government *opponents* in high-performance regions were reasonably satisfied with the government's performance, as opposed to only 33 percent of government *loyalists* in low-performance regions.[32] Controlling for performance, party loyalty makes a difference of about 14 percentage points in satisfaction, whereas controlling for party loyalty, performance makes a difference of about 24 percentage points. In other words, objective differences in performance are nearly twice as important as partisan loyalties in accounting for the satisfaction of Italian voters with their regional governments.

Yet another perspective on the operations of the regional governments comes from our 1982 nationwide survey of community leaders—that is, provincial presidents, mayors of large cities and small towns, bankers, trade union leaders, journalists, and representatives of industry, commerce, artisanry, agriculture and the cooperative movement. More than half of these leaders report meeting regularly with regional officials, and 59 percent say that the regional government has had a "very important" or

FIGURE 3.3
Satisfaction with Regional Government,
by Government Performance and Party Support

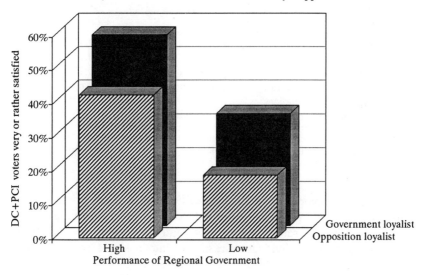

"rather important" impact on the interests of the organization they represent. Thus, most of these men and women have direct, personal knowledge from which to render judgments about the performance of their regional governments.

These community leaders deal regularly with their regional government. Mayors seek approval of zoning ordinances. Farm leaders inquire about irrigation projects. Business people discuss regional economic planning with regional officials. Labor leaders consult about job training programs. Thus we were able to elicit detailed evaluations of the activities of the regional institution from these men and women. As described in Chapter 2, we inquired about the accessibility of regional officials, about the programmatic directions of regional policies, about the feasibility of particular regional projects, about the dispatch with which the regional bureaucracy processed specific cases, about coordination between the regional and local governments, and about the technical qualifications and conscientiousness of regional administrators. Most community leaders were very critical about the region's inability to implement policies, although they were more complimentary about the programmatic choices and accessibility of the new government.[33]

Judgments about these several different aspects of institutional performance turned out to be rather closely intercorrelated, in the sense that any given regional government tended to be rated consistently favorably (or

TABLE 3.3

Community Leaders' Evaluations of Regional Government, 1982

Aspects of Regional Government Activities[a]	Factor Loading
Feasibility of regional projects	0.735
Time required to process a case	0.714
Coordination with local government	0.700
Qualifications and diligence of personnel	0.697
Programmatic choices	0.676
Openness to consultation with your organization	0.657

[a] Summary Index based on responses to the following question: "How satisfied are you with these six aspects of the activities of the regional government in this region?"

consistently unfavorably) on all six specific aspects of governmental performance. Those regions that were judged to be most creative programmatically were also said to act most promptly and listen most carefully. We combined the individual assessments into a single comprehensive index of the community leaders' evaluations, as outlined in Table 3.3. Their responses provide yet another measure of the efficacy and efficiency of the regional governments.

The size of each regional sample in this survey was quite small, averaging only fifteen leaders per region, so the score for any specific region may be marred by sampling error.[34] It is nevertheless instructive to compare these evaluations, region by region, with our Index of Institutional Performance. Figure 3.4 shows that the two are quite closely correlated, particularly given the attenuating effects of the small samples. Our evaluation of institutional performance generally conforms to the judgments of people who deal with these governments day to day.[35]

The close correlation between our impersonal, "objective" assessment of these governments and the evaluation offered by their own constituents is not merely methodologically gratifying. It also underlines the risks of *excessive* cultural relativism, as well as the perils of the so-called "revealed preference" approach to government outcomes: the assumption that people get the kind of government that they want. It is sometimes said that government in some parts of Italy—and in many other parts of the world, for that matter—is lethargic, inefficient, and corrupt "because the people like it that way there." Figures 3.2 and 3.4 are strong evidence to the contrary. At least in Italy, people everywhere recognize the distinction between good government and bad, using essentially the same basic standards of efficiency, creativity, coherence, responsiveness, and practical achievement. They like good government, and they dislike bad. This

FIGURE 3.4
Institutional Performance (1978–1985) and
Community Leaders' Satisfaction (1982)

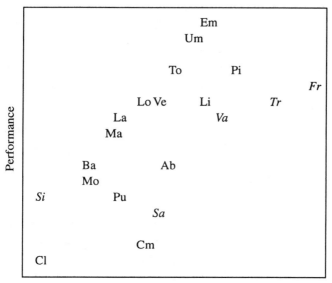

Community Leaders' Satisfaction
Correlation: $r = .66$

Ordinary regions only: $r = .77$
Special regions only: $r = .84$
Special regions are shown in italics.

does *not* mean, of course, that everyone agrees on what policy priorities should be pursued or how those policies should be implemented, that there is "one best way" to govern or that government can be reduced to technique. It does mean that the difference between better and worse is widely appreciated.

CONCLUSIONS

What have we learned from this chapter? Some regional governments have been consistently more successful than others—more efficient in their internal operations, more creative in their policy initiatives, more effective in implementing those initiatives. These differences in performance have been stable over more than a decade. They are widely recognized by constituents of the regional governments, both ordinary citizens and community leaders.

Some places are better governed than others, even when the governments involved have identical structures and equivalent legal and financial resources.[36] Moreover, it is general institutional effectiveness that varies consistently from region to region, not merely whether one government has a superior day-care program this year or a more efficient budget planner.

If this is so, then one of the most urgent priorities of political scientists, as well as concerned citizens, should be to understand why. Doubtless, certain interests are served by the activities we have labeled poor performance. Weak zoning, for example, may favor construction firms and land developers. Nevertheless, better government—government that serves the interests of most of the people most of the time—can be identified. Some of these new institutions are working well, while others are not. What explains these differences in institutional performance? That is the question to which we turn next.

CHAPTER 4

Explaining Institutional Performance

IT IS BEST to begin a journey of exploration with a map. Figure 4.1 shows the level of institutional performance of each of Italy's twenty regions. The most striking feature of this map is the strong North-South gradient. Although the correlation between latitude and institutional performance is not perfect, the northern regional governments as a group have been more successful than their southern counterparts. To be sure, this discovery is not unexpected. In the words of a thousand travelogues, "the South is different."

We shall have occasion to return to this conspicuous contrast between North and South in Chapters 5 and 6. However, if our purpose is not simply description, but understanding, this observation merely reformulates our problem. What is it that differentiates the successful regions in the North from the unsuccessful ones in the South, and the more from the less successful within each section? As adumbrated in Chapter 1, we shall concentrate here on two broad possibilities:

- Socioeconomic modernity, that is, the results of the industrial revolution.
- "Civic community," that is, patterns of civic involvement and social solidarity.

Toward the end of this chapter we shall also explore briefly several other plausible explanations, which turn out to be less powerful.

SOCIOECONOMIC MODERNITY

The most important social and economic development in Western society in the last several centuries has been the industrial revolution and its aftermath, that colossal watershed in human history that has fascinated social theorists, Marxists and non-Marxists alike, for more than one hundred years. Vast populations moved from the land to the factory. Standards of living increased almost beyond belief. Class structures were transformed. Capital stocks, both physical and human, deepened. Levels of education and standards of public health rose. Economic and technological capabilities multiplied.

Political sociologists have long argued that the prospects for stable democratic government depend on this social and economic transforma-

FIGURE 4.1
Institutional Performance in the Italian Regions, 1978–1985

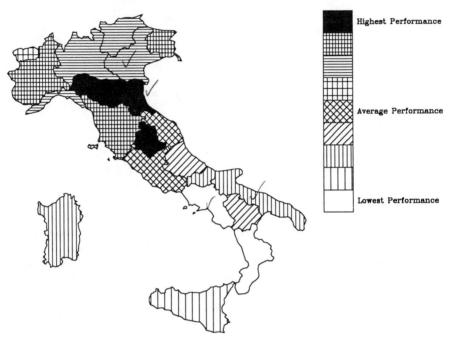

tion. Empirically speaking, few generalizations are more firmly established than that effective democracy is correlated with socioeconomic modernization.[1] Reviewing the incidence of successful democracies around the world, for example, Kenneth Bollen and Robert Jackman report that "the level of economic development has a pronounced effect on political democracy, even when noneconomic factors are considered. . . . GNP is the dominant explanatory variable."[2] Wealth eases burdens, both public and private, and facilitates social accommodation. Education expands the number of trained professionals, as well as the sophistication of the citizenry. Economic growth expands the middle class, long thought to be the bulwark of stable, effective democracy. After examining the successes and failures of urban governments around the world, Robert C. Fried and Francine Rabinovitz concluded that "of all the theories to explain the performance differences, the most powerful one is modernization."[3]

In Italy much of this transformation has occurred within the last generation, although it had begun at the end of the last century. Change has touched all parts of the peninsula but, as our trip from postindustrial Seveso to preindustrial Pietrapertosa reminded us, the North is much

FIGURE 4.2
Economic Modernity and Institutional Performance

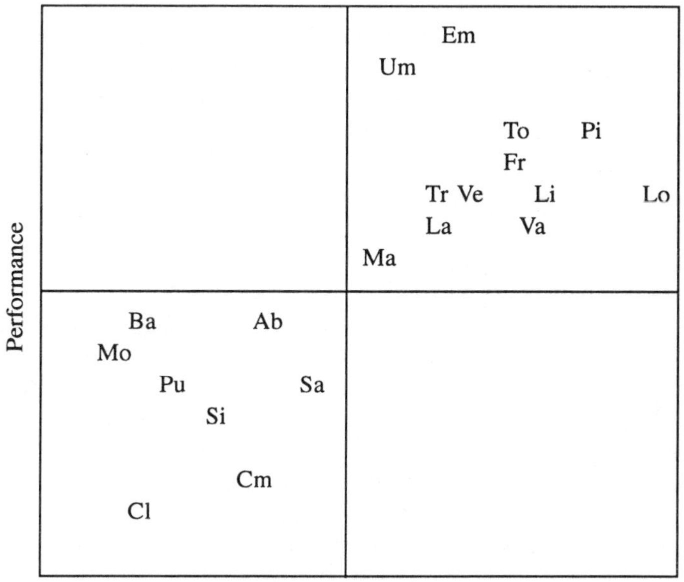

Economic Modernity
Correlation: $r = .77$

more advanced than the South. It is hard to believe that this stark contrast in levels of affluence and economic modernity is not an important part of the explanation—perhaps even the sole explanation—for the differences we have discovered in the performance of regional governments.

Figure 4.2, which arrays the Italian regions according to their degree of economic modernity and institutional performance, illustrates both the power and the limitations of this interpretation of our puzzle.[4]

The wealthier, more modern regions of the North (concentrated in the upper right quadrant of Figure 4.2) have a head start over their poorer counterparts in material and human resources. Their advantage is symbolized by the headquarters of the respective regional governments. Contrast the nondescript structures on dusty piazzas in several southern regions with the thirty-story skyscraper in the heart of Milan housing the Lombardia government, built originally for the Pirelli multinational corporation. Public health officers or public works managers in northern regions can call on the full resources of one of the most advanced economies in the world. Their southern counterparts face the daunting problems of under-development with little local help. Take a single but revealing example: in the 1970s there were hundreds of data-processing firms in Milan, but scarcely any in Potenza. Regional administrators seeking help in measuring their problems or managing their personnel are clearly better off in Lombardia than in Basilicata.[5]

To be sure, it cannot be merely the financial resources available to the regional governments that account for the North-South disparity in performance. Funding for the regional governments is provided by the central authorities according to a redistributive formula that favors poorer regions. Indeed, our survey of institutional performance showed that many of the most backward regions have more funds available than they have been able to expend. Figure 4.2, however, suggests that this fiscal redistribution apparently cannot compensate for the immense differences in socioeconomic and technological infrastructure.

Yet the more closely one examines the patterns in Figure 4.2, the more evident are the limitations of this interpretation. The regions appear divided into two quadrants, the haves and the have-nots, with governments in the latter regions displaying consistently lower levels of performance. The marked differences in performance *within* each quadrant, however, are wholly inexplicable in terms of economic development.[6] Campania, the region around Naples, is more advanced economically than Molise and Basilicata, at the very bottom of the developmental hierarchy, but the two latter governments are visibly more effective than Campania's. Lombardia, Piemonte, and Liguria—the three corners of the famed industrial triangle of the North—are all wealthier than Emilia-Romagna and Umbria (or at least they were in the early 1970s), but the latter two governments were distinctly more successful. Wealth and economic development cannot be the entire story.

Economic modernity is somehow associated with high-performance public institutions—that much is clear. What our simple analysis so far cannot reveal is whether modernity is a cause of performance (perhaps one among several), whether performance is perhaps in some way a cause of modernity, whether both are influenced by a third factor (so that the association between the two is in some sense spurious), or whether the link between modernity and performance is even more complex. We shall return to those more complicated—and more interesting—questions later in this chapter and in the following two chapters.

THE CIVIC COMMUNITY: SOME THEORETICAL SPECULATIONS

In sixteenth-century Florence, reflecting on the unstable history of republican institutions in ancient times as well as in Renaissance Italy, Nicolò Machiavelli and several of his contemporaries concluded that whether free institutions succeeded or failed depended on the character of the citizens, or their "civic virtue."[7] According to a long-standing interpretation of Anglo-American political thought, this "republican" school of civic humanists was subsequently vanquished by Hobbes, Locke, and their liberal successors. Whereas the republicans had emphasized community and the obligations of citizenship, liberals stressed individualism and individual rights.[8] Far from presupposing a virtuous, public-spirited citizenry, it was said, the U.S. Constitution, with its checks and balances, was designed by Madison and his liberal colleagues precisely to make democracy safe for the unvirtuous. As a guide to understanding modern democracy, civic republicans were passé.

In recent years, however, a revisionist wave has swept across Anglo-American political philosophy. "The most dramatic revision [of the history of political thought] of the last 25 years or so," reports a not-uncritical Don Herzog, is "the discovery—and celebration—of civic humanism."[9] The revisionists argue that an important republican or communitarian tradition descended from the Greeks and Machiavelli through seventeenth-century England to the American Founders.[10] Far from exalting individualism, the new republicans recall John Winthrop's eloquent, communitarian admonition to the citizens of his "city set upon a hill": "We must delight in each other, make others' conditions our own, rejoyce together, mourn together, labor and suffer together, always having before our eyes our community as members of the same body."[11]

The new republican theorists have not gone unchallenged. The defenders of classical liberal individualism argue that the notion of community lauded by the new republicans is a "dangerous and anachronistic ideal."[12] Remarkably, this wide-ranging philosophical debate has so far taken place almost entirely without reference to systematic empirical research, whether within the Anglo-American world or elsewhere. Nevertheless, it contains the seeds for a theory of effective democratic governance: "As the proportion of nonvirtuous citizens increases significantly, the ability of liberal societies to function successfully will progressively diminish."[13] We want to explore empirically whether the success of a democratic government depends on the degree to which its surroundings approximate the ideal of a "civic community."[14]

But what might this "civic community" mean in practical terms? Reflecting upon the work of republican theorists, we can begin by sorting out some of the central themes in the philosophical debate.

Civic Engagement

Citizenship in a civic community is marked, first of all, by active participation in public affairs. "Interest in public issues and devotion to public causes are the key signs of civic virtue," suggests Michael Walzer.[15] To be sure, not all political activity deserves the label "virtuous" or contributes to the commonweal. "A steady recognition and pursuit of the public good at the expense of all purely individual and private ends" seems close to the core meaning of civic virtue.[16]

The dichotomy between self-interest and altruism can easily be overdrawn, for no mortal, and no successful society, can renounce the powerful motivation of self-interest. Citizens in the civic community are not required to be altruists. In the civic community, however, citizens pursue what Tocqueville termed "self-interest properly understood," that is, self-interest defined in the context of broader public needs, self-interest that is "enlightened" rather than "myopic," self-interest that is alive to the interests of others.[17]

The absence of civic virtue is exemplified in the "amoral familism" that Edward Banfield reported as the dominant ethos in Montegrano, a small town not far from our Pietrapertosa: "Maximize the material, short-run advantage of the nuclear family; assume that all others will do likewise."[18] Participation in a civic community is more public-spirited than that, more oriented to shared benefits. Citizens in a civic community, though not selfless saints, regard the public domain as more than a battleground for pursuing personal interest.

Political Equality

Citizenship in the civic community entails equal rights and obligations for all. Such a community is bound together by horizontal relations of reciprocity and cooperation, not by vertical relations of authority and dependency. Citizens interact as equals, not as patrons and clients nor as governors and petitioners. To be sure, not all classical republican theorists were democrats. Nor can a contemporary civic community forgo the advantages of a division of labor and the need for political leadership. Leaders in such a community, however, must be, and must conceive themselves to be, responsible to their fellow citizens. Both absolute power and the absence of power can be corrupting, for both instill a sense of irresponsibility.[19] The more that politics approximates the ideal of political equality among citizens following norms of reciprocity and engaged in self-government, the more civic that community may be said to be.

Solidarity, Trust, and Tolerance

Citizens in a civic community, on most accounts, are more than merely active, public-spirited, and equal. Virtuous citizens are helpful, respectful, and trustful toward one another, even when they differ on matters of substance. The civic community is not likely to be blandly conflict-free, for its citizens have strong views on public issues, but they are tolerant of their opponents. "This is probably as close as we can come to that 'friendship' which Aristotle thought should characterize relations among members of the same political community," argues Michael Walzer.[20] As Gianfranco Poggi has noted of Tocqueville's theory of democratic governance, "Interpersonal trust is probably the moral orientation that most needs to be diffused among the people if republican society is to be maintained."[21]

Even seemingly "self-interested" transactions take on a different character when they are embedded in social networks that foster mutual trust, as we shall see in more detail in Chapter 6. Fabrics of trust enable the civic community more easily to surmount what economists call "opportunism," in which shared interests are unrealized because each individual, acting in wary isolation, has an incentive to defect from collective action.[22] A review of community development in Latin America highlights the social importance of grass-roots cooperative enterprises and of episodes of political mobilization—even if they are unsuccessful in immediate, instrumental terms—precisely because of their indirect effects of "dispelling isolation and mutual distrust."[23]

Associations: Social Structures of Cooperation

The norms and values of the civic community are embodied in, and reinforced by, distinctive social structures and practices. The most relevant social theorist here remains Alexis de Tocqueville. Reflecting on the social conditions that sustained "Democracy in America," Tocqueville attributed great importance to the Americans' propensity to form civil and political organizations:

> Americans of all ages, all stations in life, and all types of disposition are forever forming associations. There are not only commercial and industrial associations in which all take part, but others of a thousand different types—religious, moral, serious, futile, very general and very limited, immensely large and very minute. . . . Thus the most democratic country in the world now is that in which men have in our time carried to the highest perfection the art of pursuing in common the objects of common desires and have applied this new technique to the greatest number of purposes.[24]

Civil associations contribute to the effectiveness and stability of democratic government, it is argued, both because of their "internal" effects on individual members and because of their "external" effects on the wider polity.

Internally, associations instill in their members habits of cooperation, solidarity, and public-spiritedness. Tocqueville observed that "feelings and ideas are renewed, the heart enlarged, and the understanding developed only by the reciprocal action of men one upon another."[25] This suggestion is supported by evidence from the *Civic Culture* surveys of citizens in five countries, including Italy, showing that members of associations displayed more political sophistication, social trust, political participation, and "subjective civic competence."[26] Participation in civic organizations inculcates skills of cooperation as well as a sense of shared responsibility for collective endeavors. Moreover, when individuals belong to "cross-cutting" groups with diverse goals and members, their attitudes will tend to moderate as a result of group interaction and cross-pressures.[27] These effects, it is worth noting, do not require that the manifest purpose of the association be political. Taking part in a choral society or a bird-watching club can teach self-discipline and an appreciation for the joys of successful collaboration.[28]

Externally, what twentieth-century political scientists have called "interest articulation" and "interest aggregation" are enhanced by a dense network of secondary associations. In Tocqueville's words:

> When some view is represented by an association, it must take clearer and more precise shape. It counts its supporters and involves them in its cause; these supporters get to know one another, and numbers increase zeal. An association unites the energies of divergent minds and vigorously directs them toward a clearly indicated goal.[29]

According to this thesis, a dense network of secondary associations both embodies and contributes to effective social collaboration. Thus, contrary to the fear of faction expressed by thinkers like Jean-Jacques Rousseau, in a civic community associations of like-minded equals contribute to effective democratic governance.[30]

More recently, an independent line of research has reinforced the view that associationism is a necessary precondition for effective self-government. Summarizing scores of case studies of Third World development, Milton Esman and Norman Uphoff conclude that local associations are a crucial ingredient in successful strategies of rural development:

> A vigorous network of membership organizations is essential to any serious effort to overcome mass poverty under the conditions that are likely to prevail in most developing countries for the predictable future. . . . While other components—infrastructure investments, supportive public policies, appropriate technologies, and bureaucratic and market institutions—are necessary, we cannot visualize any strategy of rural development combining growth in productivity with broad distribution of benefits in which participatory local organizations are not prominent.[31]

Unhappily from the point of view of social engineering, Esman and Uphoff find that local organizations "implanted" from the outside have a high failure rate. The most successful local organizations represent indigenous, participatory initiatives in relatively cohesive local communities.[32]

Although Esman and Uphoff do not say so explicitly, their conclusions are quite consistent with Banfield's interpretation of life in Montegrano, "the extreme poverty and backwardness of which is to be explained largely (but not entirely) by the inability of the villagers to act together for their common good or, indeed, for any end transcending the immediate material interest of the nuclear family."[33] Banfield's critics have disagreed with his attribution of this behavior to an "ethos," but they have not dissented from his description of the absence of collaboration in Montegrano, the striking lack of "deliberate concerted action" to improve community conditions.[34]

Both defenders and critics of civic republicanism have made intriguing philosophical points. We wish to confront the question that has so far remained unaddressed in any empirical way: Is there any connection between the "civic-ness" of a community and the quality of its governance?

THE CIVIC COMMUNITY: TESTING THE THEORY

Lacking detailed ethnographic accounts of hundreds of communities throughout the regions of Italy, how can we assess the degree to which social and political life in each of those regions approximates the ideal of a civic community? What systematic evidence is there on patterns of social solidarity and civic participation? We shall here present evidence on four indicators of the "civic-ness" of regional life—two that correspond directly to Tocqueville's broad conception of what we have termed the civic community, and two that refer more immediately to political behavior.

One key indicator of civic sociability must be the vibrancy of associational life. Fortunately, a census of all associations in Italy, local as well as national, enables us to specify precisely the number of amateur soccer clubs, choral societies, hiking clubs, bird-watching groups, literary circles, hunters' associations, Lions Clubs, and the like in each community and region of Italy.[35] The primary spheres of activity of these recreational and cultural associations are shown in Table 4.1.

Leaving aside labor unions for the moment, sports clubs are by far the most common sort of secondary association among Italians, but other types of cultural and leisure activities are also prominent. Standardized for population differences, these data show that in the efflorescence of their associational life, some regions of Italy rival Tocqueville's America

TABLE 4.1
Local Associations in Italy: Spheres of Activity

Sphere of Activity	Percentage of Associations
Sports clubs	73
Other associations	27
Of which:	
Leisure time	42
Cultural and scientific activities	21
Music and theater	19
Technical or economic	4
Health and social services	4
Other	10

Source: *Le Associazioni Italiane*, ed. Alberto Mortara (Milan: Franco Angeli, 1985), p. 57.

of congenital "joiners," whereas the inhabitants of other regions are accurately typified by the isolated and suspicious "amoral familists" of Banfield's Montegrano. In Italy's twenty regions, the density of sports clubs ranges from one club for every 377 residents in Valle d'Aosta and 549 in Trentino-Alto Adige to one club for every 1847 residents in Puglia. The figures for associations other than sports clubs range from 1050 inhabitants per group in Trentino-Alto Adige and 2117 in Liguria to 13,100 inhabitants per group in Sardinia. These are our first clues as to which regions most closely approximate the ideal of the civic community.[36]

Tocqueville also stressed the connection in modern society between civic vitality, associations, and local newspapers:

> When no firm and lasting ties any longer unite men, it is impossible to obtain the cooperation of any great number of them unless you can persuade every man whose help is required that he serves his private interests by voluntarily uniting his efforts to those of all the others. That cannot be done habitually and conveniently without the help of a newspaper. Only a newspaper can put the same thought at the same time before a thousand readers. . . . So hardly any democratic association can carry on without a newspaper.[37]

In the contemporary world, other mass media also serve the function of town crier, but particularly in today's Italy, newspapers remain the medium with the broadest coverage of community affairs. Newspaper readers are better informed than nonreaders and thus better equipped to participate in civic deliberations. Similarly, newspaper readership is a mark of citizen interest in community affairs.

The incidence of newspaper readership varies widely across the Italian regions.[38] In 1975, the fraction of households in which at least one member read a daily newspaper ranged from 80 percent in Liguria to 35 percent in Molise. This, then, is the second element in our assessment of the degree to which political and social life in Italy's regions approximates a civic community.

One standard measure of political participation is electoral turnout. Turnout in Italian general elections, however, is marred as a measure of civic involvement for several reasons:

· Until recently Italian law required all citizens to vote in general elections, and although enforcement of this law was uneven, it presumably brought many people to the polls whose motivation was scarcely "civic."
· Party organizations have an obvious incentive to influence elections, and thus electoral turnout presumably varies with party organizational strength and activity, independently of the voters' own civic engagement.
· In many parts of the peninsula where patron-client networks are rampant, voting in general elections represents a straightforward *quid pro quo* for immediate, personal patronage benefits, hardly a mark of "civic" involvement.

Since 1974, however, a previously unused constitutional provision for national referenda has been repeatedly employed to resolve a wide range of controversial issues. Some of these deliberations, like the 1974 vote on the legalization of divorce, aroused deeply held religious beliefs. Others, like the 1985 referendum on escalator clauses in national wage contracts, affected the pocketbooks of many voters and engaged class cleavages. Still others, like the 1981 vote on anti-terrorism laws or the 1987 vote on nuclear power, triggered cross-cutting, "new politics" alignments. Each referendum invited citizens to express their views on a major issue of public policy.

Turnout in these referenda has been significantly lower than in general elections, no doubt because of the absence of the "uncivic" motivations enumerated above. Electoral turnout in recent decades has averaged above 90 percent, whereas turnout in successive referenda has dropped steadily from 86 percent in the first referendum in 1974 to 64 percent in the latest referendum in 1987. As Italy's leading student of referenda turnout has observed, "Those who use the vote as an occasion for 'exchange' have scant motivation to go to the polls when the election (as in the case of the referendum) does not offer the possibility of obtaining immediate, personal benefits."[39] The primary motivation of the referendum voter is concern for public issues, perhaps enhanced by a keener than average sense of civic duty, so that turnout for referenda offers a relatively "clean" measure of civic involvement.

Regional differences in turnout in the successive referenda have been strong and stable, even as the nationwide averages have diminished. Turnout in five key referenda between 1974 and 1987 for which region-

TABLE 4.2
Index of Referenda Turnout, 1974–1987

Year	Subject Matter	Factor Loading
1974	Divorce legalization	0.990
1978	Public financing of parties	0.988
1981	Public security and anti-terrorism	0.996
1985	Wage escalator clauses	0.991
1987	Nuclear power	0.976

by-region returns are available averaged 89 percent in Emilia-Romagna, as contrasted with 60 percent in Calabria. Moreover, the regional ranking with respect to turnout has been virtually identical across the whole range of issues: divorce (1974), public financing of parties (1978), terrorism and public security (1981), wage escalator clauses (1985), and nuclear power (1987). In short, citizens in some parts of Italy choose to be actively involved in public deliberations on a wide spectrum of public issues, whereas their counterparts elsewhere remain disengaged. As our third indicator of civic involvement, therefore, we have constructed a summary indicator of turnout in five of these referenda (see Table 4.2).[40]

Although turnout itself in general elections is not a good measure of citizen motivation, one special feature of the Italian ballot does provide important information on regional political practices. All voters in national elections must choose a single party list, and legislative seats are allocated to parties by proportional representation. In addition, however, voters can, if they wish, indicate a preference for a particular candidate from the party list they have chosen. Nationally speaking, only a minority of voters exercise this "preference vote," but in areas where party labels are largely a cover for patron-client networks, these preference votes are eagerly solicited by contending factions. In such areas, the preference vote becomes essential to the patron-client exchange relationship.

The incidence of preference voting has long been acknowledged by students of Italian politics as a reliable indicator of personalism, factionalism, and patron-client politics, and we shall shortly present additional confirmation of this interpretation.[41] In that sense, preference voting can be taken as an indicator for the absence of a civic community. Regional differences in the use of the preference vote have been highly stable for decades, ranging from 17 percent in Emilia-Romagna and Lombardia to 50 percent in Campania and Calabria. Table 4.3 summarizes a composite index of preference voting in six national elections from 1953 to 1979, which serves as the fourth element in our evaluation of the "civic-ness" of the Italian regions.[42]

TABLE 4.3

Index of Preference Voting, 1953–1979

Year of Election	Factor Loading
Preference voting, 1953	0.971
Preference voting, 1958	0.982
Preference voting, 1963	0.984
Preference voting, 1972	0.982
Preference voting, 1976	0.970
Preference voting, 1979	0.978

If our analysis of the motivations and political realities that underlie referenda turnout and preference voting is correct, then the two should be negatively correlated—one reflecting the politics of issues; the other, the politics of patronage. Figure 4.3 shows that this is so. Citizens in some regions turn out in large numbers to declare their views on a wide range of public questions, but forgo the use of personalized preference votes in

FIGURE 4.3

Referenda Turnout and Preference Voting

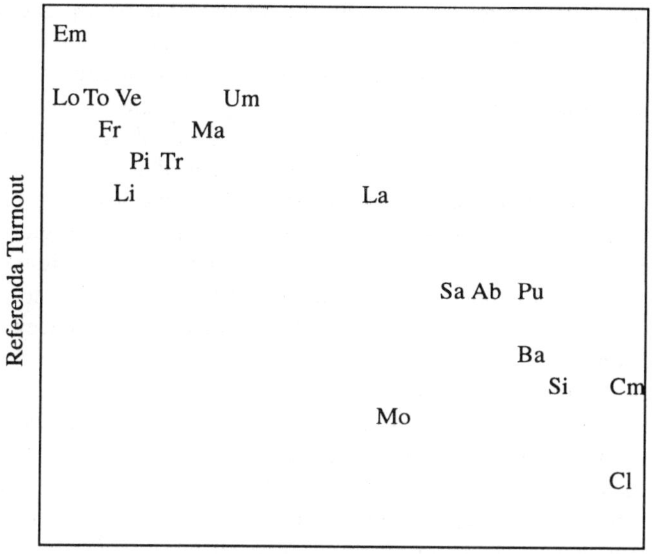

Preference Voting

Correlation: $r = -.91$

TABLE 4.4
The Civic Community Index

Component Measure	Factor Loading
Preference voting, 1953–1979	–0.947
Referendum turnout, 1974–1987	0.944
Newspaper readership, 1975	0.893
Scarcity of sports and cultural associations, 1981	–0.891[a]

[a] As indicated in the text, this variable is scored so that a higher number corresponds to a lower density of associations.

	Intercorrelations (r) among Components of the Civic Community Index			
	PrefV	*Refrn*	*Newsp*	*Assns*
PrefV	1.00	–0.91	–0.77	0.82
Refrn	–0.91	1.00	0.79	–0.76
Newsp	–0.77	0.79	1.00	–0.73
Assns	0.82	–0.76	–0.73	1.00

Note: All of the above correlations are statistically significant at the .001 level or better.

general elections. Elsewhere, citizens are enmeshed in patron-client networks. They typically pass up the chance to express an opinion on public issues, since for them the ballot is essentially a token of exchange in an immediate, highly personalized relationship of dependency.

Both groups are, in some sense, "participating in politics." It is not so much the *quantity* of participation as the *quality* that differs between them. The character of participation varies because the nature of politics is quite different in the two areas. Political behavior in some regions presumes that politics is about collective deliberation on public issues. By contrast, politics elsewhere is organized hierarchically and focused more narrowly on personal advantage. *Why* these regional differences exist, and what consequences they have for regional governance, are questions to which we shall shortly turn.

As our image of the civic community presumes, our four indicators are in fact highly correlated, in the sense that regions with high turnout for referenda and low use of the personal preference ballot are virtually the same regions with a closely woven fabric of civic associations and a high incidence of newspaper readership. Consequently, we can conveniently combine the four into a single Civic Community Index, as summarized in Table 4.4. Any single indicator of "civic-ness" might be misleading,

FIGURE 4.4
The Civic Community in the Italian Regions

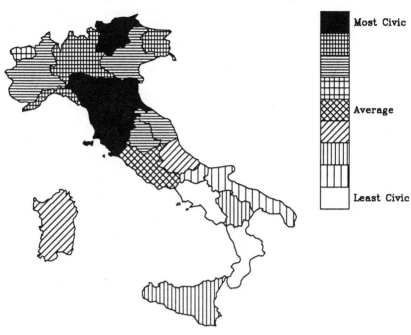

of course, but this composite index reflects an important and coherent syndrome.

Figure 4.4, in turn, charts the levels of "civic-ness" of each of Italy's twenty regions. In the most civic regions, such as Emilia-Romagna, citizens are actively involved in all sorts of local associations—literary guilds, local bands, hunting clubs, cooperatives and so on. They follow civic affairs avidly in the local press, and they engage in politics out of programmatic conviction. By contrast, in the least civic regions, such as Calabria, voters are brought to the polls not by issues, but by hierarchical patron-client networks. An absence of civic associations and a paucity of local media in these latter regions mean that citizens there are rarely drawn into community affairs.

Public life is very different in these two sorts of communities. When two citizens meet on the street in a civic region, *both* of them are likely to have seen a newspaper at home that day; when two people in a less civic region meet, probably *neither* of them has. More than half of the citizens in the civic regions have *never* cast a preference ballot in their lives; more than half of the voters in the less civic regions say they *always* have.[43]

FIGURE 4.5
The Civic Community and Institutional Performance

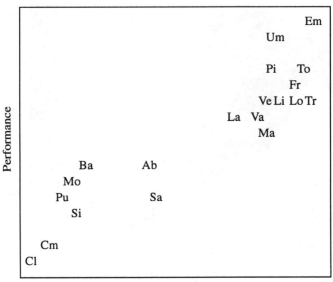

Civic Community
Correlation: $r = .92$

Membership in sports clubs, cultural and recreational groups, community and social action organizations, educational and youth groups, and so on is roughly twice as common in the most civic regions as in the least civic regions.[44]

Even a casual comparison of Figure 4.4 with Figure 4.1 indicates a remarkable concordance between the performance of a regional government and the degree to which social and political life in that region approximates the ideal of a civic community. The strength of this relationship appears with stark clarity in Figure 4.5. Not only does "civic-ness" distinguish the high performance regions in the upper right-hand quadrant from the laggards in the lower left-hand quadrant, but even the more subtle differences in performance *within* each quadrant are closely tied to our measure of community life.[45] In this respect, the predictive power of the civic community is greater than the power of economic development, as summarized in Figure 4.2. The more civic a region, the more effective its government.

So strong is this relationship that when we take the "civic-ness" of a region into account, the relationship we previously observed between economic development and institutional performance entirely vanishes.[46] In other words, economically advanced regions appear to have more successful regional governments merely because they happen to be more civic. To be sure, the link between the civic community and economic development is itself interesting and important, and we shall pay close attention to that link in Chapters 5 and 6. For the moment, it is enough to recognize that the performance of a regional government is somehow very closely related to the civic character of social and political life within the region. Regions with many civic associations, many newspaper readers, many issue-oriented voters, and few patron-client networks seem to nourish more effective governments. What's so special about these communities?

SOCIAL AND POLITICAL LIFE IN THE CIVIC COMMUNITY

Life in a civic community is in many respects fundamentally distinctive. We can deepen our understanding of the social and political implications of "civic-ness" by drawing on our surveys of regional politicians, community leaders, and the mass public.

Consider first some independent evidence in support of our assertion that political involvement in less civic regions is impelled and constrained by personalistic, patron-client networks, rather than by programmatic commitments on public issues. Our 1982 nationwide sample of community leaders was asked whether they would describe political life in their respective regions as relatively "programmatic" or relatively "clientelistic." The fraction of respondents describing politics in their region as clientelistic ranged from 85 percent in Molise to 14 percent in Friuli-Venezia Giulia. Figure 4.6 shows that these self-descriptions of regional politics are very closely correlated with our Civic Community Index (particularly if one bears in mind the statistical attenuation produced by very small samples and consequent sampling error). Regions where citizens use personal preference votes, but do not vote in referenda, do not join civic associations, and do not read newspapers are the same regions whose leaders describe their regional politics as clientelistic, rather than programmatic.

Evidence from both citizens and politicians helps us trace the incidence of personalized patronage politics. Citizens in the less civic regions report much more frequent personal contact with their representatives than in the civic north.[47] Moreover, these contacts involve primarily personal matters, rather than broader public issues. In our 1988 survey, 20 percent of voters in the least civic regions acknowledged that they occasionally "seek personal help about licenses, jobs, and so on from a politician," as contrasted with only 5 percent of the voters in the most civic regions. This "particularized contacting" is *not* predicted by the demographic character-

FIGURE 4.6
"Clientelism" and the Civic Community

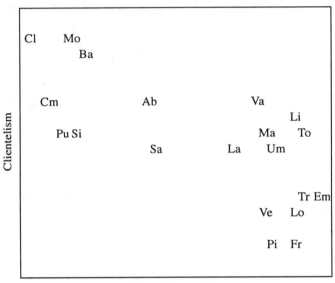

Civic Community
Correlation: $r = -.71$

FIGURE 4.7
"Particularized Contacting" and the Civic Community

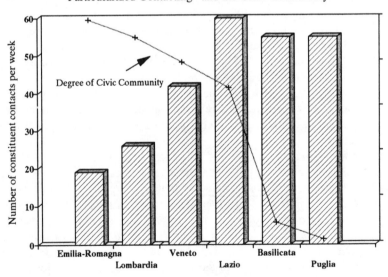

istics normally associated with political participation, such as education, social class, income, political interest, partisanship, or age, but it is much more common in *all* social categories in less civic regions. This form of participation seems to depend less on *who* you are than on *where* you are.[48]

Evidence from our surveys of regional councilors is wholly consistent with this picture. We asked each councilor how many citizens had approached him in the previous week and for what reasons. The results from all four waves of interviews were virtually identical. Councilors in Emilia-Romagna, the most civic of regions, reported seeing fewer than twenty constituents in an average week, as compared with fifty-five to sixty contacts per week for councilors in the least civic regions. (Figure 4.7 shows the results for all six regions.)

In the less civic regions, these encounters overwhelmingly involve requests for jobs and patronage, whereas Emilians are more likely to be contacted about policy or legislation. The average councilor in Puglia or Basilicata gets roughly eight to ten requests every day for jobs and other favors, compared to about one such request a day in Emilia-Romagna. On the other hand, the Emilian councilor also reports about one citizen inquiry a day on some public issue, the sort of topic virtually never raised with a councilor in Puglia or Basilicata. In short, citizens in civic regions contact their representatives much less often, and when they do, they are more likely to talk about policy than patronage.

Our exploration of the distinctive features of civic and less civic communities so far has concentrated on the behavior of ordinary citizens, but there are also revealing differences in the character of political elites in the two types of region. Politics in less civic regions, as we have seen, is marked by vertical relations of authority and dependency, as embodied in patron-client networks. Politics in those regions is, in a fundamental sense, more elitist. Authority relations in the political sphere closely mirror authority relations in the wider social setting.[49]

It is not surprising, therefore, to discover that political leaders in the less civic regions are drawn from a narrower slice of the social hierarchy. Educational levels among ordinary citizens in the less civic South are faintly lower than in the North; in 1971 only 2.6 percent of southern residents were university graduates, as contrasted to 2.9 percent of northern residents. Among regional political elites, however, educational levels are significantly *higher* in the South. All but 13 percent of the councilors in Puglia and Basilicata have a university education, as compared to 33–40 percent in the northern, more civic regions. In other words, the regional elite in the less civic regions is drawn almost entirely from the most privileged portion of the population, whereas a significant number of political leaders in the more civic regions come from more modest backgrounds.[50]

Political leaders in the civic regions are more enthusiastic supporters of political equality than their counterparts in less civic regions. From our first encounters with the newly elected regional councilors in 1970, those in the more civic regions, such as Emilia-Romagna and Lombardia, have been consistently more sympathetic to the idea of popular participation in regional affairs, whereas the leaders in the less civic regions have been more skeptical.[51]

In those early years, political leaders in the more civic regions lauded the regional reform as an opportunity to enlarge grass-roots democracy in Italy, but leaders in the less civic regions were perplexed by this populist, "power to the people" rhetoric. As the new institution matured during the 1970s and the initial euphoria faded, regional leaders throughout Italy who had once expressed aspirations for direct democracy became more circumspect. Efforts to encourage greater popular involvement in the regional government waned, and attention everywhere shifted instead to administrative efficiency and effectiveness. Nevertheless, clear differences in sympathy for political equality persisted among the leaders of different regions.

Some of these differences in outlook are captured by four "agree-disagree" items that we posed to regional councilors in each of our four surveys from 1970 to 1988, which we have combined into a single Index of Support for Political Equality. Councilors who score high on this Index are avowed egalitarians. Conversely, low scorers on the Index of Support for Political Equality express skepticism about the wisdom of the ordinary citizen and sometimes even have doubts about universal suffrage. They stress the desirability of strong leadership, especially from traditional elites.

Figure 4.8 shows the sharp differences in support for political equality across the six regional elites, mirroring almost perfectly the "civic-ness" of the regional community. Where associationism flourishes, where citizens attend to community affairs and vote for issues, not patrons, there too we find leaders who believe in democracy, not social and political hierarchy.

These regional differences in authority patterns have had a powerful and enduring impact on popular attitudes toward the very structure of Italian government. Two striking illustrations of this fact, nearly half a century apart, are provided by the 1946 balloting on whether to retain the Italian monarchy and a 1991 referendum on electoral reform, a far-reaching package of proposals designed to inhibit "vote-buying" and other forms of patron-clientelism. As shown in Figures 4.9 and 4.10, the more civic the social and political life of a region in the 1970s, the more likely it was to have voted for the republic and against the monarchy thirty years earlier, and the more likely it was to support egalitarian electoral reform

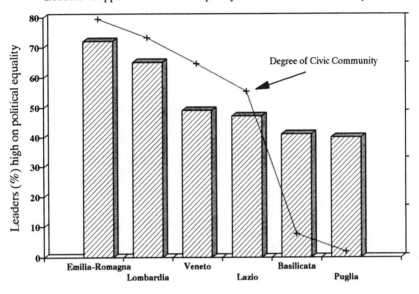

FIGURE 4.8
Leaders' Support for Political Equality and the Civic Community

Index of Support for Political Equality

1. People should be permitted to vote even if they cannot do so intelligently.

2. *Few people really know what is in their best interests in the long run.

3. *Certain people are better qualified to lead this country because of their traditions and family background.

4. *It will always be necessary to have a few strong, able individuals who know how to take charge.

* Scoring on these items is reversed.

FIGURE 4.9
The Civic Community and Republicanism, 1946

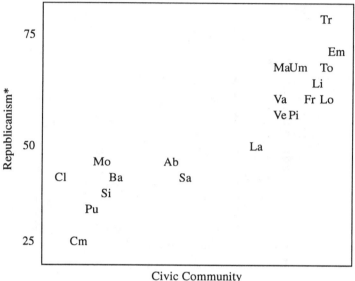

Civic Community
Correlation: $r = .90$

*Percentage of electorate voting against the monarchy in 1946.

more than a decade later. Citizens in the more civic regions, like their leaders, have a pervasive distaste for hierarchical authority patterns.

In short, civics is about equality as well as engagement. It is impossible to sort out the complex causal connections that underlie these patterns of elite-mass linkages. It is fruitless to ask which came first—the leaders' commitment to equality or the citizens' commitment to engagement. We cannot say in what measure the leaders are simply responding to the competence and civic enthusiasm (or lack of it) of their constituents, and in what measure civic engagement by citizens has been influenced by the readiness (or reluctance) of elites to tolerate equality and encourage participation. Elite and mass attitudes are in fact two sides of a single coin, bound together in a mutually reinforcing equilibrium.

In Chapter 5 we shall present evidence that these distinctive elite-mass linkages have evolved over a very long time. Under these circumstances, it would be surprising if elite and mass attitudes were not congruent. A situation of authoritarian elites and assertive masses cannot be a stable equilibrium, and a pattern of obeisant leaders and complaisant followers is hardly more permanent. The more stable syndromes of elite-mass linkages that we have actually found deepen our understanding of the dynam-

FIGURE 4.10
The Civic Community and Electoral Reformism, 1991

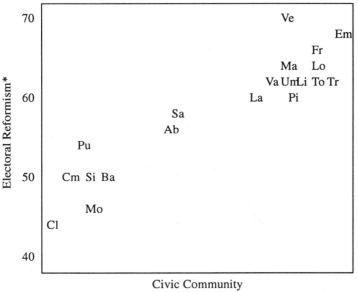

Civic Community
Correlation: $r = .92$

*Percentage of electorate voting for electoral reform in 1991.

ics of politics in civic and less civic regions. The effectiveness of regional government is closely tied to the degree to which authority and social interchange in the life of the region is organized horizontally or hierarchically. Equality is an essential feature of the civic community.[52]

Political leaders in civic regions are also readier to compromise than their counterparts in less civic regions. As we shall shortly see, there is no evidence at all that politics in civic regions is any less subject to conflict and controversy, but leaders there are readier to resolve their conflicts. Civic regions are characterized, not by an absence of partisanship, but by an openness of partisanship. This important contrast between civic and less civic politics is reflected in Figure 4.11, which reports the responses of councilors in our four surveys over two decades to the following proposition: "To compromise with one's political opponents is dangerous because that normally leads to the betrayal of one's own side." Of political leaders in the most civic region, only 19 percent agreed—less than half the rate among politicians in the least civic regions. Politicians in civic regions do not deny the reality of conflicting interests, but they are unafraid of creative compromise.[53] This, too, is part of the tapestry of the civic community that helps explain why government there works better.

FIGURE 4.11

Leaders' Fear of Compromise and the Civic Community

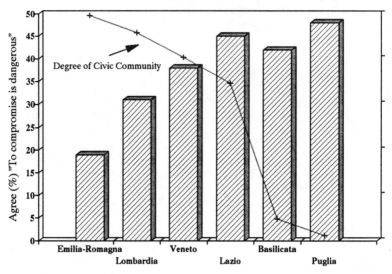

The civic community is defined operationally, in part, by the density of local cultural and recreational associations. Excluded by that definition, however, are three important affiliations for many Italians—unions, the Church, and political parties. The civic context turns out to have distinctive effects on membership in these three different sorts of organizations.

Unions

In many countries (particularly those with "closed shop" provisions), union membership is essentially involuntary, and thus has little civic significance. In Italy, however, union membership is voluntary and signifies much more than merely holding a particular job.[54] The ideological fragmentation of the Italian labor movement offers a wide choice of political affiliations—Communist, Catholic, neo-Fascist, socialist, and none-of-the-above. White collar and agricultural unions are more important in Italy than in many other countries, expanding further the opportunities for membership. Salvatore Coi concludes that "political motivation and ideological tradition" are more important than economic structure in determining union membership in Italy.[55] As a result, union membership has greater civic significance in Italy than it might elsewhere.

Union membership is much more common in the more civic regions. In fact, union membership is roughly twice as high in the more civic regions, *controlling for* the respondent's occupation: *Among* blue-collar workers, *among* farmers, *among* professionals, *among* self-employed businessmen, and so on, membership in unions is consistently higher in the more civic regions. By contrast, union membership is unrelated to education, age, and urbanization, and the differences by social class are less than one might expect. Union membership is almost as common among professionals and executives in civic regions as among manual workers in less civic regions.[56] The civic context is almost as important as socioeconomic status in accounting for union membership in Italy. In the civic regions, solidarity in the workplace is part of a larger syndrome of social solidarity.[57]

The Church and Religiosity

Organized religion, at least in Catholic Italy, is an alternative to the civic community, not a part of it. Throughout Italian history, the presence of the Papacy in Rome has had a powerful effect on the Italian Church and its relationship with civic life. For more than thirty years after Unification, the Papal *non expedit* forbade all Catholics from taking part in national political life, although after World War II the Church became a senior partner of the Christian Democratic party. Despite the reforms of the Second Vatican Council and the flowering of many divergent ideological tendencies among the faithful, the Italian Church retains much of the heritage of the Counter-Reformation, including an emphasis on the ecclesiastical hierarchy and the traditional virtues of obedience and acceptance of one's station in life.[58] Vertical bonds of authority are more characteristic of the Italian Church than horizontal bonds of fellowship.

At the regional level, all manifestations of religiosity and clericalism— attendance at Mass, religious (as opposed to civil) marriages, rejection of divorce, expressions of religious identity in surveys—are negatively correlated with civic engagement. (Figure 4.12 summarizes this pattern.) At the individual level, too, religious sentiments and civic engagement seem to be mutually incompatible. Of those Italians who attend Mass more than once a week, 52 percent say they rarely read a newspaper and 51 percent say they never discuss politics; among their avowedly irreligious compatriots, the equivalent figures are 13 percent and 17 percent.[59] Churchgoers express greater contentment with life and with the existing political regime than other Italians. They seem more concerned about the city of God than the city of man.

In the first two decades after World War II, many Italians joined Catholic Action, a federation of Catholic lay associations reinvigorated by the Church as it sought to stay in tune with newly democratic Italy. The larg-

FIGURE 4.12
Clericalism and the Civic Community

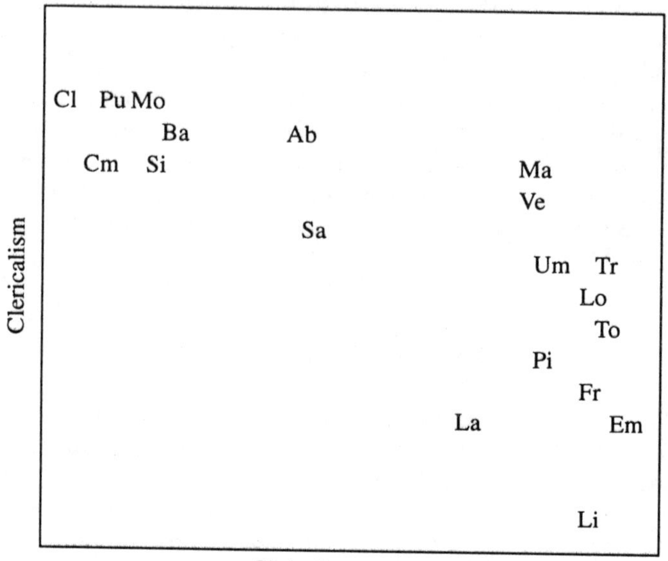

Civic Community
Correlation: $r = -.76$

Note: Clericalism is a composite factor-score index, based on the following eight indicators:

Component measure	Loading
Church marriage rate, 1976	0.952
Divorce rate, 1986	−0.915
Church marriage rate, 1986	0.862
Anti-Divorce Referendum, 1974	0.842
Divorce rate, 1973	−0.796
Survey: "Are you a religious person?"	0.792
Survey: "How often do you attend Church?"	0.783
Survey: "Is religion important to you?"	0.767

est mass organization in Italy at that time, Catholic Action at its peak enrolled nearly a tenth of all Italian men, women, and children in its network of cultural, recreational, and educational activities. This membership had a regional distribution almost the *reverse* of that depicted for clericalism in Figure 4.12. Catholic Action was two or three times stronger in the northern, civic, more association-prone regions of the North than in the less civic areas of the Mezzogiorno. In that geographic sense, Catholic Action represented the "civic" face of Italian Catholicism. In the 1960s, however, with the rapid secularization of Italian society and turmoil within the Church following the Second Vatican Council, Catholic Action collapsed catastrophically, losing two-thirds of its members in just five years and leaving hardly a trace by the period of our study.[60] In today's Italy, as in the Italy of Machiavelli's civic humanists, the civic community is a secular community.

Parties

Italian political parties have ably adapted to the contrasting contexts within which they operate, uncivic as well as civic. As a result, citizens of less civic regions are as engaged in party politics and as interested in politics as citizens of more civic regions.[61] Membership in political parties is virtually as common in the least civic regions as in the most civic. Voters in less civic regions are as likely to feel close to a party as those in more civic regions. They talk politics as often as citizens in civic regions, and as we have seen, they are actually much more likely to have personal contacts with political leaders. Citizens of the less civic regions are not less partisan or "political."[62]

Party membership and political involvement, however, have a distinctive meaning in the less civic regions. It was above all in the Mezzogiorno that the "PNF" printed on party cards in the Fascist era was commonly said to stand not for *Partito Nazionale Fascista* [National Fascist Party], but *per necessità familiare* ["for family necessity"]. Winning favor from the powerful remains more important in less civic regions. "Connections" are crucial to survival here, and the connections that work best are vertical ones of dependence and dominion rather than horizontal ones of collaboration and solidarity. As Sidney Tarrow describes the impoverished, uncivic Mezzogiorno: "Political capacity in southern Italy is *highly developed*. . . . [The individual] is at once both highly political and resistant to horizontal secondary association. In this sense, all his social relations are 'political.'"[63] Political parties are salient organizationally even in the less civic regions, despite the paucity of secondary associations, because all parties in that context have tended to become vehicles for patron-client politics. As we observed earlier, it is not the degree of political participation that distinguishes civic from uncivic regions, but its character.

Civic Attitudes

For all their politicking, citizens of less civic regions feel exploited, alienated, powerless. Figure 4.13 shows that (against a reasonably high background level of alienation among all Italians) both low education and uncivic surroundings accentuate feelings of exploitation and powerlessness.

FIGURE 4.13

Citizens' Feelings of Powerlessness, Education, and the Civic Community

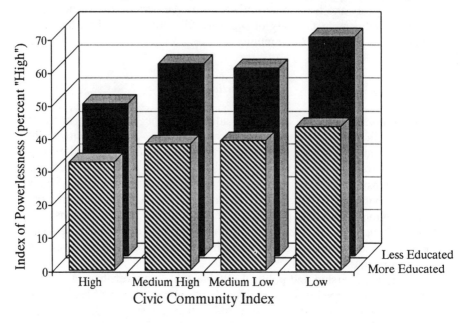

Index of Powerlessness

("High" = agreement with all four of the following items)

1. Most people in positions of power try to exploit you.
2. You feel left out of what is happening around you.
3. What you think doesn't count very much.
4. The people who run the country are not really concerned
   with what happens to you.

In every community, the more educated feel more efficacious, for education represents social status, personal skills, and connections. Nevertheless, even these advantages cannot fully compensate for the cynicism and alienation that pervade the less civic regions of Italy. Educated citizens in the least civic regions feel almost as impotent as less educated citizens in the most civic regions. Figure 4.13 also shows that community context has an even sharper effect on efficacy among the less educated than among the more educated. Class differences in powerlessness are heightened in the less civic regions.[64] We do not need to construct tortured psychodynamic interpretations of this disaffection. By contrast with the more egalitarian, cooperative civic community, life in a vertically structured, horizontally fractured community produces daily justification for feelings of exploitation, dependency, and frustration, especially at the bottom of the social ladder, but also on somewhat higher rungs.

Honesty, trust, and law-abidingness are prominent in most philosophical accounts of civic virtue. Citizens in the civic community, it is said, deal fairly with one another and expect fair dealing in return. They expect their government to follow high standards, and they willingly obey the rules that they have imposed on themselves. In such a community, writes Benjamin Barber, "Citizens do not and cannot ride for free, because they understand that their freedom is a consequence of their participation in the making and acting out of common decisions."[65] In a less civic community, by contrast, life is riskier, citizens are warier, and the laws, made by higher-ups, are made to be broken.

This account of the civic community sounds noble, perhaps, but also unrealistic and even mawkish, echoing some long-forgotten high school civics text. Remarkably, however, evidence from the Italian regions seems consistent with this vision. The least civic regions are the most subject to the ancient plague of political corruption. They are the home of the Mafia and its regional variants.[66] Although "objective" measures of political honesty are not easily available, we did ask our nationwide sample of community leaders to judge whether politics in their respective regions was more honest or more corrupt than the average region. Leaders in the less civic regions were much more likely to describe their regional politics as corrupt than were their counterparts in more civic regions. Analogous contrasts emerged from our 1987 and 1988 surveys of mass publics throughout the peninsula, as illustrated in Table 4.5. Citizens in civic regions expressed greater social trust and greater confidence in the law-abidingness of their fellow citizens than did citizens in the least civic regions.[67] Conversely, those in the less civic regions were much more likely to insist that the authorities should impose greater law-and-order on their communities.[68]

These remarkably consistent differences go to the heart of the distinction between civic and uncivic communities. Collective life in the civic regions is eased by the expectation that others will probably follow the rules. Knowing that others will, *you* are more likely to go along, too, thus fulfilling *their* expectations. In the less civic regions nearly everyone expects everyone else to violate the rules. It seems foolish to obey the traffic laws or the tax code or the welfare rules, if you expect everyone else to cheat. (The Italian term for such naive behavior is *fesso*, which also

TABLE 4.5

Honesty, Trust, Law-Abidingness, and the Civic Community

	Civic Community Index			
	High	Medium High	Medium Low	Low
Which better describes politics in this region: "honest" or "corrupt"?				
Percentage of leaders who say "honest"	89	76	67	44
Some people say that you usually can trust people. Others say that you must be very wary in relations with people. Which is your view?				
Percentage of public who say "trust"	33	32	28	17
People in this town strictly obey the laws, even the traffic code.				
Percentage of public who "agree"	60	47	39	25
Support for stricter law-and-order				
Percentage of public who endorse all four items[a]	37	46	49	60

[a] Composite index of support for stricter law-and-order:
   1. The police should have greater power to defend the law.
   2. The government doesn't do enough to assure public order.
   3. In these days there is not enough respect for authority.
   4. The police have too much power in Italy. (Disagree fully)

means "cuckolded.") So you cheat, too, and in the end everyone's dolorous, cynical expectations are confirmed.

Lacking the confident self-discipline of the civic regions, people in less civic regions are forced to rely on what Italians call "the forces of order," that is, the police. For reasons we shall explore in greater detail in Chapter 6, citizens in the less civic regions have no other resort to solve the fundamental Hobbesian dilemma of public order, for they lack the horizontal bonds of collective reciprocity that work more efficiently in the civic regions. In the absence of solidarity and self-discipline, hierarchy and force provide the only alternative to anarchy.

In the recent philosophical debate between communitarians and liberals, community and liberty are often said to be inimical. No doubt this is sometimes true, as it was once in Salem, Massachusetts. The Italian case suggests, however, that because citizens in civic regions enjoy the benefits of community, they are able to be more liberal. Ironically, it is the amoral individualists of the less civic region who find themselves clamoring for sterner law enforcement.

FIGURE 4.14
Satisfaction with Life and the Civic Community

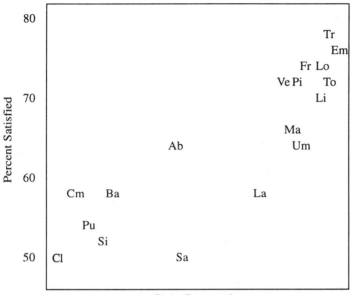

Civic Community
Correlation: $r = .87$

Yet the vicious circle winds tighter still: In the less civic regions even a heavy-handed government—the agent for law enforcement—is itself enfeebled by the uncivic social context. The very character of the community that leads citizens to demand stronger government makes it less likely that any government can be strong, at least if it remains democratic. (This is a reasonable interpretation, for example, of the Italian state's futile anti-Mafia efforts in Sicily over the last half century.) In civic regions, by contrast, light-touch government is effortlessly stronger because it can count on more willing cooperation and self-enforcement among the citizenry.

The evidence we have reviewed strongly suggests that public affairs are more successfully ordered in the more civic regions. It is not surprising, therefore, that citizens in civic regions are happier with life in general than are their counterparts in less civic regions. In a series of nationwide surveys between 1975 and 1989, roughly twenty-five thousand people were asked whether they were "very satisfied, fairly satisfied, not very satisfied, or not at all satisfied with the life you lead." Figure 4.14 shows that citizens of civic regions are much more satisfied with life. Happiness is living in a civic community.

At the individual level, life satisfaction is best predicted by family income and by religious observance, but the correlation with the civic community is virtually as strong as these personal attributes.[69] Civic community is so closely correlated with both institutional performance and regional affluence that it is statistically difficult to distinguish among them although, of the three, civic-ness is marginally the best predictor of life satisfaction. In any event, as we shall discuss in more detail in succeeding chapters, these three features of community life have come to form a closely interconnected syndrome. Figure 4.14 shows that the character of one's community in this sense is as important as personal circumstance in producing personal happiness.

The contrast between more civic and less civic communities that emerges from these serried rows of data is, in many respects, quite consistent with the speculations of political philosophers. In one important respect, however, our story contradicts most classical accounts. Many theorists have associated the civic community with small, close-knit, premodern societies, quite unlike our modern world—the civic community as a world we have lost.[70]

Contemporary social thought has borrowed from the nineteenth-century German sociologist Ferdinand Tönnies the distinction between *Gemeinschaft* and *Gesellschaft*—that is, between a traditional, small-scale, face-to-face *community* resting on a universal sense of solidarity and a modern, rationalistic, impersonal *society* resting on self-interest. This perspective leads readily to the view that the civic community is an atavism destined to disappear. In its place arise large, modern agglomerations, technologically advanced, but dehumanizing, which induce civic passivity and self-seeking individualism. Modernity is the enemy of civility.

Quite the contrary, our studies suggest. The least civic areas of Italy are precisely the traditional southern villages. The civic ethos of traditional communities must not be idealized. Life in much of traditional Italy today is marked by hierarchy and exploitation, not by share-and-share-alike. James Watson, a close observer of Calabria, the toe of Italy's boot and the least civic of all twenty regions, stresses the lack of civic trust and associations:

> The first quality that strikes an observer in Calabria is diffidence; not just diffidence towards the outsider but also within the community, even in small villages. Trust is not a commodity in great supply. . . . Historically, civil society has been almost totally lacking in associations apart from the occasional village or town social club (*Circolo della Caccia, dei Nobili* etc.).[71]

Conversely, at the top of the civic scale Emilia-Romagna is far from a traditional "community" in the classic sense—an intimate village as idealized in our folk memory. On the contrary, Emilia-Romagna is among the most modern, bustling, affluent, technologically advanced societies on the face of the earth. It is, however, the site of an unusual concentration of overlapping networks of social solidarity, peopled by citizens with an unusually well developed public spirit—a web of civic communities. Emilia-Romagna is not populated by angels, but within its borders (and those of neighboring regions in north-central Italy) collective action of all sorts, including government, is facilitated by norms and networks of civic engagement. As we shall see in Chapter 5, these norms and networks have vital roots in deep regional traditions, but it would be nonsense to classify Emilia-Romagna as a "traditional" society. The most civic regions of Italy—the communities where citizens feel empowered to engage in collective deliberation about public choices and where those choices are translated most fully into effective public policies—include some of the most modern towns and cities of the peninsula. Modernization need not signal the demise of the civic community.

We can summarize our discoveries so far in this chapter rather simply. Some regions of Italy have many choral societies and soccer teams and bird-watching clubs and Rotary clubs. Most citizens in those regions read eagerly about community affairs in the daily press. They are engaged by public issues, but not by personalistic or patron-client politics. Inhabitants trust one another to act fairly and to obey the law. Leaders in these regions are relatively honest. They believe in popular government, and they are predisposed to compromise with their political adversaries. Both citizens and leaders here find equality congenial. Social and political networks are organized horizontally, not hierarchically. The community values solidarity, civic engagement, cooperation, and honesty. Government works.[72] Small wonder that people in these regions are content!

At the other pole are the "uncivic" regions, aptly characterized by the French term *incivisme*.[73] Public life in these regions is organized hierarchically, rather than horizontally. The very concept of "citizen" here is stunted. From the point of view of the individual inhabitant, public affairs is the business of somebody else—*i notabili*, "the bosses," "the politicians"—but not me. Few people aspire to partake in deliberations about the commonweal, and few such opportunities present themselves. Political participation is triggered by personal dependency or private greed, not by collective purpose. Engagement in social and cultural associations is meager. Private piety stands in for public purpose. Corruption is widely regarded as the norm, even by politicians themselves, and they are cynical about democratic principles. "Compromise" has only negative overtones. Laws (almost everyone agrees) are made to be broken, but fearing others' lawlessness, people demand sterner discipline. Trapped in these interlocking vicious circles, nearly everyone feels powerless, exploited, and unhappy. All things considered, it is hardly surprising that representative government here is less effective than in more civic communities.

This discovery poses two new and important questions: *How did the civic regions get that way?* and *How do norms and networks of civic engagement undergird good government?* We shall address those questions in the two chapters that follow, but first a few words about other potential explanations for the success and failure of the regional governments.

OTHER EXPLANATIONS FOR INSTITUTIONAL SUCCESS?

Social disharmony and political conflict are often thought inimical to effective governance. Consensus is said to be a prerequisite for stable democracy. This view has a distinguished lineage. Cicero wrote that "the commonwealth, then, is the people's affair; and the people is not every group of men, associated in any manner, but is the coming together of a considerable number of men who are united by a common agreement about law and rights and by the desire to participate in mutual advantages."[74] Shaken by the specter of social conflict in revolutionary France, Edmund Burke suggested that the well ordered society must be considered a partnership, "a partnership in all science, a partnership in all art, a partnership in every virtue, and in all perfection."[75]

This viewpoint has commanded many distinguished advocates among twentieth-century social scientists as well. Gabriel Almond praised the "homogeneous" political culture of "Anglo-American" political systems and described the fragmented "Continental" type of political system as "associated with immobilism" and ever threatened by "Caesaristic breakthrough."[76] Giovanni Sartori argued that ideological polarization and fragmentation are characteristic of ineffective, "breakdown-prone" democracies.[77] The greater the cleavages in a society or polity, the more difficult it will be to compose a stable government resting on the consent of the governed. The greater the disagreement on issues of substance, the less likely that any coherent program will be pursued: "If everyone had the same political preferences, the task of making policy would be much easier."[78]

This presumed association between social cohesion, political harmony, and good government appears, often implicitly, in many accounts of the civic community:

> For Rousseau and for classical republicans generally, [patriotic feeling and political participation] rested and could only rest on social, religious, and cultural unity. They were the political expressions of a homogeneous people. One might say that, for them, citizenship was only possible where it was least necessary, where politics was nothing more than the extension into the public arena of a common life that began and was sustained outside.[79]

Such sentiments suggested for our research a variety of hypotheses about how social unity and political consensus might be linked to institutional performance. Sad to say, our expectations were thoroughly confounded. The success or failure of Italy's regional governments was wholly uncorrelated with virtually all measures of political fragmentation, ideological polarization, and social conflict:

- We examined the ideological polarization of the party system—measured both by party strength and by the views of regional leaders—suspecting that the greater the gulf between left and right, and the more powerful the voices of extremism, the more difficult it might be to compose an effective government.
- We examined the distribution of voters' views on key social and economic issues, presuming that the weaker the consensus on important policy matters, the more difficult government leaders might find it to forge a coherent strategy.
- We examined the fragmentation of the regional party system, believing that a multiplicity of small, fractious parties might impede government stability.
- We examined data on economic conflicts, such as strike rates, expecting that social tensions might thwart government effectiveness.
- We examined the geographic disparities in economic development and demography within each region, thinking that extremes of modernity and backwardness, or tensions between a large metropolis and surrounding rural areas, might make governing more difficult.
- We asked community leaders to rate their regions from "conflictful" to "consensual," and we matched their reports against our measures of institutional performance, presuming that where conflicts were salient, cooperation for common purposes would be arduous and governance might suffer.

None of these investigations, however, offered the slightest sustenance for the theory that social and political strife is incompatible with good government. We observed regions of high performance and low conflict, such as Veneto, but we also found successful, conflictful regions, such as Piedmont. We observed unsuccessful, conflict-ridden regions, such as Campania, but we also discovered consensual regions whose governments have performed below the national average, such as Basilicata.

Implicit in these conclusions is also the fact that we found no correlation between conflict and the civic community. The civic community is by no means harmonious and distinctively strife-free. Benjamin Barber's vision of "strong democracy" captures the character of the civic community as it emerges from our Italian explorations:

Strong democracy rests on the idea of a self-governing community of citizens who are united less by homogeneous interests than by civic education and who are made capable of common purpose and mutual action by virtue of their civic attitudes and participatory institutions rather than their altruism or their good nature. Strong democracy is consonant with—indeed it depends upon—the politics of conflict, the sociology of pluralism, and the separation of private and public realms of action.[80]

Several other possible explanations for institutional performance also failed to pass muster when confronted with evidence from the Italian regional experiment:

- *Social stability* has sometimes been associated with effective governance. Rapid social change, it has been argued, increases social strain, dissolves social solidarity, and disrupts existing norms and organizations that buttress government. Our preliminary analysis of regional performance through 1976 had found tentative evidence that demographic instability and social change inhibited performance,[81] but this relationship disappeared in our subsequent, fuller analysis of performance and social change.

- *Education* is one of the most powerful influences on political behavior almost everywhere, including Italy. Nevertheless, contemporary educational levels do not explain differences in performance among the Italian regions. The correlation between institutional performance and the fraction of the regional population who attended school beyond the minimum school-leaving age of fourteen is insignificant. Emilia-Romagna, the highest-performing, most civic region, and Calabria, the lowest-performing, least civic region, have virtually identical scores on this measure of educational attainment (46 percent vs. 45 percent).[82] Historically, education may have played an important role in strengthening the foundations for the civic community, but it seems to have no direct influence on government performance today.

- *Urbanism* might be thought relevant, in some form, to institutional performance. One version of this hypothesis recalls Marx's epithet about the idiocy of rural life and suggests that successful institutions might be positively associated with urbanization. An alternative folk theory, already alluded to, sees civic virtue in traditional villages and vice in the city. This theory implies that institutional performance should be lower in more urban regions. A more subtle theory would tie institutional performance (and perhaps the civic community) specifically to medium-sized cities, spared the anonymity of the modern metropolis, as well as the isolation of the countryside. In fact, however, we found no association of any sort between city size or population density and the success or failure of the regional governments.[83]

- *Personnel stability* marks the high-performance institution, according to some theories of institutionalization. Low turnover signifies that the members are committed to the institution and its success. Personnel stability also ensures a supply of experienced policymakers. High personnel turnover, especially in the early years of an institution, is said to engender precarious transitions.[84] After examining detailed records for our six selected regions, however, we found no positive correlation between institutional success and personnel stability in either the regional council or the cabinet. The two regional councils with the lowest mean tenure over the entire 1970–1988 period were Emilia-Romagna and Veneto, which achieved virtually the highest ratings on our evaluation of institutional performance. "Fresh" leadership may be as important as "seasoned" leadership in explaining which institutions succeed.

· *The Italian Communist party (PCI)* has sometimes been given credit for the strong performance of certain regions. Certainly in a descriptive sense, our evidence is consistent with the judgment, widely held across party lines in Italy, that Communist regions are better governed than most others. Sometimes this is attributed to a rational, competitive calculation on the part of the PCI that it could best establish its credentials as a national party of government by showing how well it could rule regionally and locally. A more cynical alternative sometimes offered is that the PCI has, despite itself, been spared the corrupting effects of national power. Communists themselves attribute their "businesslike" successes to a systematic effort to recruit competent cadres or even to superior morality. Each of these interpretations contains a grain of truth, although we are most attracted by the first.

Our initial analysis covering the 1970–1976 period suggested that this difference was due entirely to the fact that the Communists had come to power in unusually civic regions. "Communist regional governments were more successful [we argued] because they tilled more fertile soil, not because of their techniques of plowing. It is not *who* they were, but *where* they were, that counted."[85] Our subsequent analysis, however, suggests that this might not be the whole story.

After 1975, Communists joined ruling coalitions in several regions less favored by civic tradition, and performance in those regions tended in fact to improve. By the time of our later, fuller evaluation of institutional performance, the correlation between PCI power and institutional performance was not entirely attributable to covariance with the civic community.[86] On the other hand, during the period of our research, the Communists remained in opposition in virtually all those regions, mainly in the South, where the civic and economic conditions are most detrimental to effective governance. Only when the PCI (now re-baptized the "Democratic Party of the Left") gains power in adverse circumstances of that sort will it be possible finally to evaluate the claim that party control makes a difference for good government.[87]

With the possible, partial exception of PCI rule, none of these supplementary explanations adds anything at all to our understanding of why some governments work and others do not. The evidence reviewed in this chapter is unambiguous: Civic context matters for the way institutions work. By far the most important factor in explaining good government is the degree to which social and political life in a region approximates the ideal of the civic community. Civic regions are distinctive in many respects. The next question is this: Why are some regions more civic than others?

CHAPTER 5

Tracing the Roots of the Civic Community

OUR INQUIRY into the performance of Italian regional governments in the 1970s and 1980s has pinpointed the unique character of civic life in some regions. Following that thread now draws us deep into the contrasting pasts of Italy's regions. Our story begins with a momentous time of transition on the Italian peninsula nearly a thousand years ago, as Italians were emerging from that obscure era justly termed the Dark Ages. Early medieval Italy, when our story opens, was closer to ancient Rome than to our own times, not only chronologically but also in everyday ways of life. Nevertheless, social patterns plainly traceable from early medieval Italy to today turn out to be decisive in explaining why, on the verge of the twenty-first century, some communities are better able than others to manage collective life and sustain effective institutions.[1]

THE CIVIC LEGACIES OF MEDIEVAL ITALY

Although the regional governments were established in 1970 against the backdrop of a national administration that had been highly centralized for a hundred years, the regions themselves had far deeper historical roots. For a millennium and a half, from the fall of Rome until the middle of the nineteenth century, Italy was, in the dismissive words of the Austrian statesman Metternich, merely "a geographical expression," a congeries of many small city-states and semi-colonial dominions of foreign empires. In a world of modernizing European nation states, this fragmentation condemned Italians to economic backwardness and political marginality.

It had not always been so. In the medieval period, Italians had created political structures more advanced than any other in Christendom. Indeed, two strikingly distinctive political regimes, both innovative and both destined to have far-reaching social, economic, and political consequences, appeared around 1100 in separate parts of the peninsula:

> Throughout the peninsula during the eleventh century, the time-honoured imperial system of government—Byzantine in the south, German in the north—passed through a time of strain and weakness, ending in virtual collapse, which handed the initiative to local forces. In the south the breakdown of the central government was relatively short-lived and a powerful Norman

kingdom built upon Byzantine and Arab foundations emerged; in the north, on the other hand, the attempts to revive imperial power all ended in failure and local particularism triumphed all but completely. It was in this region, stretching from Rome to the Alps, that the characteristic Italian society of the Middle Ages was free to evolve most fully; here the communes became in effect city-states, so that the area may be conveniently described as communal Italy.[2]

The new regime in the South, founded by Norman mercenaries from northern Europe and centered in Sicily, was singularly advanced, both administratively and economically. "The great Norman ruler, Roger II, who united Sicily, Apulia, and Calabria in 1130, retained the institutions of his Byzantine and Muslim predecessors, particularly their efficient system of taxation."[3] After a period of turbulence, his successor Frederick II re-established his dominion over all Italy south of the emerging Papal States and imposed an enlightened and widely admired "blend of Greek bureaucracy and Norman feudalism, but more fully integrated into a united state than it had been under his predecessors."[4] In 1231 Frederick issued a new constitution, which included the first codification of administrative law in Europe in seven centuries and foreshadowed many of the principles of the centralized, autocratic state that would later spread across the continent. Frederick's *Constitutiones* represented the monarchy's assertion of a monopoly over the provision of justice and public order, as well as an emphatic endorsement of the privileges of the feudal nobility.[5] In a Hobbesian world of widespread violence and anarchy, as afflicted all of Europe in the early Middle Ages, the imposition of social order was the supreme issue of governance.

Quite remarkably for the times, the Norman kingdom practiced religious toleration and gave freedom of worship to Moslems and Jews. Norman kings patronized an extraordinary flowering of Greek, Arabic, Jewish, Latin, and Italian vernacular arts, architecture, and learning so renowned that from Roger II to Frederick II the court was sometimes termed "a republic of scholars." In 1224 Frederick founded at Naples the first state university in Europe, where candidates were trained for the civil service he had elaborated, building on the foundations laid by Roger in the previous century. "At its zenith Norman Sicily had possessed the most highly developed bureaucracy of any western kingdom."[6]

Economically, the kingdom boasted several flourishing commercial towns, including Palermo, Amalfi, and Naples, Messina, Bari, and Salerno. Frederick enlarged their harbors and established a navy and merchant fleet, although (true to his autocratic mission) he insisted on state monopolies of much of the kingdom's commerce, a policy which would not serve the realm well in the future. A bold soldier-diplomat, a talented ornithologist, a gifted poet, as well as a creative ruler, Frederick was regarded by his contemporaries as *stupor mundi*, "the wonder of the world."[7] "By the end of the 12th century, Sicily, with its control of the Mediterranean sea routes, was the richest, most advanced, and highly organized State in Europe."[8]

In its social and political arrangements, however, the South was, and would remain, strictly autocratic, a pattern of authority that was reinforced by Frederick's reforms. His *Constitutiones* reaffirmed the full feudal rights of the barons and declared it "sacrilege" to question the ruler's decisions. "In their comprehensiveness and detail, and above all in their concept of royal authority, Frederick's laws illustrate the singularity of Sicily in western Europe. The *regnum* was held by the Emperor from God himself."[9] Like his great predecessor Roger II, Frederick had a mystical, semidivine conception of the monarch's role, and his rule rested on awe, coupled with terror and occasional cruelty. When he launched a military campaign against the northern communes, it was, he said, to teach a lesson to those who "preferred the luxury of a certain imprecise freedom to stable peace."[10]

Southern towns showed some signs of desire for self-government, but they were soon incorporated within the Norman kingdom and subjugated by a network of central and local officials responsible only to the king. Although the barons, like the townsmen, were controlled by the royal administration, the barons provided the military strength that lay at the core of the regime. Historians debate whether the kingdom is best labelled "feudal," "bureaucratic," or "absolutist," but the best judgment is that it had strong elements of all three. In any event, any glimmerings of communal autonomy were extinguished as soon as they appeared. The civic life of artisans and merchants was regulated from the center and from above, not (as in the North) from within. As Denis Mack Smith concludes,

> Sicily was still a fairly rich country where one might have expected a vigorous town life, but in fact she never knew anything like the independent communes which existed in northern Italy; and although this may reflect a simple lack of civic enterprise, it also derived from the fact that the Norman monarchy was too authoritarian and too strong to need to encourage the cities against the baronage. . . . Frederick tied the cities to the state, even though this may have seemed to sacrifice economics to politics. Sicilian history had taught him that prosperity came from a strong kingship, and up to a point he was right: only later events were to show that economic development was arrested in Sicily just when the free maritime communities elsewhere in Italy were becoming adventurous and rich.[11]

As royal power began to fade after Frederick's death, the southern barons gained power and autonomy, but southern towns and cities did not. As the centuries passed, the steep social hierarchy came to be ever more dominated by a landed aristocracy endowed with feudal powers, while at the bottom masses of peasants struggled wretchedly close to the limits of physical survival. Between these two social formations cowered a small, largely impotent middle class of administrators and professionals. Although southern Italy in the next seven centuries was to be the subject of much bitter contention between various foreign dynasties (especially Spain and France), this hierarchic structure would endure essentially unchanged. The regime remained a feudal monarchy, no matter how enlightened its incumbent, and among Frederick II's successors, enlightenment would turn out to be much rarer than rapacity.

Meanwhile, in the towns of northern and central Italy—"oases amidst the feudal forest"[12]—by contrast, an unprecedented form of self-government was emerging. This communal republicanism gradually came to constitute the major alternative to the manor-based, lord-and-serf feudalism of the rest of medieval Europe. Of this part of Italy, the eminent historian Frederic Lane has written, "From the twelfth to the sixteenth century the feature which most distinguished Italian society from that in other regions in Europe was the extent to which men were able to take part in determining, largely by persuasion, the laws and decisions governing their lives."[13]

Like the autocratic regime of Frederick II, the new republican regime was a response to the violence and anarchy endemic in medieval Europe, for savage vendettas among aristocratic clans had laid waste to the towns and countryside in the North as in the South. The solution invented in the North, however, was quite different, relying less on vertical hierarchy and more on horizontal collaboration. The communes sprang originally from voluntary associations, formed when groups of neighbors swore personal oaths to render one another mutual assistance, to provide for common defense and economic cooperation. "While it would be going too far to describe the early communes as private associations, for they must have been involved in public order from the start, it remains true that they were primarily concerned with the protection of their members and their common interests, and they had no organic connection with the public institutions of the old regime."[14] By the twelfth century communes had been established in Florence, Venice, Bologna, Genoa, Milan, and virtually all the other major towns of northern and central Italy, rooted historically in these primordial social contracts.

The emerging communes were not democratic in our modern sense, for only a minority of the population were full members.[15] Indeed, one distinctive feature of the republican synthesis was the absorption of the rural nobility into the urban patriciate to form a new kind of social elite. However, the extent of popular participation in government affairs was extraordinary by any standard: Daniel Waley describes the communes as "the paradise of the committee-man" and reports that Siena, a town with roughly 5000 adult males, had 860 part-time city posts, while in larger towns the city council might have several thousand members, many of them active participants in the deliberations.[16] In this context, "the success of communal republicanism depended on the readiness of its leaders to share power with others as equals."[17] The executive leaders of the commune were elected according to procedures that varied from town to town.[18] Those who governed the communal republics acknowledged legitimate limits on their rule. "Elaborate legal codes were promulgated to confine the violence of the overmighty."[19] In this sense, the structure of authority in the communal republics was fundamentally more liberal and egalitarian than in contemporary regimes elsewhere in Europe, including, of course, the South of Italy itself.

As communal life progressed, guilds were formed by craftsmen and tradesmen to provide self-help and mutual assistance, for social as well as for strictly occupational purposes.[20] "The oldest guild-statute is that of Verona, dating from 1303, but evidently copied from some much older statute. 'Fraternal assistance in necessity of whatever kind,' 'hospitality towards strangers, when passing through the town' . . . and 'obligation of offering comfort in the case of debility' are among the obligations of the members."[21] "Violation of statutes was met by boycott and social ostracism."[22]

Soon these groups, along with other townsmen, began to press for broader political reform, "some system of representation and control which would secure order: 'the tranquil and peaceful state of the city'."[23]

> During the first half of the thirteenth century the guilds became the backbone of radical political movements which sought the distribution of power within the communes on a wider basis than before. . . . [T]hey appropriated the old name of *popolo* ["the people"] with its powerful democratic overtones. By 1250 the *popolo* had secured a dominant position in the constitutions of the major communes.[24]

Thus, at the very moment when Frederick II was strengthening feudal authority in the South, political power in the North had begun to diffuse well beyond the traditional elite. For example, "Modena's town council already in 1220 had many artisans and shopkeepers, including fishmongers and clothes-repairers or rag merchants . . . , as well as the always numerous smiths."[25] The practices of civic republicanism provided a breadth of popular involvement in public decision making without parallel in the medieval world.

These political changes were part of "the burgeoning of associative life with the rise of communes, guilds, business partnerships, . . . new forms of solidarity [that] expressed a more vivid sense of equality."[26] Beyond the guilds, local organizations, such as *vicinanze* (neighborhood associations), the *populus* (parish organizations that administered the goods of the local church and elected its priest), confraternities (religious societies for mutual assistance), politico-religious parties bound together by solemn oath-takings, and *consorterie* ("tower societies") formed to provide mutual security, were dominant in local affairs.[27]

The oaths of mutual assistance sworn by members of these associations in all sectors of society sounded remarkably like that of the Veronese guild we cited earlier. In 1196 members of a *consorteria* of Bolognese magnates swore "to help each other without fraud and in good faith . . . with our tower and common house and swear that none of us will act against the others directly or through a third party." The statutes of the *Spade* ["Sword"] *compagnia* (1285), one of many voluntary associations in the neighborhoods of Bologna, recorded that its members "should maintain and defend each other against all men, within the commune and outside it." In each case, these broad commitments were followed by elaborate descriptions of the procedures of the association, including the practical assistance to be provided to members, such as legal aid, as well as procedures for resolving disputes among members.[28] "The inevitable conflicts generated within and between these more complex communities called for skilled advocates, mediators and statesmen, and even for a renewed civic morality to prevent the new society from tearing itself apart in internecine strife."[29] This rich network of associational life and the new mores of the republics gave the medieval Italian commune a unique character precisely analogous to what (in the previous chapter) we termed a "civic community."

Public administration in the communal republics was professionalized. A corps of experts in municipal government developed remarkably advanced systems of public finance (including a market in negotiable long-term public securities), land reclamation, commercial law, accounting, zoning, public hygiene, economic development, public education, policing, and government by committee, often sharing ideas with colleagues in neighboring cities. Bologna, with its renowned school of law, played the role of "capital of communal Italy, with an informal pre-eminence based not on force or wealth, but on intellectual leadership."[30] The figure of the *podestà*, an itinerant, professionally trained jurist-administrator elected for a limited term, came to play a key part in communal affairs.[31]

Covenants and contracts were central to all aspects of life in the republics, and the ranks of notaries, lawyers, and judges burgeoned to record, interpret, and enforce these agreements. Bologna, a town of roughly 50,000 inhabitants, is estimated to have had 2000 professional notaries![32] Such figures could, of course, be seen as an index of the contentiousness of the republics, but more fundamentally, they signify an unusual confidence in written agreements, in negotiation, and in the law. Nothing signals more clearly the unique contribution of the communal republics than this: At a time when force and family were the only solutions to dilemmas of collective action elsewhere in Europe, citizens of the Italian city-states had devised a new way of organizing collective life.

Ecclesiastical authority in the communal republics was minimal, not because religiosity was replaced by secularism, but because Church hierarchy was supplanted by lay associations:

> Without attacking the theoretical supremacy of the pope, townsmen tended to regard the church, like their secular governments, as for all practical purposes a local affair. . . . They saw priests not as superior to other men but as primarily the servants of the communities whose spiritual needs they were supposed to meet. . . . This should not be taken, however, as a sign of any decline in religious fervour. The 14th and 15th centuries were, in fact, a peculiarly devout age in the history of Italy, but Italian devotion now took on a special quality. It found expression in spontaneous and local confraternities of laymen for the purposes of performing pious works and devotional exercises together.[33]

One result of all these developments was a powerful and unparalleled degree of civic commitment:

> Along the banks of the Arno and near the Po, in the Veneto as in Liguria, citizens had a first and fervent allegiance to their own cities, to the local shaping of their own political destinies, and this feeling survived the Renaissance. . . . From the day of the commune's emergence, men had found order and protection by grouping together. As the commune had expanded, the life of urban residents came to turn more and more around the decisions and fortified buildings of local government. The feeling that men had their earthly and family fortunes tied to the fortunes of the commune became such as to arouse the most intense loves and hatreds.[34]

Intimately associated with the expansion of civic republicanism was a rapid growth in commerce. As civil order was established, bold and ambitious merchants expanded their trading networks, first in the regions around each city-state and then gradually to the farthest reaches of the known world. "These merchants, masters of the commerce of the world, founders of European capitalism, extended their empire of trade from China to Greenland."[35] For markets of this complexity to evolve, closely integrated communities of traders were crucial, able to sustain legal or quasi-legal institutions to settle disputes, exchange information, and share risks.[36] The prosperity produced by trade helped in turn to shape and sustain the civic institutions of the republics. "Of the ten 'Major Arts' (or guilds) which largely took over the government of Florence in the thirteenth century, seven were in export trades."[37]

Mercantile development was vital for the economies of the republics. Its fundamental institutions—markets, money, and law—represented a revival of practices that had been relatively well developed in the classical world. Another economic institution hardly less fundamental than these was, however, quite novel: *Credit* was invented in the medieval Italian republics.[38] At the same time that the Norman kingdom in the Mezzogiorno was enjoying a new prosperity based on social and political hierarchy, the civic republicanism of the northern cities laid the foundations for one of the great economic revolutions in world history, comparable (according to some historians) only to the Neolithic emergence of permanent settlements and the later industrial revolution.

"At the heart of this transformation was an exponential increase in credit."[39] Earlier epochs, no matter how grand or how mean, had had only the most rudimentary mechanisms for linking savings and investment, and hence their prospects for economic development were limited. Without credit, individual families might accumulate great fortunes, or the state might enforce savings through taxation and invest in massive public works, like the pyramids or the Parthenon, but until some means of efficient intermediation between individual savers and independent investors could be devised, the immense power of private capital accumulation could not be harnessed to economic growth. For this momentous social invention to succeed, the unique context provided by the communal republics proved crucial.

Unlike the wealth of the Sicilian kingdom, based on land, the growing prosperity of the northern Italian city-states was rooted in finance and commerce.[40] Banking and long-distance trade depended on credit, and credit, if it were to be provided efficiently, required mutual trust and confidence that contracts and the laws governing them would be impartially enforced. (Etymologically, "credit" derives from *credere*, "to believe.") For reasons we shall explore more fully in the next chapter, the institutions of civic republicanism, the networks of associations, and the extension of solidarity beyond the bonds of kinship that had emerged in the northern communes were crucial for this trust and confidence to flourish.

In this rich civic soil sprouted numerous innovations in business practice, which helped generate the affluence, public and private, of Renaissance Florence and her neighbors:

> The extension of credit and the increased use of the contract were prominent features of the takeoff in the towns of north and central Italy in the eleventh and twelfth centuries. In Genoa, Pisa, Venice, and a bit later in Florence, new legal strategies for raising capital and creating partnerships were coming

into vogue. Not surprisingly, the bonds of partnership were grafted onto family ties. . . . By the twelfth century, however, more flexible contractual arrangements were being entered into and the contributions of outsiders welcomed. These changes were manifested in the rise of the *compagnia*, the *commenda* [long-distance shipping enterprises], deposit banking, fiduciary money, and letters of credit. In the new practices and organization of business activity, risks were minimized, whereas opportunities for cooperation and profit were enhanced. . . . We can discern a measure of this expanded trust in the decline of interest rates and the rise of deposit and transfer banking. A *collaborative* attitude between borrower and lender was becoming pervasive in the cities of north and central Italy."[41]

Through these and other mechanisms, even small savers were enabled to invest in larger commercial enterprises:

> The basic fact in the economic history of Europe from the eleventh century onward was that savings were activated for productive purposes to a degree inconceivable in previous centuries. . . . It was the widespread sense of honesty, strengthened by the sense of belonging to an integrated community, quite apart from definite legal obligations, which made possible the participation of all kinds of people with their savings in the productive process.[42]

In sum, in the communal republics of northern medieval Italy, vast improvements in economic life, as well as in governmental performance, were made possible by the norms and networks of civic engagement. Revolutionary changes in the fundamental institutions of politics and economics arose out of this unique social context, with its horizontal ties of collaboration and civic solidarity, and in turn, those political and economic advances reinforced the civic community.

We must not exaggerate the egalitarianism of the communes nor their success in resolving social conflict and controlling violence. Perhaps as many as half of the population were indigent slum-dwellers.[43] Throughout the period the nobility remained an important part of society, even though they were increasingly integrated within, and subordinated to, the life of the republics. Oligarchic families played an essential role in the life of republics like Venice and Florence, even though their power was less untrammeled than in the South. The nobility kept retinues of clients around them. Factionalism was rife. Clan vendettas and violence (including a kind of low-level guerilla warfare) never disappeared from public life. The battle towers and fortified palaces that still adorn Bologna and Florence recall both the social inequalities and the pervasive insecurity that characterized even the most successful of communes.

Nevertheless, social mobility within the republics was higher than anywhere else in Europe at the time. Moreover, the role of collective solidarity in maintaining the civic order marked the northern cities as *sui generis*. One anonymous chronicler in 1291, for instance, reported laconically, "There was a certain disturbance in Parma, and so four trades, that is, the butchers, the smiths, the shoemakers, and furriers, together with the judges and notaries and the other trades of the city, took oath together to maintain themselves, and having made certain provisions, all disturbance immediately stopped."[44]

Thus, by the beginning of the fourteenth century, Italy had produced, not one, but two innovative patterns of governance with their associated social and cultural features—the celebrated Norman feudal autocracy of the South and the fertile communal republicanism of the North. "The Italians were the pacesetters in the art of government, and the Italian states generally developed a greater bureaucratic power to intervene in the lives of their citizens, for good or ill, than was to be found in the other states of the time."[45] In economic and social life, as well as in politics, both the monarchy and the republics had surmounted the dilemmas of collective action and the problems of collective life that still stifled progress elsewhere in Europe. Italy's leading role in Europe could be measured not just politically and economically and artistically, but also demographically: Palermo in the South and Venice and Florence in the North, each with populations over 100,000, were the three largest cities of Europe.[46]

But the systems that had been invented in the North and in the South were quite different, both in their structure and in their consequences. "Two different societies and ways of life here faced other," concludes the historian John Larner.[47] In the North, feudal bonds of personal dependence were weakened; in the South, they were strengthened. In the North, the people were citizens; in the South, they were subjects. Legitimate authority in the North was "only delegated [by the community] to public officials, who remain responsible to those with whose affairs they are entrusted."[48] Legitimate authority in the South was monopolized by the king, who (though he might delegate administrative tasks to officials and might confirm the nobles in their privileges) was responsible only to God. In the North, while religious sentiments remained profound, the Church was only one civil institution among many; in the South, the Church was a powerful and wealthy proprietor in the feudal order.[49] In the North the crucial social, political, and even religious allegiances and alignments were horizontal, while those in the South were vertical. Collaboration, mutual assistance, civic obligation, and even trust—not universal, of course, but extending further beyond the limits of kinship than anywhere else in Europe in this era—were the distinguishing features in the North. The chief virtue in the South, by contrast, was the imposition of hierarchy and order on latent anarchy.

The pre-eminent social issue of the Middle Ages, the *sine qua non* for all progress, was public order. Theft and plunder were common. Protection and refuge might be provided, as in the Norman kingdom, by an autocratic sovereign or the strongest local baron. Or security could be sought instead through interweaving pacts of mutual assistance among rough equals, the more complex strategy followed in the communal republics. As compared to the rest of Christendom, both regimes produced prosperity and efficient government, but the limits of the southern, hierarchic solution to the dilemmas of collective action were already becoming manifest by the thirteenth century. Whereas a hundred years earlier the South generally had been reckoned no less advanced than the North, the communal republics were now pulling rapidly ahead, and the North's lead would continue to widen for the next several centuries. Gradually the full consequences of the differences in community life and social structure between feudal and republican Italies were becoming manifest.

> In the feudal world, a vertical arrangement typically prevailed, where relations between men were dictated by the concepts of fief and service; investiture and homage; lord, vassal, and serf. In the cities, a horizontal arrangement emerged, characterized by cooperation among equals. The *gild*; the *confraternity*; the *university*; and above all of them, that gild of gilds, the sworn union among all the burghers, the *Commune*, were institutions created by the new outlook and which reflected the new ideals.[50]

During the fourteenth century, factionalism and famine, the Black Death and the Hundred Years War began to undermine the spirit of the civic community and the stability of republican government. The devastation of the Black Death was extraordinary: More than one third of the entire population of Italy—and probably more than half of the urban population—perished during the savage summer of 1348, and this was followed by recurrent epidemics that severely depressed economic activity for more than a century. Nor was political leadership in the communal republics spared: of the Council of Seven elected in Orvieto at the end of June, 1348, six were dead by August—a decimation that was by no means unique. The cathedral of Siena, only half-finished when the plague struck, remained so—mute evidence of how thoroughly the Black Plague sapped civic energies and shattered civic life.[51]

Moreover, the clamor of clashes among broader religious and military forces beyond the city walls echoed increasingly within the republics themselves. "The history of the communes could hardly be other than tumultuous, for they were trying to practice government on conciliar principles in a society which remained intensely hierarchical."[52] Nearly everywhere, Guelphs, Ghibellines, and a hundred other clans struggled in constant intrigue and often bloody strife. Relying on mercenary armies, individual despots [*signori*] and their families gained political dominance. These new tyrannies were "very long lasting, the medieval *signoria* evolving imperceptibly into the renaissance principate."[53]

By the beginning of the fourteenth century, more than two hundred years after they had been founded, republican communal governments had begun to succumb to signorial domination, although the despots often continued to pay homage to the forms and ideals of republican government.[54] A significant exception to this spectacle of decay, however, was provided by a belt of cities extending across north-central Italy from Venice on the Adriatic across Emilia and Tuscany to Genoa on the Tyrrhenian Sea, where republican traditions proved hardier than elsewhere further north.[55]

Just as Minerva's owl of wisdom flies only at dusk, political philosophers began to articulate the essential virtues of the *vita civile* [civic life] of the communal republics only at their demise. The fate of the communes inspired Renaissance political theorists, Machiavelli above all, to reflect on the preconditions for stable republican government, focusing especially on the character of the citizens, their *virtù civile*.

Machiavelli, in a passage of remarkable relevance to our own task of understanding institutional success and failure, argued that republican government (though the most desirable form of government where it could be achieved) was destined to fail where social conditions were unsuitable. In particular, where men lack civic virtue and where social and economic life is organized in feudal fashion, "there has never arisen any republic or any political life, for men born in such conditions are entirely inimical to any form of civic government. In provinces thus organized [like Naples, he added] no attempt to set up a republic could possibly succeed." In his native Tuscany, by contrast, social conditions were so favorable "that a wise man, familiar with ancient forms of civic government, should easily be able to introduce there a civic constitution." Machiavelli's chapter title aptly summarizes what we might term the "iron law of civic community": "That it is very easy to manage Things in a State in which the Masses are not Corrupt; and that, where Equality exists, it is impossible to set up a Principality, and, where it does not exist, impossible to set up a Republic."[56]

The works of Machiavelli, Guicciardini, and others "express a feeling for the particular political community as a concrete and continuing entity that is independent of the men and governments in power at any given time and worthy of human affection, loyalty, and support."[57] At the core of this ideology of the *vita civile* was the ideal of "the model citizen, governing his own affairs in town and country and dutifully participating in the affairs of the state."[58]

Meanwhile, by the thirteenth century, the Papacy had acquired tempo-ral sway over the territory between the Kingdom of Sicily in the South and the domain of the communal republics in the North. The Pope ruled over these lands as a feudal monarch, appointing princes to fiefdoms in return for fealty, but his control was less centralized and efficient than that of the Norman regime to the south.[59] Given the somewhat ambiguous temporal authority of the Pope, further weakened during the period of the Avignon papacies between 1305 and 1377, the Papal States encompassed a wide variety of social structure and political practice. In some towns local ty-rants resisted Papal interference, while elsewhere "the nobility fought each other, terrorized the countryside, and did as they pleased, and ban-dits made the region everywhere unsafe."[60] To the north, on the other hand, the papal territories nominally included several cities with strong communal traditions, such as Ferrara, Ravenna, Rimini, and above all, Bologna.

Figure 5.1 shows the various regimes that characterized Italy at the beginning of the fourteenth century.[61] The map clearly reveals four bands across the peninsula, corresponding to differing degrees of republicanism and autocracy. From south to north, they are as follows:

- The feudal monarchy founded by the Normans in the Mezzogiorno;
- The Papal States with their variegated mixture of feudalism, tyranny, and republicanism;
- The heartland of republicanism, those communes which had retained re-publican institutions into the fourteenth century; and
- The erstwhile republican areas further north that had, by this time, fallen prey to signorial rule.

The parallel between this pattern and the distribution of civic norms and networks in the 1970s, as displayed in Figure 4.4, is remarkable. The southern territories once ruled by the Norman kings constitute exactly the seven least civic regions in the 1970s. Almost as precisely, the Papal States (minus the communal republics that lay in the northern section of the Pope's domains) correspond to the next three or four regions up the civic ladder in the 1970s. At the other end of the scale, the heartland of republicanism in 1300 corresponds uncannily to the most civic regions of today, followed closely by the areas still further north in which medieval republican traditions, though real, had proved somewhat weaker. To de-termine whether this intriguing correlation represents a genuine historical continuity or merely a curious coincidence, we shall need to scrutinize the evolution of Italian social and political life during the intervening seven centuries.

During the fifteenth and early sixteenth centuries, further miseries were inflicted on the peninsula, as Spain, France, and the other ascendant pow-

FIGURE 5.1
Republican and Autocratic Traditions: Italy, c. 1300

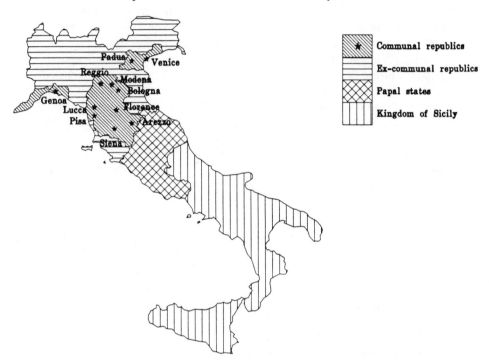

Sources: *The Times Atlas of World History*, 3rd edition, eds. Geoffrey Barraclough and Norman Stone (London: Times Books, 1989), p. 124; J. K. Hyde, *Society and Politics in Medieval Italy: The Evolution of the Civil Life, 1000–1350* (London: Macmillan, 1973), Map 4; and John Larner, *Italy in the Age of Dante and Petrarch: 1216–1380* (New York: Longman, 1980), pp. 137–150.

ers of Europe fought their bloody dynastic duels in the Italian arena. The demographic and economic consequences of these foreign invasions, together with the devastating plagues and trade disruptions of the previous century, were especially traumatic for the communes of the North. The populations of Brescia and Pavia, for instance, each fell by two-thirds during the early years of the sixteenth century, as a result of repeated assaults and sacking. Not until the nineteenth century would the cities of the North reach once again their medieval population levels. The South, by contrast, escaped much of this destruction. The population of Naples, for example, doubled during the fifteenth century and more than redoubled during the first half of the sixteenth century, becoming (after Paris) the second largest city in Europe. Contrary to the population flows of the twentieth century, many northerners migrated southwards during the sixteenth century, drawn by the relative prosperity of the South, coupled with the dismal downfall of the North. In the first half of the seventeenth century, just as the glimmerings of economic revival began to appear, new waves of epidemics swept across Italy. In 1630–31 and again in 1656–57, up to half of the population of the cities of the Center and North perished from the plague.[62]

By the seventeenth century, all the cities of central and northern Italy had ceased to be republican or even, in many cases, independent. The collapse of communal republicanism led to a kind of "re-feudalization" of the Italian peninsula. Mercantile and financial innovation was replaced by a preoccupation with land ownership and parasitic indolence. Local conflicts, factional struggles, and convoluted conspiracies signified the dissolution of the social fabric, just as the other states of Europe were moving toward national unity.[63]

Throughout Italy, North and South, autocratic politics were now embodied in patron-client networks. However, among the northern heirs to the communal tradition, patrons, no matter how autocratic, still accepted civic responsibilities—a usage echoed in our expression "patron of the arts." Careful anthropological reconstruction of this epoch in the life of a central Italian hill town has confirmed that although the local gentry monopolized political power, they also subsidized civic life by endowing hospitals and roads, local choirs and bands, and even municipal offices and the salaries of town clerks. The ethic of mutual responsibility persisted in the northern countryside, as well, as, for example, in the *aiutarella*, a traditional practice of work exchange among neighbors.[64] Thus, despite the spread of inequality, exploitation, and factional conflict, the northern heritage of communal republicanism, although no longer embodied in political institutions, was transmitted in the form of an ethic of civic involvement, social responsibility, and mutual assistance among social equals.

Patterns of authority in the North were no longer so distinct from the feudal structures of the Mezzogiorno. Nevertheless, something of the glorious experience of the communes, and of the intense economic activity that civic engagement had generated, survived in the Po Valley and Tuscany, so that these regions would be more receptive to the first breezes of renewed progress, first cultural and then economic, that whispered along the peninsula in the second half of the eighteenth century. Despite the social and economic gloom provoked by several centuries of foreign depredation, pestilence, and domestic strife, the ideal of the *vita civile* persisted in the regions of communal republican traditions.

Meanwhile, the medieval heritage of governance in the South provided an enduring contrast. Frederick II's sovereign had offered a solution of a sort to problems of collective action, but this solution was soon corrupted by the proverbial effects of absolute power: King and barons became predatory autocrats. Government remained feudal and autocratic, tempered only by episodic, ephemeral rebellion. Authoritarian political institutions were reinforced by the tradition of vertical social networks, embodying power asymmetries, exploitation and dependence, in contrast to the northern tradition of horizontal associations, joining rough equals in mutual solidarity. Patron-client politics in the South was more personalistic, more exploitative, more transitory, less "civil."

By the eighteenth century, "the Kingdom of Naples, with its two sections, one on the mainland and the other in Sicily, was by far the biggest State in Italy with its five million inhabitants, but for a long time it was possibly also the worst administered, the most routine-bound and negligent."[65] As had been true in the earliest medieval period, and as remains true today—contrary to a common misapprehension—the South was no less urban than the North during much of this period.[66] In 1791 Naples' population was twice that of Rome, three times that of Milan, four times that of Turin or Florence; but Naples was "a grotesque parasite, many of whose inhabitants were royal employees, priests, domestic servants, and beggars. She lived on the back of a desperately overworked, desperately poor, peasantry, who were given no civic rights."[67] In the southern cities, the power of the nobility remained paramount, with "little of that mingling of nobles and townsmen so characteristic of society in the north."[68]

In the North the aristocracy's power, which had long been challenged, was already beginning to erode. By contrast, "in the south 'during the first decades of the eighteenth century the political jurisdictional and economic power of the barony [was] still virtually intact.' There, the process of overthrowing feudalism was particularly slow: at the end of the century the power of the barons was still extremely strong."[69] The gulf between rulers and ruled was exacerbated in the Mezzogiorno by the fact that virtually all the successive dynasties that controlled the South were alien. From 1504 until 1860, all of Italy south of the Papal States was ruled by the Hapsburgs and the Bourbons, who (as Anthony Pagden has recently described in detail) systematically promoted mutual distrust and conflict among their subjects, destroying horizontal ties of solidarity in order to maintain the primacy of vertical ties of dependence and exploitation.[70]

Despite the eclipse of communal republicanism in the North after the fourteenth century, as the democratic revolutions that were to sweep Europe in the nineteenth century approached the Italian peninsula, the discerning observer could detect the continuing regional differences of culture and social structure that had appeared in the medieval era seven centuries earlier. As we shall see, those enduring differences would powerfully condition how the various regions would respond to the new challenges and opportunities that loomed ahead, as Italy achieved national unification.

CIVIC TRADITIONS AFTER UNIFICATION

The nineteenth century was a time of unusual ferment in the associational life of much of Western Europe, particularly among the so-called "popular" classes—that is, the great bulk of the population. Older forms of organized sociability, such as the medieval guilds and religious societies, had gradually lost vitality over the preceding centuries, and were mere remnants from that earlier age when they had genuinely engaged popular interests and passions. Winds of change, spawned by the French Revolution, now swept away much of this moldering social underbrush. Inspired by the astringent doctrine of *laissez faire*, liberal governments in France, Italy, and elsewhere abolished guilds, dissolved religious establishments, and discouraged the revival of any similar social or economic "combinations." To enforce this new order, officials in France and Italy kept close surveillance over (and often tried to suppress) even such innocuous signs of organized sociability as workingmen's drinking clubs.

This attempted eradication of association—the contemporary background, incidentally, against which Tocqueville was writing his encomium of associationism in America—was not borne lightly in the villages and towns of the continent. Soon, the first stirrings of the industrial revolution made the creation of new forms of organized social and economic solidarity even more urgent. To the ancestral hazards of illness, accident, and old age were now added the unaccustomed perils of unemployment and the unpleasant anonymity of the new industrial centers. Nor were those who remained on the land immune to novel ills, as the agricultural panics of the second half of the century made plain. In a time of turbulence and uncertainty many people sought aid and solace in organized camaraderie. Like a verdant second growth following a forest conflagration, new and more vital associations began to spring up to replace those that had decayed or been destroyed earlier in the century.

This "great surge in popular sociability" (in the words of the eminent French social historian Maurice Agulhon) arose in France in the first half of the nineteenth century.[71] It was manifested in Masonic lodges and *cercles*, in popular drinking clubs (*chambree*) and choral societies, in religious fraternities and peasant clubs, and most especially in mutual aid societies, created to provide self-help insurance against the costs of sickness, accidents, old age, and burial. Many of the associations had extremely detailed written statutes, "remarkable for their preoccupation with financial rigour, the fair distribution of tasks and political and moral guarantees—in short, with efficiency in the widest sense of the term."[72]

Although many of the associations were formed predominantly by members of the lower classes, membership often cut across conventional social boundaries within the local community; one *cercle*, for example, "was, for the most part, composed of 'workers and artisans,' 'masons, locksmiths and cobblers' with, at their head, a number of bourgeois or rather petits bourgeois who were also intellectuals."[73] Although social inequalities were clearly still important within the village, the social structure encouraged by the new associationism was difficult to classify,

> somewhere between, on the one hand, the old-style patronage and, on the other, the new egalitarianism. . . . It looks as though there was a progress from right to left, that is from a structure of patronage, which was conservative, to an egalitarian structure which was democratic and that this passed through an intermediary phase of democratic patronage.[74]

Although these groups were not overtly political, they often came to have political affinities with one or another of the *tendences* of French political life. Social interaction and the exercise of organizational skills widened the cultural horizons of the participants and quickened their political awareness and (eventually) their political involvement. "For the lower classes of Provence at this period, to set themselves up as a *chambree* was, just as much and perhaps even more than learning to read, to become accessible to whatever was new, to change and to independence."[75] Agulhon's painstaking reconstruction of life in several southern French villages of this era has shown how this cultural mobilization in the years after 1830 contributed directly to the great political mobilizations of 1848.

Italian social historiography of this period awaits its Agulhon, so we lack any similarly evocative portrait of social life in the early nineteenth-century Italian town. Nevertheless, it seems likely that similar trends appeared during the *Risorgimento* (or "resurgence") that roused Italians to political action and led in 1870 to the political unification of Italy.[76] In fact, much of the argument for unification was based on claims for the "principle of association" which all the various nationalist movements (Mazzinians, neo-Guelphs, Cavourian moderates) stressed. Scientific congresses, professional associations, and reformist groups (especially in Piedmont, Tuscany and Lombardy) pressed for major social, economic, and political reforms. Newly formed associations (including the renowned "secret societies") and newspapers were central to the abortive revolutions of 1848 and to the nationalist agitation that led to the plebiscites of 1860 that ratified unification. New civic, charitable, and educational associations were founded in most cities and towns.[77]

A particularly important manifestation of this "principle of association" in post-unification Italy was the development of mutual aid societies, directly analogous to their French counterparts and to the "friendly societies" of Britain, also founded in this period. In the aftermath of the suppression of the Italian guilds and "pious societies," particularly after 1850, these mutual aid societies—"the first embryo of an associative process"[78]—were founded to alleviate the social and economic hardships of urban artisans and craftsmen.

The functions of the mutual aid societies included benefits to aged and incapacitated members and those otherwise unable to work; aid to families of deceased members; compensation for industrial accidents; payments to unemployed workers; monetary encouragement to members traveling in search of jobs; funeral expenses; nursing and maternity care; and the provision of educational opportunities for members and their families, including night schools, elementary instruction, arts and crafts, and circulating libraries. Although the mutual aid societies responded particularly to the needs of the urban working classes, their membership and their appeal cut across conventional boundaries of class, economic sector, and politics.[79] In effect, mutual aid societies provided a locally organized, underfunded, self-help version of what the twentieth century would call the welfare state.

These voluntary associations signified less an idealistic altruism than a pragmatic readiness to cooperate with others similarly placed in order to surmount the risks of a rapidly changing society. At the core of the mutual aid societies was practical reciprocity: I'll help you if you help me; let's face these problems together that none of us can face alone. In this sense, these new forms of sociability were directly reminiscent of the formation of the medieval communes more than seven centuries earlier, with their fabric of organized collective action for mutual benefit. Just as the earliest medieval self-help associations represented voluntary cooperation to address the elemental insecurity of that age—the threat of physical violence—so mutual aid societies represented collective solidarity in the face of the economic insecurities peculiar to the modern age.

At about this same time and often under the aegis of mutual aid societies, cooperative organizations also began to spring up among both producers and consumers. "Like mutual aid societies, Italian cooperatives grew out of the conservative principle of self-help and endeavored to better the lot of their members without seeking drastic changes in existing economic arrangements."[80] The new organizations spread through all sectors of the economy; there were agricultural cooperatives, labor cooperatives, credit cooperatives, cooperative rural banks, producer cooperatives, and consumer cooperatives, the latter comprising more than half of all cooperatives by 1889. In fact, concludes one close student of working class organization, "the variety of cooperatives in Italy made that country unique in the world of cooperation."[81]

Although cooperatives were becoming common in much of Europe in this period, one of the distinguishing features of the Italian movement was its strength among unlettered peasants in the countryside. Many cooperatives were founded in the 1880s in the North "to carry out public works schemes during winter unemployment."[82] For example, in 1883 a group of landless *braccianti* in Emilia-Romagna formed a cooperative to bid for contracts for land drainage.

> There were co-operative dairies and wine factories, as well as co-operative rural banks, and for perishable truck-garden produce a joint sales organization was most necessary. Agricultural experts were employed by a society and sent around to give demonstrations on market days, to teach pruning and wine production and the use of vegetables in the rotation of crops.[83]

These forms of organized but voluntary social solidarity grew rapidly in the last decades of the nineteenth century. Membership in the mutual aid societies more than quadrupled in the three decades after 1870 and peaked at the turn of the century. "The period from 1860 to 1890 must be characterized as the golden age of mutual aid societies," concludes one scholar.[84] The comparable surge in cooperatives occurred a decade or so later.

The ancestry of these organizational initiatives in prior forms of organized sociability, particularly in northern Italy, was often quite conscious and explicit. The first of the new cooperatives, for example, was the Society of Artistic Glassware in the glassmaking center of Altare in Liguria:

> On Christmas night of 1856, Giuseppe Cesio took the lead in bringing together 84 artisans of this ancient craft in Altare. They proposed to better their lot, greatly threatened by economic depression and the aftermath of the cholera epidemic, through the formation of a cooperative association. The ritual which elaborated this declaration of purpose suggested the revival of the medieval tradition of this region of Liguria where, around the year 1000, there sprang up the famous guild of Altare which survived until its suppression by King Carlo Felice on June 6, 1823.[85]

Although the manifest purposes of these organizations were nonpolitical, they served important latent political functions. Like their French counterparts, the Italian mutual aid societies were formally nonpartisan, although some were vaguely radical and republican, and others were variously liberal, socialist, or Catholic in inspiration. The cooperative movement, too, remained independent of political parties, though collaborating with mutual aid societies and the nascent trade union movement. Despite this nonpartisanship, however, participation in these activities must have had what a later generation would term "consciousness-raising" effects, for many leaders in the newly emerging labor unions and political movements came from the world of mutual aid societies and cooperatives. Union activity in both agriculture and industry expanded rapidly during the first two decades of the twentieth century. The largest of the union federations was socialist in orientation, but there was also a strong Catholic-inspired federation, along with a number of independent organizations.

Meanwhile, from the 1870s to the 1890s, the "Social Catholicism" movement spawned numerous lay associations, particularly in the strongly Catholic Northeast. By 1883–84 the most influential lay organization, the *Opera dei Congressi e dei Comitati Cattolici*, had 993 parish committees in the North, 263 in Central Italy, though only 57 in the South; and "by 1897 the '*Opera*' claimed 3,892 parish committees, 708 youth sections, 17 university circles, 688 workers' associations, 588 rural banks, 24 daily newspapers, 105 periodicals, and many other organizations and activities."[86] Although the South was no less devoutly Catholic than the North, it was notably less represented in the civic associations of Social Catholicism, as it would be in Catholic Action after World War II.[87]

The incipient socialist counterparts to these Catholic organizations were centered in the Chambers of Labor:

> The Chambers, or their offshoots, organized housing co-operatives, co-operative shops, and educational associations. They often produced their own magazines and ran their own recreational facilities. . . . They illustrate how the allegedly 'modern', Socialist labour movement was deeply impregnated with the older, Mazzinian ideals of local co-operatives and self-help, of laicism and mutual aid.[88]

Although universal manhood suffrage was not established in Italy until World War I, several mass-based political movements were formed around the turn of the century. The socialist movement constituted the largest and most active of these new parties, with growing strength both in areas of incipient industrialization and in some parts of the countryside, where it drew on local traditions of collective peasant and sharecropper protest. The new political mobilization also included an important and growing progressive Catholic movement, especially in the Northeast, where the lay associations of Social Catholicism had been most active in the preceding two decades. In 1919, on the eve of the first postwar elections, the Catholic movement was formally constituted as the *Partito popolare*, or Popular party. The electoral strength of these two parties, the socialists and the *popolari*, jointly representing organized mass opposition to the traditional regime, reached a peak just after World War I in the few years of universal male suffrage before the advent of Fascism.

Both the socialists and the *popolari* drew on the heritage of social mobilization, the organizational infrastructure, and the energies of the mutual aid societies, the cooperatives, and the labor unions. Sesto San Giovanni, for example, an industrial suburb of Milan, was the site of two strong and rivalrous community networks, one Catholic and one socialist, each of which included housing and consumer cooperatives, educational and athletic associations, bands and choral groups, and so forth.[89] The two parties were natural rivals for the allegiance of the masses of the Italian electorate, and each had particular regional strongholds. Generally speaking, the socialist party and its labor affiliates flourished in the industrializing areas around Milan, Turin, and Genoa, whereas the *popolari* and their associated unions were stronger in agricultural areas. This rivalry would provide the basis for the dominant image of Italian political society after World War II, centered on the conflict between two "institutionalized traditions" or "subcultures," the red (socialist) and the white (Catholic).[90]

This red/white image is in some respects misleading, however, for despite their rivalry, the two mass-based parties had common sociological roots in ancient traditions of collective solidarity and horizontal collaboration. At the turn of the century they also shared opposition to the existing authorities. Both were weakest where the established conservative alliance, based on clientelist ties with established social elites of landowners and officeholders, was strongest. At the grass-roots of Italian politics, the main alternative to the socialists and the *popolari* was the labyrinth of vertical patron-client networks that for nearly half a century had provided the basis of the system of *trasformismo*, in which state patronage was bartered (via local notables) for electoral support. After World War II these same patron-client networks, now increasingly organized within the framework of the mass parties themselves, would persist as the primary structure of power in the less civic regions of Italy.[91]

Although mutual aid societies, cooperatives, and other manifestations of civic solidarity were established in all sectors of the economy and in all parts of the peninsula, they were not equally extensive or equally successful everywhere. In north-central Italy, mirroring almost precisely that area where the communal republics had longest endured five centuries earlier (and where the most civic regions would be found in the 1970s), the medieval traditions of collaboration persisted, even among poor peasants. "A significant network of social and economic obligations, particularly in the countryside, is formed by the recognition of neighborhoodship. Between *vicini* [neighbors] there is continuous mutual aid and exchange of services."[92]

> Sharecropping families had in fact developed a rich network of exchanges and mutual aid: typical of these was the *aiutarella*, the exchange of labour

between families at crucial moments in the agricultural calendar, such as at threshing time. On a cultural level there was also the important practice of the *veglia*. During the long winter evenings, families would gather in the stables or kitchens of the farmhouses, to play cards and games, to knit and to mend, to listen to and tell stories. Participation in the *veglia* was not segregated family by family. Rather, . . . it involved rotating hospitality and a complex system of visiting.[93]

By stark contrast, an 1863 report concluded that in Calabria, a desolate land locked in the southern traditions of authoritarian rule (and destined to rank as the least civic of all the regions in the 1970s), there were "no associations, no mutual aid; everything is isolation. Society is held up by the natural civil and religious bonds alone; but of economic bonds there is nothing, no solidarity between families or between individuals or between them and the government."[94]

In areas of Italy long subjected to autocratic rule, national unification did little to inculcate civic habits:

In all classes the absence of a community sense resulted from a habit of insubordination learned in centuries of despotism. Even the nobles had become accustomed to obstruction, and thought that governments could be fairly cheated without moral obliquity so long as the cheating were successful. . . . Instead of recognizing that taxes had to be paid, the attitude was rather that if one group of people had discovered a profitable evasion, then other groups had better look to their own interests. Each province, each class, each industry thus endeavored to gain at the expense of the community.[95]

Southern agriculture, although complicated by a crazy-quilt patchwork of landholding, was typified by the *latifondo*,[96] or large estate, worked by impoverished peasants:

The peasants were in constant competition with each other for the best strips of land on the *latifondo*, and for what meagre resources were available. Vertical relationships between patron and client, and obsequiousness to the landlord, were more important than horizontal solidarities. As Bevilacqua has written for the period 1880–1920: 'The peasant classes were more at war amongst themselves than with the other sectors of rural society; a war which fed off a terrain of recurring and real contrasts, both economic, psychological and cultural.' That such attitudes triumphed can only be understood in the context of a society which was dominated by distrust. . . . [T]he weight of the past, when combined with the failures of state authority after 1860 and the disastrous peasant-landlord relations . . . produced a society where *fede pubblica* (civic trust) had been reduced to a minimum: '*chi ara diritto, muore disperato*' (he who behaves honestly comes to a miserable end) was a noted Calabrian proverb.[97]

The primeval mistrust that rent the social fabric in these regions was, in fact, captured in innumerable proverbs:

- "Damned is he who trusts another."
- "Don't make loans, don't give gifts, don't do good, for it will turn out bad for you."
- "Everyone thinks of his own good and cheats his companion."
- "When you see the house of your neighbor on fire, carry water to your own."[98]

In the Mezzogiorno, above all, observed Pasquale Villari in 1883, "One feels too much the 'I' and too little the 'we'."[99]

The combination of impoverishment and mutual distrust forestalled horizontal solidarity and fostered what Banfield has called "amoral familism."[100] "In an overcrowded latifundia economy," recalls Sidney Tarrow, "the village square was an employment bureau where the fortunate few found a day's labor while their bitter neighbors looked on."[101] "Each became different from the other; he came to find himself ever more involved in a bitter battle of competition to obtain work or to be able to cultivate a little land, and thus participated less in class solidarity and in the life of the collectivity, and appeared exclusively interested in the progress of himself and his family."[102] Mark the contrast with those landless *braccianti* of civic Emilia-Romagna who, facing a similar dilemma, formed a voluntary cooperative to seek shared work.

As Tarrow, among other scholars, has emphasized, the South *was not* (and *is not*) apolitical or asocial.[103] On the contrary, political cunning and social connections have long been essential to survival in this melancholy land. The relevant distinction is not between the presence and absence of social bonds, but rather between horizontal bonds of mutual solidarity and vertical bonds of dependency and exploitation. The southerner—whether peasant or city-dweller, whether in the old Hapsburg kingdom of the sixteenth century, the new Italian kingdom of the nineteenth century, or (as we saw in the previous chapter) the regional politics of the late twentieth century—has sought refuge in vertical bonds of patronage and clientelism, employed for both economic and political ends:

> Clientelism is the product of a disorganic society and tends to preserve social fragmentation and disorganization. . . . Turiello [a close observer of the Mezzogiorno in the 1880s] refers again and again to the 'excessive isolation (*scioltezza*) of individuals' who feel no moral bond outside the family, and views the clientele as the specific remedy for a disjointed society. The clientele, he wrote, are 'the only associations which actually show real operative energy in a civil society which has been divided within itself for centuries' and in which people unite not on the basis of mutual trust but only when forced by necessity.[104]

The new institutions of the unified nation-state, far from homogenizing traditional patterns of politics, were themselves pulled ineluctably into conformity with those contrasting traditions, just as the regional governments after 1970 would be remolded by these same social and cultural contexts:

In the 1870s, one can say that the most advanced provinces of Italy already were expressing their preferences through free institutions or associations—agrarian associations, mutual aid societies, chambers of commerce, savings banks—while the southern ones were more inclined to make use of personal contacts or parliamentary and municipal clienteles.[105]

The southern feudal nobility—along with elements of the urban professional classes who had acquired common land and Church properties expropriated by the newly-forged Italian state—used private violence, as well as their privileged access to state resources, to reinforce vertical relations of dominion and personal dependency and to discourage horizontal solidarity.[106] Leopoldo Franchetti, a civic-minded Tuscan landowner who in 1876 authored a remarkable analysis of social conditions in Sicily, concluded:

The landed classes ruled from on high the network of clientelistic structures at various levels and maintained contact for their own advantage with the supreme representative organs of the country. . . . Every local notable in his jurisdiction of power was the head of a network of persons of the most diverse social conditions, who depended on him for their economic survival and social prestige and who furnished him legal support in terms of electoral suffrage and illegal support in the recourse to private violence in defense of his particular interests, in a rigorously hierarchical relationship of para-feudal dependence.[107]

For wretchedly vulnerable peasants, recourse to patron-client ties was a sensible response to an atomized society. One recent account of the "moral economy" of life on a *latifondo* estate in Calabria in the first half of the nineteenth century recounts that peasants in fact feared exclusion from the patron-client system, for it alone assured their physical subsistence, along with the necessary intermediation with distant state authorities and a primitive kind of private welfare program (pensions for widows and orphans and occasional "gratuities"), so long as the peasant-client remained obedient, "faithful" to the estate, and "available" to perform chores as required by the landlord-patron.[108] In the absence of horizontal solidarity, as exemplified by mutual aid societies, vertical dependence is a rational strategy for survival—even when those who are dependent recognize its drawbacks.[109]

The dispossessed southern peasantry did not always endure their fate in silence. Violent protest movements, including chronic brigandage, flared like heat lightning across the Mezzogiorno landscape throughout the late nineteenth century. However, these anarchic episodes (unlike the contemporary urban and rural strike waves in the center and north of the country) produced no permanent organization and left little residue of collective solidarity.[110] The South remained, as the great Communist intellectual Antonio Gramsci lamented, "a great social disaggregation."[111] Despite the occasional violent revolts, "it is more important to emphasize the more usual passive reaction of resigned submission. For it is this submission that provides the historical background to the acceptance of the arrogation of power by individuals, viz. the *mafiosi*, by the rest of the population."[112]

Organized criminality bears different labels in various parts of the Mezzogiorno—*Mafia* in Sicily, *Camorra* in Campania, *'Ndrangheta* in Calabria, and so on, but the phenomenon everywhere has a broadly similar structure. Historians, anthropologists, and criminologists debate its specific historical origins, but most agree that it is based on traditional patterns of patron-clientelism, and that it burgeoned in response to the weaknesses of the administrative and judicial structures of the state, in turn further undermining the authority of those structures. "The chronic weakness of the State resulted in the emergence of self-help institutions, and the exclusive power position of informal groups subsequently made it impossible for the State to win the loyalty of the public, while its resultant weakness again strengthened the family, the clientage, and *mafiosi* positions."[113]

If the absence of credible state enforcement of laws and contracts was one precondition for the emergence of the Mafia, a second, no less important, was the ancient culture of mistrust. Diego Gambetta emphasizes this prerequisite for *mafioso* power: "Distrust percolates through the social ladder, and the unpredictability of sanctions generates uncertainty in agreements, stagnation in commerce and industry, and a general reluctance towards impersonal and extensive forms of cooperation."[114] As Franchetti, the aristocratic Tuscan visitor to Sicily, observed in 1876:

> Matters naturally reached a point where the instinct of self-preservation made everyone ensure the help of someone stronger; since no legitimate authority in fact existed, it fell to clientelism to provide the force which held society together. . . . A very unequal distribution of wealth; a total absence of the concept of equality before the law; a predominance of individual power; the exclusively personal character of all social relations; all this [was] accompanied (as was inevitable) by the bitterest of hatreds, by a passion for revenge, by the idea that whoever did not provide justice for himself lacked honor.[115]

Given this pervasive lack of trust and security, ensured neither by the state nor by civic norms and networks, *mafiosi* (and their counterparts elsewhere in the South) provided a kind of privatized Leviathan. "The Mafia offered protection against bandits, against rural theft, against the inhabitants of rival towns, above all against itself."[116] Mafia "enforcers" enabled economic agents to negotiate agreements with a modicum of confidence that those agreements would be kept. "The most specific activity of *mafiosi* consists in producing and selling a very special commodity, intangible, yet indispensable in a majority of economic transactions. Rather than producing cars, beer, nuts and bolts, or books, they produce and sell trust."[117]

As one *mafioso* explained his role, "One man will come and say: 'I have a problem with Tizio, do see if you can settle the matter for me.' I summon the person concerned to me or else I go and visit him—according to what terms we are on—and I reconcile them."[118] (The *mafioso*, of course, also has an interest in increasing demand for his services by judicious injections of distrust into the system, to prevent his customers from establishing independent mutual trust.) Despite the manifold costs of this system—social, economic, political, psychic, and moral—from the point of an individual trapped, powerless, in the desolate anarchy of the Mezzogiorno, "to choose to obtain the mafioso's protection can hardly be considered irrational."[119]

Only a romantic idealization of the Mafia, however, could ignore its fundamentally hierarchic, exploitative nature. In the nineteenth century, *mafiosi* served as violent middlemen between absentee landlords and their clients.[120] As older forms of feudalism began to break down, "the ancient *bravi* [underlings] of the feudal lords went into business for themselves and continued to exercise violence for private purposes. . . . These malefactors, freed from the pure system of feudal relations, became thus an essential factor in the clientelistic system that took its place."[121] Like the conventional clientelism it mirrored, the Mafia adjusted quickly to the new institutions of the Italian state, and inexorably reshaped the practices of representative democracy into conformity with traditional patterns of exploitation and dependence.

The structure of the Mafia itself is classically based on vertical (often unstable) relations of authority and dependence, with little or no horizontal solidarity among equals. According to Hess's detailed account, the basic organizational unit of the Mafia, the *cosca*, is not a group:

> Interaction and an awareness of 'we', a consciousness of an objective to be jointly striven for, are absent or slight. Essentially it is a multitude of dyadic relationships maintained by the *mafioso* (m) with persons independent of each other $(X_1 - X_n)$. . . . None of the X persons regards himself as a member of an organization, in a way that a bandit or partisan regards himself as belonging to a gang or to a resistance group, i.e., to groups which can survive even after the elimination of the leader.[122]

Organized criminality is an organic element in the pattern of horizontal mistrust and vertical exploitation/dependence that has characterized southern culture and social structure for at least a millennium.[123]

MEASURING THE DURABILITY OF CIVIC TRADITIONS

Standard historical accounts are unambiguous in their contrasting descriptions of civic engagement in the North and in the South. However, this broad contrast obscures important and enduring differences within each of these two broad sections of the country, differences from region to region and even from province to province. For example, Pino Arlacchi's careful description of life in three areas within nineteenth-century Calabria contrasts the naked authoritarianism of Crotone and the clan violence of Gioia Tauro with the unexpected tradition of cooperatives and mutual aid in nearby Cosentino. To these contrasting traditions, Arlacchi traces the marked differences in social stability and economic progress that have characterized these three areas in the postwar period.[124] We have already noted some variation in the tenacity of civic traditions among the various regions of the North. If we are to establish more systematically the fine-grained linkages between these traditions and the incidence of the civic community profiled in the previous chapter, we must move beyond qualitative sketches to quantitative assessments. We must discipline our tale by careful counting.

The available statistical evidence confirms the stark differences from region to region in associationism and collective solidarity a century ago. By 1904, for example, Piedmont had more than seven times as many mutual aid societies as Puglia, in proportion to population. By 1915, cooperative membership per capita was eighteen times greater in Emilia-Romagna than in Molise. These regional concentrations depended in turn on the pre-existing traditions of collaboration and sociability. Often an ancient guild found reincarnation in a "pious society" in the eighteenth century, which in turn evolved into a mutual aid society, which encouraged cooperatives, which subsequently formed the basis for labor unions and mass-based political parties.

All these modern manifestations of social solidarity and political mobilization, stretching over the six decades between 1860 and 1920—mutual aid societies, cooperatives, and mass-based political parties—were closely intercorrelated. They were associated as well with other manifestations of civic involvement and sociability, including electoral participation and cultural and recreational associations. The available nationwide quantitative indicators of civic engagement in the late nineteenth century thus include the following:

- Membership in mutual aid societies;[125]
- Membership in cooperatives;[126]
- Strength of the mass parties;[127]
- Turnout in the few relatively open elections before Fascism brought authoritarian rule to Italy;[128]
- The longevity of local associations.[129]

The impressive intercorrelations among these several metrics (shown in detail in Appendix F) demonstrate that, in the nineteenth and early twentieth centuries, the same Italian regions that sustained cooperatives and choral societies also provided the most support for mutual aid societies and mass parties, and that citizens in those same regions were the most eager to make use of their newly granted electoral rights. Elsewhere, by contrast, apathy and ancient vertical bonds of clientelism restrained civic involvement and inhibited voluntary, horizontally organized manifestations of social solidarity.

In order to explore the historical antecedents of "civic-ness" in contemporary Italy, we have combined these five indicators into a single factor score, representing nineteenth-century traditions of civic involvement, as summarized in Table 5.1.[130] Figure 5.2 charts how these traditions of civic involvement varied across the regions that Italy comprised in the half century between roughly 1860 and 1920.

Even a cursory comparison of Figure 5.2 with Figure 4.4 attests to the astonishing constancy of regional traditions of civic involvement through more than a century of vast social change. A more convenient way of visualizing this continuity is provided in Figure 5.3, which arrays the almost perfect correlation between our Civic Community Index for the 1970s and 1980s and our comparable measure of civic involvement a century earlier.[131] Despite the massive waves of migration, economic change, and social upheaval that have swept along the peninsula in the intervening decades, contemporary civic norms and practices recapitulate regional traditions that were well established long ago.[132]

Where Italians a century ago were most actively engaged in new forms

TABLE 5.1
Traditions of Civic Involvement, 1860–1920

Component	Loading
Strength of mass-based parties, 1919–1921	0.97
Incidence of cooperatives, 1889–1915	0.93
Membership in mutual aid societies, 1873–1904	0.91
Electoral turnout, 1919–1921	0.78
Local associations founded before 1860	0.56

FIGURE 5.2
Civic Traditons in the Italian Regions, 1860–1920

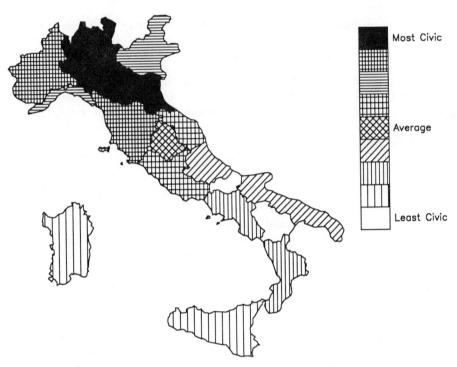

of social solidarity and civic mobilization, exactly there Italians today are the most thoroughly civic in their political and social life. And in these very regions public life was distinctively civic nearly a millennium ago, with an equally impressive flowering of community life, including tower societies, guilds, neighborhood associations, and other forms of civic engagement. The absence of adequate statistical records prevents us from demonstrating this longer continuity with the same quantitative precision that is possible for the more recent period, although Figure 5.1, Figure 5.2, and Figure 4.4 provide glimpses of this continuity in c. 1300, c. 1900, and c. 1970. In any event, the rituals performed at the Christmas Eve founding of that first cooperative in Altare in 1865 suggest that these historical continuities did not escape the participants themselves.

How important are these deep traditions of civic life for institutional performance today? Figure 5.4 presents the correlation between institutional performance in the 1980s and civic traditions in 1860–1920. The pattern is stark: One could have predicted the success or failure of regional government in Italy in the 1980s with extraordinary accuracy from patterns of civic engagement nearly a century earlier.[133]

FIGURE 5.3

Civic Traditions and the Civic Community Today

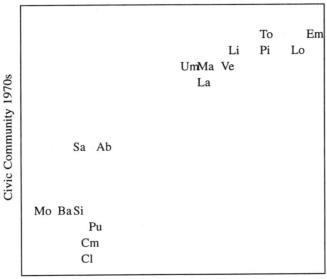

Civic Traditions, 1860–1920
Correlation: $r = .93$

FIGURE 5.4

Traditions of Civic Involvement, 1860–1920, and
Institutional Performance, 1978–1985

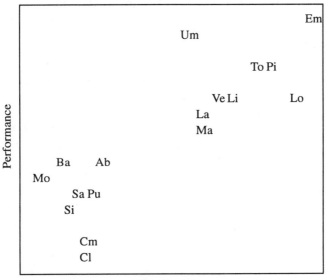

Civic Traditions
Correlation: $r = .86$

ECONOMIC DEVELOPMENT AND CIVIC TRADITIONS

In quantitative social science, it is rare indeed to discover patterns as powerful—almost mesmerizing—as those we have just examined. An important omission from our argument, however, will already have occurred to
the prudent reader. In contemporary Italy, the civic community is closely
associated with levels of social and economic development. Generally
speaking, regions today that are civic are also healthy, wealthy, and industrial. That could easily mean, a skeptic might suspect, that the civic
community is merely epiphenomenal—that only economic well-being
can sustain a culture of civic involvement. It is difficult today for poor,
sickly peasants to engage in civic-minded participation, and so it must
have been a century ago. Might not continuities in economic and social
structure account for the apparent continuities in civic life? Perhaps the
mesmerizing correlations are spurious. Economics matters, not civics.

The historical saga we have recounted casts some doubt on this claim,
for the long-term patterns of continuity and change are not consistent with
any simple economic determinism. In the first place, the emergence of
communal republicanism does not seem to have been the consequence of
unusual affluence. The level of economic development in northern Italy in
that period was quite primitive, far less advanced than the Mezzogiorno
today, and perhaps even less advanced than the South in that epoch.[134] As
we have seen, the prosperity of the communal republics was arguably the
consequence, as much as the cause, of the norms and networks of civic
engagement.[135]

In the second place, civic differences between the North and South over
this millennium appear to have been more stable than economic differences. The North-South economic gap seems to have waxed and waned
and even reversed direction in several periods, especially in response to
external developments. In the twelfth century the Norman kingdom was
nearly as advanced as the North, but, with the advent of communal republicanism, the North (and especially the towns of the Center-North, the
heartland of civic engagement) grew more rapidly for several centuries.
Beginning in the fifteenth century, however, in the aftermath of pestilence, foreign invasion, shifts in world trading patterns, and other exogenous shocks, the North's advantage faded and perhaps disappeared
entirely by the sixteenth century. Recall those sixteenth century migrants,
fleeing the debilitated North in search of a better life in booming Naples.
By contrast, although the cultural gap is hard to measure precisely across
these centuries, we have encountered no evidence that at any point over
these ten centuries the South was ever as civic in its norms and patterns of
association as the North.

TABLE 5.2
Civic Traditions and Socioeconomic Development

| Decade | *Correlation (r) between Civic Traditions (1860-1920) and Measures of Socioeconomic Development (1870s–1970s)* | | |
	Agricultural Share of Workforce	*Industrial Share of Workforce*	*Infant Mortality*
1870s	−0.02	−0.15	−0.07
1880s	−0.22	0.14	−0.22
1890s	—	—	−0.26
1900s	−0.43	0.52	−0.20
1910s	−0.52	0.64	−0.44
1920s	−0.56	0.66	−0.58
1970s	−0.84	0.84	−0.67

The civic regions did not begin wealthier, and they have not always been wealthier, but so far as we can tell, they have remained steadfastly more civic since the eleventh century. These facts are hard to reconcile with the notion that civic engagement is simply a consequence of prosperity.

For the period since Unification, we can draw on more quantitative evidence to assess the notion that economic development is the cause or precondition for civic norms and networks. The first bit of statistical data contrary to simple economic determinism is this: the powerful contemporary correlation between economics and civics did not exist a century ago. We can demonstrate this notable fact with indicators both of industrialization (as measured by agricultural and industrial employment) and of social well-being (as measured by infant mortality), for which reliable data are available on the Italian regions over the last century. (Table 5.2 offers the relevant evidence.)

Throughout this period, economic structure and social well-being have become ever more closely aligned with the virtually unchanging patterns of civic involvement. Like a powerful magnetic field, civic conditions seem gradually but inexorably to have brought socioeconomic conditions into alignment, so that by the 1970s socioeconomic modernity is very closely correlated with the civic community.[136]

To appreciate this pattern, contrast two regions that at the turn of the century seemed in many respects comparable in terms of economic structure and social well-being. In 1901 Emilia-Romagna ranked just at the national median in terms of industrialization, with 65 percent of its workforce on the land and only 20 percent in factories. By way of comparison, Calabria was slightly more industrial than Emilia-Romagna (with 63 percent of its workforce in agriculture, 26 percent in industry). To be sure, Calabria's economy was "paleo-industrial," for the region's industry was primitive, and its citizens were poorer and less educated, while Emilian agriculture was relatively prosperous. On the other hand, Emilia-Romagna's infant mortality rate in the first decade of this century was worse than the national average, whereas Calabria's figure was slightly better than the national average, though still appalling in absolute terms.[137] Whatever the marginal socioeconomic differences between them, both were backward regions.

In terms of political participation and social solidarity, on the other hand, Emilia-Romagna was blessed at the turn of the century (as it remains today and as it apparently had been almost a millennium ago) with virtually the most civic culture in all of Italy. By contrast, Calabria was cursed (and still is) by perhaps the least civic of Italian regional cultures—feudal, fragmented, alienated, and isolated.

Over the next eight decades, a social and economic gap of remarkable proportions opened between the two regions. Between 1901 and 1977, the fraction of the Emilian workforce in industry doubled (from 20 percent to 39 percent), whereas the fraction of Calabria's workforce in industry actually declined over those eight decades (from 26 percent to 25 percent), the only region in all of Italy for which that was true. Thanks to advances in medicine and public health, infant mortality had fallen substantially throughout Italy, but Calabria had trailed well behind Emilia-Romagna.[138] By the 1980s, Emilia-Romagna, with one of the most dynamic economies in the world, was on its way to becoming the wealthiest region in Italy and among the most advanced in Europe, while Calabria was the poorest region in Italy and among the most backward in Europe. Among the eighty regions of the European Community, ranked by GDP per capita, Emilia-Romagna jumped from 45th to 17th place between 1970 and 1988, the biggest jump recorded by any region in Europe, while Calabria remained locked in last place throughout the period.[139]

This pattern of correlations raises an intriguing possibility: Perhaps regional traditions of civic involvement in the last century help account for contemporary differences in levels of development. In other words, perhaps civics helps to explain economics, rather than the reverse.

Despite the frailties of these historical statistics, we can exploit the available data to explore more directly the interdependencies between socioeconomic development and traditions of civic involvement.[140] One simple empirical test is to compare two sets of predictions, using the same set of independent variables in each case:

   1. Predicting level of economic development in the 1970s from development and civic involvement around 1900.

FIGURE 5.5
Possible Effects among Civic Involvement, Socioeconomic Development,
and Institutional Performance: Italy, 1900s–1980s

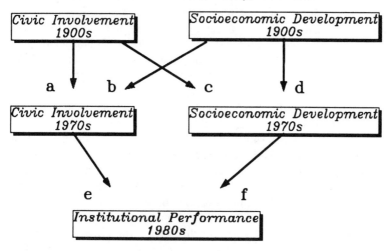

2. Predicting civic involvement in the 1970s from the same earlier measures of development and civic involvement.

If the economic determinist is correct, economics at time one should predict civics at time two. If, on the other hand, patterns of civic involvement have economic consequences, then civics at time one should help to predict economics at time two. (In both cases, we need to control for the earlier levels of the dependent variable, since presumably the best single predictor of a variable at time two is that same variable at time one—the so-called "auto-regressive" effect.) In principle, of course, both effects might operate simultaneously, implying some reciprocal influence between civics and economics. Figure 5.5 illustrates the several possible causal paths.

Theories that give priority to socioeconomic structure imply that arrows *b* and *d* should be quite strong (especially *b*), whereas the theory that civics has socioeconomic consequences emphasizes arrows *a* and *c* (especially *c*). Both theories can be tested with pairs of multiple regressions, using civic traditions and a given socioeconomic variable as measured around 1900 to predict civic patterns and the same socioeconomic variable as measured in the 1970s.[141]

The results of this statistical horse race turn out to be straightforward and startling. In the first place, civic traditions (as measured in the 1860–1920 period) are a very powerful predictor of contemporary civic community, and (controlling for civic traditions) such indicators of socioeconomic development as industrialization and public health have no impact whatsoever on civics. That is, arrow *a* is very strong and arrow *b* is uniformly nonexistent. When civics and socioeconomic structure were inconsistent at the turn of the century (a region that was civic, but relatively poor, rural, and sickly; or a region that was uncivic, but relatively wealthy, healthy, and industrial), there was no subsequent tendency for the civic traditions to be remolded to fit the "objective conditions." [142]

By contrast, civic traditions turn out to be a uniformly powerful predictor of present levels of socioeconomic development, even when we hold constant earlier levels of development. Consider each of our socioeconomic variables in turn.

The most direct measures of social structure and economic development are *agricultural* and *industrial employment*. These data clearly reflect the industrial revolution that swept over Italy during this century. Over the period from 1901 to 1977, the average fraction of the workforce engaged in industry rose from 19 percent to 34 percent, while the average fraction employed in agriculture across the twenty regions fell from 66 percent to 19 percent. Throughout this period the cross-regional differences were quite marked: In 1977, agricultural employment ranged from 5 percent in Lombardia to 43 percent in Molise, while industrial employment ranged from 22 percent in Molise to 54 percent in Lombardia. Over the period between 1901 and 1977, the rankings of the regions were modestly stable, with correlations of approximately $r = .4$; conventionally, this figure would be interpreted as a measure of economic (or perhaps center-periphery) determinism.

But when we use both civic traditions and past socioeconomic development to predict present socioeconomic development, we discover that civics is actually a much better predictor of socioeconomic development than is development itself. For example, when predicting the proportion of a region's workforce in agriculture in 1977, we are much better off knowing the cultural conditions of that region in 1860–1920 than the agricultural workforce of that region in 1901–1911. In fact, nineteenth-century civic traditions are such a powerful predictor of twentieth-century industrialization that when cultural traditions are held constant, there is simply *no correlation at all* between industrial employment in 1901–1911 and industrial employment in 1977. In other words, arrow *c* is quite strong and arrow *d* is quite weak.[143]

In the case of *public welfare*, the conclusion is identical: civic traditions, as measured in 1860–1920, predict infant mortality in the late 1970s much better than infant mortality in 1901–1910 does; in fact, holding civic culture constant, the correlation between infant mortality across those six decades is insignificant. In other words, for infant mortality, arrow *d* is negligible, while arrow *c* is rather strong.[144]

FIGURE 5.6

Actual Effects among Civic Involvement, Socioeconomic Development,
and Institutional Performance: Italy, 1900s–1980s

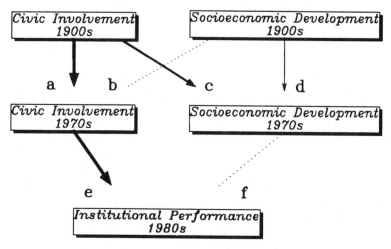

In summary, economics does not predict civics, but civics does predict
economics, better indeed than economics itself.[145] Figure 5.6 synthesizes our findings. Arrow *b* (the effect of economics on civics) is nonexistent, while arrow *c* (the effect of civics on economics) is strong—
stronger even than arrow *d*. Moreover, arrow *a* (civic continuity) is very
strong, while arrow *d* (socioeconomic continuity) is generally weak. A
region's chances of achieving socioeconomic development during this
century have depended less on its initial socioeconomic endowments than
on its civic endowments. Insofar as we can judge from this simple analysis, the contemporary correlation between civics and economics reflects
primarily the impact of civics on economics, not the reverse.[146]

Civic traditions have remarkable staying power. Moreover, as the discoveries of the previous chapter showed, it is contemporary civic engagement (arrow *e*), not socioeconomic development (arrow *f*), that directly
affects the performance of regional government. We now see further evidence that that effect is not spurious. On the contrary, these results suggest, civic traditions may have powerful consequences for economic development and social welfare, as well as for institutional performance.

Union membership, we noted in the previous chapter, is best seen as a
concomitant of civic engagement, rather than as merely a response to economic circumstance. This interpretation is strengthened by examining regional patterns of union membership just after the first World War.[147]
Aggregate union membership rates in 1921 are very strongly correlated

with prior civic traditions ($r = .84$). So strong is this link that, controlling for civic traditions, there is *no correlation at all* between industrialization and union membership. Union strength followed patterns of civic solidarity, rather than patterns of economic development.[148]

These unexpected, elemental links between civics and economics cast new light on the long-standing debate about the North-South development gap, not only within Italy but also globally. The widening gulf between North and South is *the* central issue of modern Italian history, and it is worth recalling the stark facts that have aroused such passion among scholars and activists. At Unification, neither the North nor the South had really been touched by the industrial revolution. As late as 1881, roughly 60 percent of Italians worked on the land (slightly *more* in the North), while fewer than 15 percent (slightly *more* in the South) worked in manufacturing, including cottage industry. However, northern farms were more productive, and thus per capita income was probably 15–20 percent higher in the North at the time of Unification. After 1896, however, industrialization began to move the North sharply ahead, whereas the South actually became less urban and less industrial between 1871 and 1911. Thus, by 1911 the North-South gap had widened appreciably: northern incomes were about 50 percent higher.[149]

Throughout the twentieth century the North-South gap has grown relentlessly, despite swings in world conditions (war and peace, the Great Depression and the postwar boom), fundamental constitutional changes (monarchy, Fascism, and parliamentary democracy), and great changes in economic policy (the Fascist attempt at autarky, European integration, and, not least, a massive program of public investments in the Mezzogiorno over the last forty years). Even though the South has experienced some modest, welcome development in recent decades, at the same time the North has enjoyed one of the most remarkable growth spurts in Western economic history, pulling further and further ahead of the South. By the mid-1980s, per capita income was more than 80 percent higher in the North.[150]

Few topics in Italian historiography have aroused such debate as this steadily increasing dualism—the so-called "Southern Question." Conventional economic theory, in fact, predicts gradual convergence in levels of regional development within a single country, only heightening the puzzle of Italian dualism.[151] Many possible answers have been offered:

- Physical disadvantages of the South, including distance from markets, unfavorable terrain, and lack of natural resources.
- Misguided government policies, especially in the late nineteenth century, including, in particular,

> (1) trade policy (first, free trade that killed off fledgling southern industry and later protection that encouraged northern industry);

(2) fiscal policy (high taxes on the South, and spending to benefit the North, on education, defense industries, and land reclamation—although by the end of the nineteenth century total taxes were proportionally no higher in the South[152] and the national government had already begun investing substantial sums in public works there); and

(3) industrial policy (which served northern interests by promoting an alliance between heavy industry and large banks).

- Market externalities, the "economics of agglomeration," and "learning by doing" that magnified the North's modest initial advantages.[153]
- The "moral poverty" and absence of human capital in the Mezzogiorno, along with the culture of patron-clientelism.[154]

Both the North-South gap in Italy, and the range of theories that have been offered to account for it, mirror the broader debate about development in the Third World. Why do so many countries remain underdeveloped: inadequate resources? government mistakes? center-periphery *dependencia*? market failures? "culture"? Precisely for that reason, studies of the Italian case have the potential to contribute importantly to our understanding of why many (but not all) Third World countries remain inextricably and inexplicably mired in poverty.

As Toniolo recently observed about the Italian debate, however, "this great flourishing of ideas and interpretations has not been supported—either then or later—by an adequate commitment to quantitative analysis. . . . Although the works dedicated to [the 'southern question'] would fill an entire library, many of the economist's questions as to the size and causes of Italian economic dualism . . . remain unanswered."[155]

The historical record, both distant and recent, leads us (like others) to suspect that sociocultural factors are an important part of the explanation.[156] To be sure, any single-factor interpretation is surely wrong. Civic traditions alone did not trigger (nor, in that sense, "cause") the North's rapid and sustained economic progress over the last century; that takeoff was occasioned by changes in the broader national, international, and technological environment. On the other hand, civic traditions help explain why the North has been able to respond to the challenges and opportunities of the nineteenth and twentieth centuries so much more effectively than the South.

How might this "macro" link between civics and economics be manifested at the "micro" level? Through what mechanisms might the norms and networks of the civic community contribute to economic prosperity? This key question merits more work (and we shall return to it in the next chapter), but some important insights are provided by an independent body of research carried out in recent years by Italian and American political economists. Arnaldo Bagnasco first called attention to the fact that, alongside the familiar "two Italies" of the northern industrial triangle and the backward Mezzogiorno, existed a "third Italy," based on a "diffuse economy"—small-scale, but technologically advanced, and highly productive.[157] Michael Piore and Charles Sabel extended this analysis, pointing to numerous examples in north-central Italy of craft-like "flexible specialization"—high-fashion textile firms around Prato, the Brescia mini-mill steel producers, the motorbike industry of Bologna, the ceramic tile makers of Sassuolo, and so on. Borrowing a concept from one of the founders of modern economics, Alfred Marshall, scholars have come to term such areas "industrial districts."[158]

Among the distinguishing features of these decentralized, but integrated industrial districts is a seemingly contradictory combination of competition and cooperation. Firms compete vigorously for innovation in style and efficiency, while cooperating in administrative services, raw materials purchases, financing, and research. These networks of small firms combine low vertical integration and high horizontal integration, through extensive subcontracting and "putting out" of extra business to temporarily underemployed competitors. Active industrial associations provide administrative and even financial aid, while local government plays an active role in providing the necessary social infrastructure and services, such as professional training, information on export markets and world fashion trends, and so on. The result is a technologically advanced and highly flexible economic structure, which proved precisely the right recipe for competing in the fast-moving economic world of the 1970s and 1980s. Not surprisingly, these regions of flexible specialization have enjoyed above average prosperity during these two decades.[159]

At the heart of this peculiarly productive economic structure is a set of institutional mechanisms that enable competition to coexist with cooperation by forestalling opportunism. "A rich network of private economic associations and political organizations . . . have constructed an environment in which markets prosper by promoting cooperative behavior and by providing small firms with the infrastructural needs that they could not afford alone."[160]

Social mobility is high in these industrial districts, as workers move from salaried jobs to self-employment and back again. Although labor unions are often well developed and strikes are not rare, the practice of "social compromise" encourages flexibility and innovation. Mutual assistance is common, and technical innovations diffuse quickly from firm to firm. The importance of cooperative horizontal networks among small firms and worker-owners contrasts with the salience of vertical authority and communication in large, conventional firms elsewhere in Italy. In short, by contrast with the "internal" economies of scale highlighted in classical theories of the firm, Marshallian industrial districts rely heavily on "external economies." "Narrow economic considerations combine with less precisely calculable ideas of collective advantage to create a sense of professional solidarity which is the backdrop and limit for competition between the firms."[161]

Piore and Sabel conclude that "the cohesion of the industry rests on a more fundamental sense of community, of which the various institutional forms of cooperation are more the result than the cause. . . . Among the ironies of the resurgence of craft production is that its deployment of modern technology depends on its reinvigoration of affiliations that are associated with the preindustrial past."[162]

Typically singled out as essential for the success of industrial districts, in Italy and beyond, are norms of reciprocity and networks of civic engagement. Networks facilitate flows of information about technological developments, about the creditworthiness of would-be entrepreneurs, about the reliability of individual workers, and so on. Innovation depends on "continual informal interaction in cafes and bars and in the street." Social norms that forestall opportunism are so deeply internalized that the issue of opportunism at the expense of community obligation is said to arise less often here than in areas characterized by vertical and clientelistic networks. What is crucial about these small-firm industrial districts, conclude most observers, is mutual trust, social cooperation, and a well-developed sense of civic duty—in short, the hallmarks of the civic community.[163] It is no surprise to learn that these highly productive, small-scale industrial districts are concentrated in those very regions of north-central Italy that we have highlighted as centers of civic traditions, of the contemporary civic community, and of high-performance regional government.

We regard these discoveries about the cultural antecedents of economic development as provocative, rather than conclusive. It would be ridiculous to suppose that the civic traditions we have sketched in this chapter are the only—or even the most important—determinant of economic prosperity. In fact, as the British historical geographers John Langton and R.J. Morris point out, "Whether cultural inheritance or economic development is constructed to be an independent element will depend very much on the time-scale within which the historical process is conceived. It is obvious that they interact to change one another. There was no cause and effect but a dialectical process of reciprocation."[164] Our bivariate model (Figure 5.6) is too simple to account for all of the factors that may influence regional economic progress, such as natural resources, convenience to major markets, and national economic policies. Much finer-grained studies (including studies at the subregional level) would be necessary to substantiate the broad historical argument we have sketched.

Nevertheless, the evidence of this chapter dramatizes the power of historical continuities to affect the odds of institutional success. Even our simple findings imply that, to the extent that we have overlooked the "real" cause(s) of economic development (call that Factor X), then Factor X must be more closely correlated with civic traditions than with prior economic development. Once established, affluence may reinforce "civic-ness," while poverty probably discourages its emergence, in an interlocked pair of vicious and virtuous circles. Our evidence argues, however, that the "economics → civics" loop in these interactions is not dominant. Civic norms and networks are not simply froth on the waves of economic progress.

During the last ten centuries—and particularly in the last several decades—Italy has undergone massive economic, social, political, and demographic change. Millions of Italians migrated from one region to another, more than nine million of them (or roughly one-fifth of the entire population) in the fifteen years after 1955.[165] During the first century after Unification, regions leapfrogged one another in the socioeconomic rankings. Regions with a relatively industrial economy in 1970 had not necessarily been the industrial regions a century earlier, and regions with good public health in 1970 had not been the healthier ones in 1870.

Despite this whirl of change, however, the regions characterized by civic involvement in the late twentieth century are almost precisely the same regions where cooperatives and cultural associations and mutual aid societies were most abundant in the nineteenth century, and where neighborhood associations and religious confraternities and guilds had contributed to the flourishing communal republics of the twelfth century. And although those civic regions were not especially advanced economically a century ago, they have steadily outpaced the less civic regions both in economic performance and (at least since the advent of regional government) in quality of government. The astonishing tensile strength of civic traditions testifies to the power of the past.

But *why* is the past so powerful? What virtuous circles in the North have preserved these traditions of civic engagement through centuries of radical social, economic, and political change? What vicious circles in the South have reproduced perennial exploitation and dependence? To address such questions we must think not merely in terms of cause and effect, but in terms of social equilibria. To that task we turn in the next chapter.

CHAPTER 6

Social Capital and Institutional Success

DILEMMAS OF COLLECTIVE ACTION

Collective life in the less civic regions of Italy has been blighted for a thousand years and more. Why? It can hardly be that the inhabitants prefer solitary and submissive squalor.[1] Foreign oppression might once have been part of the explanation for their plight, but the regional experiment suggests that self-government is no panacea. One is tempted to ask in exasperation: Have people in these troubled regions learned nothing at all from their melancholy experience? Surely they must see that they would all be better off if only everyone would cooperate for the common good.[2]

David Hume, the eighteenth-century Scottish philosopher, offered a simple parable that captures the essential dilemma that confounds rational public-spiritedness:

> Your corn is ripe to-day; mine will be so to-morrow. 'Tis profitable for us both, that I shou'd labour with you to-day, and that you shou'd aid me to-morrow. I have no kindness for you, and know you have as little for me. I will not, therefore, take any pains upon your account; and should I labour with you upon my own account, in expectation of a return, I know I shou'd be disappointed, and that I shou'd in vain depend upon your gratitude. Here then I leave you to labour alone; You treat me in the same manner. The seasons change; and both of us lose our harvests for want of mutual confidence and security.[3]

Failure to cooperate for mutual benefit does not necessarily signal ignorance or irrationality. Game theorists have studied this fundamental predicament under a variety of guises.

- In *the tragedy of the commons*, no herder can limit grazing by anyone else's flock. If he limits his own use of the common meadow, he alone loses. Yet unlimited grazing destroys the common resource on which the livelihood of all depends.
- A *public good*, such as clean air or safe neighborhoods, can be enjoyed by everyone, regardless of whether he contributes to its provision. Under ordinary circumstances, therefore, no one has an incentive to contribute to providing the public good, and too little is produced, causing all to suffer.
- In the dismal *logic of collective action*, every worker would benefit if all

struck simultaneously, but whoever raises the strike banner risks betrayal by a well-rewarded scab, so everyone waits, hoping to benefit from someone else's foolhardiness.

• In *the prisoner's dilemma*, a pair of accomplices is held incommunicado, and each is told that if he alone implicates his partner, he will escape scot-free, but if he remains silent, while his partner confesses, he will be punished especially severely. If both remained silent, both would be let off lightly, but unable to coordinate their stories, each is better off squealing, *no matter what the other does*.

In all these situations, as in Hume's rustic anecdote, every party would be better off if they could cooperate. In the absence of a credible mutual commitment, however, each individually has an incentive to defect and become a "free rider." Each rationally expects the other to defect, leaving him with the "sucker's payoff." "These models are . . . extremely useful for explaining how perfectly rational individuals can produce, under some circumstances, outcomes that are not 'rational' when viewed from the perspective of all those involved."[4]

This quandary does not arise from malevolence or misanthropy, although those sentiments may be fostered by its grim denouement. Even if neither party wishes harm to the other, and even if both are conditionally predisposed to cooperate—I will, if you will—they can have no guarantee against reneging, in the absence of verifiable, enforceable commitments. Worse yet, each knows that the other faces the same predicament. "It is necessary not only to trust others before acting cooperatively, but also to believe that one is trusted *by* others."[5] In such circumstances, each finds cooperation irrational, and all end up with an outcome no one wants—unharvested corn, overgrazed commons, deadlocked government.

The principal problem for Hume's farmers is the absence of credible sanctions against defection: How can each be confident that the other will keep his word in the face of temptation to shirk? More complex contexts, like modern government (or modern markets), bring the added complication of monitoring: How can one agent know whether another did in fact make a "good faith effort" to keep his word, in the face of multiple uncertainties and countervailing pressures? Both accurate information and reliable enforcement are essential to successful cooperation.

The performance of all social institutions, from international credit markets to regional governments to bus queues, depends on how these problems are resolved. In a world of saints, perhaps, dilemmas of collective action would not arise, but universal altruism is a quixotic premise for either social action or social theory. If actors are unable to make credible commitments to one another, they must forgo many opportunities for mutual gain—ruefully, but rationally.

Hobbes, one of the first great social theorists to confront this perplexity, offered the classic solution: third-party enforcement. If both parties concede to the Leviathan the power to enforce comity between them, their reward is the mutual confidence necessary to civil life. The state enables its subjects to do what they cannot do on their own—trust one another. "Everyone for himself and the State for all," as Pietr Kropotkin, the Russian anarchist, skeptically characterized the guiding principle of modern society.[6]

Sadly, the solution is too neat. North puts the problem succinctly:

> In principle, third-party enforcement would involve a neutral party with the ability, costlessly, to be able to measure the attributes of a contract and, costlessly, to enforce agreements such that the offending party always had to compensate the injured party to a degree that made it costly to violate the contract. These are strong conditions that obviously are seldom, if ever, met in the real world.[7]

Part of the difficulty is that coercive enforcement is expensive: "Societies which rely heavily on the use of force are likely to be less efficient, more costly, and more unpleasant than those where trust is maintained by other means."[8] The more basic problem, however, is that impartial enforcement is itself a public good, subject to the same basic dilemma that it aims to solve. For third-party enforcement to work, the third party must itself be trustworthy, but what power could ensure that the sovereign would not "defect"? "Put simply, if the state has coercive force, then those who run the state will use that force in their own interest at the expense of the rest of society."[9]

History has taught southern Italians the improbability of the Hobbesian solution to dilemmas of collective action. "The classic providers of institutions—monarchs—sometimes provided institutions that were welfare enhancing; but they also provided institutions that led to economic decline."[10] In the language of game theory, impartial third-party enforcement is not generally a "stable equilibrium," that is, one in which no player has an incentive to alter his behavior.

In the classic prisoner's dilemma and related dilemmas of collective action, by contrast, defection *is* a stable equilibrium strategy for all parties. "'Defect' is the unique best reply, not only to itself, but *all* strategies, pure or mixed."[11] However unfortunate the consequences for all concerned, defection remains rational for any individual.

Yet, as others have observed, this theory proves too much, for it *under-*predicts voluntary cooperation. To Hume's very example of uncooperative neighboring farmers, for example, we must counterpose the *aiuta-rella* long practiced by sharecroppers in central Italy or the practice of barn-raising on the American frontier, which are all the more puzzling in light of the compelling logic of collective action. "We should ask why uncooperative behaviour does not emerge as often as game theory predicts."[12]

This question has engaged the creative energies of many scholars in recent years. Game theorists generally agree that cooperation should be easier when players engage in indefinitely repeated games, so that a defector faces punishment in successive rounds. This principle is fundamental to further theorizing in this field. (It is so widely recognized that one version of it is known as the Folk Theorem.)[13] Other conditions internal to the game itself that can favor cooperation, theoretically speaking, are that the number of players be limited, that information about each player's past behavior be abundant, and that players not discount the future too heavily. Each of these factors is important. They seem to imply, however, that impersonal cooperation should be rare, whereas it seems to be common in much of the modern world. How come?[14]

One important line of research, exemplified by the work of economist Oliver Williamson, has emphasized the role of formal institutions in reducing "transaction costs" (that is, the costs of monitoring and enforcing agreements), and thus in enabling agents more efficiently to surmount problems of opportunism and shirking.[15] As we noted in Chapter 1, Elinor Ostrom has recently demonstrated the value of this approach by carefully comparing cooperative attempts to manage common-pool resources, such as grazing grounds, water supplies, and fisheries. Why, she asks, have some institutions succeeded in overcoming the logic of collective action and others failed? Among the principles of institutional design suggested by her comparisons are that the boundaries of the institution be clearly defined, that affected parties participate in defining the rules, that violators be subject to graduated sanctions, that low-cost mechanisms be available for resolving conflicts, and so on.[16]

This version of "the new institutionalism" leaves open, however, a crucial question: How and why are formal institutions that help surmount collective action problems actually provided? It would seem that the participants themselves cannot create the institution, for the same reason that they need it in the first place, and an impartial "lawgiver" is as problematical as an impartial Hobbesian sovereign:[17]

> We cannot write a contract (i.e., a constitution) to abide by our constitution without falling into an infinite regress of such contracts. Formal mechanisms of social control should archetypically be subject to free riding, as ruling cliques whittle away at the constitution, otherwise well-meaning citizens let their neighbors bear the costs of policing these usurpers, and scofflaws cheat on their taxes and run traffic lights."[18]

Scofflaws, shirkers, and ruling cliques do afflict many societies, of course, as citizens in the less civic regions of Italy can testify. Yet collaborative institutions elsewhere seem to work more effectively. Why? To resolve this puzzle, some hard-nosed theorists recently have turned to what Robert Bates terms "soft" solutions, such as community and trust: "In a world in which there are prisoner's dilemmas, cooperative communities will enable rational individuals to transcend collective dilemmas."[19]

SOCIAL CAPITAL, TRUST,
AND ROTATING CREDIT ASSOCIATIONS

Success in overcoming dilemmas of collective action and the self-defeating opportunism that they spawn depends on the broader social context within which any particular game is played. Voluntary cooperation is easier in a community that has inherited a substantial stock of social capital, in the form of norms of reciprocity and networks of civic engagement.[20]

Social capital here refers to features of social organization, such as trust, norms, and networks, that can improve the efficiency of society by facilitating coordinated actions:

> Like other forms of capital, social capital is productive, making possible the achievement of certain ends that would not be attainable in its absence. . . . For example, a group whose members manifest trustworthiness and place extensive trust in one another will be able to accomplish much more than a comparable group lacking that trustworthiness and trust. . . . In a farming community . . . where one farmer got his hay baled by another and where farm tools are extensively borrowed and lent, the social capital allows each farmer to get his work done with less physical capital in the form of tools and equipment.[21]

Spontaneous cooperation is facilitated by social capital. An instructive illustration of this principle is a type of informal savings institution found on every continent called a *rotating credit association*. A rotating credit association consists of a group "who agree to make regular contributions to a fund which is given, in whole or in part, to each contributor in rotation."[22] Rotating credit associations have been reported from Nigeria to Scotland, from Peru to Vietnam, from Japan to Egypt, from West Indian immigrants in the eastern United States to Chicanos in the West, from illiterate Chinese villagers to bank managers and economic forecasters in Mexico City. Many U.S. savings and loans reportedly began life as rotating credit associations.[23]

In a typical rotating credit association, each of twenty members might contribute a monthly sum equivalent to one dollar, and each month a different member would receive that month's pot of twenty dollars to be used as he or she wished (to finance a wedding, a bicycle, a sewing machine, or new inventory for a small shop).[24] That member is ineligible for subsequent distributions, but is expected to continue making regular contributions until all members have had a turn at receiving the pot. Rotating credit associations vary widely in size, social composition, organization, and procedures for determining the payout. All combine sociability with small-scale capital formation.

Rotating credit associations, however convivial their meetings, represent something more than social entertainment or altruism. Clifford Geertz reports from Java, for example, that the *arisan* (the term literally means "cooperative endeavor" or "mutual help") reflects "not so much a general spirit of cooperativeness—Javanese peasants tend, like many peasants, to be rather suspicious of groups larger than the immediate family—but a set of explicit and concrete practices of exchange of labor, of capital, and of consumption goods which operate in all aspects of life. . . . Cooperation is founded on a very lively sense of the mutual value to the participants of such cooperation, not on a general ethic of the unity of all men or on an organic view of society."[25]

Rotating credit associations clearly violate the logic of collective action: Why shouldn't a participant drop out once he has received the pot? Seeing that risk, why would anyone else contribute in the first place? "A rotating credit association obviously cannot function unless all members continue to keep up their obligations."[26] Yet rotating credit associations flourish where no legal Leviathan stands ready to punish defection.

The risk of default is well recognized by participants, and organizers select members with some care. Thus, a reputation for honesty and reliability is an important asset for any would-be participant. One important source of reputational information, of course, is previous participation in another rotating credit association, and acquiring a sound reputation is one important side-benefit of taking part. Both reputational uncertainty and the risk of default are minimized by strong norms and by dense networks of reciprocal engagement. So strong can be the norm against defection that members on the verge of default are reported to have sold daughters into prostitution or committed suicide.[27]

In a small, highly personalized community, such as an Ibo village in Nigeria, the threat of ostracism from the socioeconomic system is a powerful, credible sanction. In the more diffuse, impersonal society of contemporary Mexico City, by contrast, more complex networks of mutual trust must be woven together to support rotating credit associations. Vélez-Ibañez has described a flourishing array of Mexican rotating credit associations extending along social networks, based on *confianza* (generalized reciprocity and mutual trust). "*Confianza* links will be both direct and indirect and will vary in quality and density. In many cases, members must trust in the trust of others to complete their obligations, since they know little about them. As one informant put it, 'mutual trust is lent'."[28]

Social networks allow trust to become transitive and spread: I trust you, because I trust her and she assures me that she trusts you.

Rotating credit associations illustrate how dilemmas of collective action can be overcome by drawing on external sources of social capital, for they "use pre-existing social connections between individuals to help circumvent problems of imperfect information and enforceability."[29] Like conventional capital for conventional borrowers, social capital serves as a kind of collateral, but it is available to those who have no access to ordinary credit markets.[30] Lacking physical assets to offer as surety, the participants in effect pledge their social connections. Thus social capital is leveraged to expand the credit facilities available in these communities and to improve the efficiency with which markets operate there.

Rotating credit associations are often found in conjunction with cooperatives and other forms of mutual aid and solidarity. In part, this is because all these forms of voluntary cooperation are fed by the same underlying stock of social capital. As Ostrom reports of small-scale common-pool resources (CPR), such as Alpine meadows, "When individuals have lived in such situations for a substantial time and have developed shared norms and patterns of reciprocity, they possess social capital with which they can build institutional arrangements for resolving CPR dilemmas."[31]

Mutual aid practices, like rotating credit associations, themselves also represent investments in social capital. The Javanese *arisan* "is commonly viewed by its members less as an economic institution than a broadly social one whose main purpose is the strengthening of community solidarity." In Japan, too, "the *ko* is but one of several traditional forms of mutual aid common in Japanese villages, including exchange labor patterns, reciprocal gift giving, communal house raising and repairing, neighborly assistance in death, illness, and other personal crises and so forth. Thus, as in rural Java, the rotating credit association is more than a simple economic institution: it is a mechanism strengthening the overall solidarity of the village."[32]

As with conventional capital, those who have social capital tend to accumulate more—"them as has, gets." "Success in starting small-scale initial institutions enables a group of individuals to build on the social capital thus created to solve larger problems with larger and more complex institutional arrangements. Current theories of collective action do not stress the process of accretion of institutional capital."[33]

Most forms of social capital, such as trust, are what Albert Hirschman has called "moral resources"—that is, resources whose supply increases rather than decreases through use and which become depleted if *not* used.[34] The more two people display trust towards one another, the greater their mutual confidence.[35] Conversely:

Deep distrust is very difficult to invalidate through experience, for either it prevents people from engaging in the appropriate kind of social experiment or, worse, it leads to behaviour which bolsters the validity of distrust itself. . . . Once distrust has set in it soon becomes impossible to know if it was ever in fact justified, for it has the capacity to be *self-fulfilling*.[36]

Other forms of social capital, too, such as social norms and networks, increase with use and diminish with disuse.[37] For all these reasons, we should expect the creation and destruction of social capital to be marked by virtuous and vicious circles.

One special feature of social capital, like trust, norms, and networks, is that it is ordinarily a public good, unlike conventional capital, which is ordinarily a private good. "As an attribute of the social structure in which a person is embedded, social capital is not the private property of any of the persons who benefit from it."[38] Like all public goods, social capital tends to be undervalued and undersupplied by private agents. For example, my reputation for trustworthiness benefits you as well as me, since it enables us both to engage in mutually rewarding cooperation. But I discount the benefits to you of my being trustworthy (or the costs to you of my being untrustworthy) and thus I underinvest in trust formation.[39] This means that social capital, unlike other forms of capital, must often be produced as a by-product of other social activities.[40]

Trust is an essential component of social capital. As Kenneth Arrow has observed, "Virtually every commercial transaction has within itself an element of trust, certainly any transaction conducted over a period of time. It can be plausibly argued that much of the economic backwardness in the world can be explained by the lack of mutual confidence."[41] Anthony Pagden recalls the insights of a shrewd eighteenth-century Neapolitan economist, Antonio Genovesi:

> In the absence of trust, [Genovesi] pointed out, "there can be no certainty in contracts and hence no force to the laws," and a society in that condition is effectively reduced "to a state of semi-savagery." . . . [In Genovesi's Naples] bonds and even money, since so much of it was false, were no longer freely accepted and the Neapolitans were reduced to the condition of the savages described by Genovesi who will only give with the right hand if they simultaneously receive with the left.[42]

In the civic regions of Italy, by contrast to Naples, social trust has long been a key ingredient in the ethos that has sustained economic dynamism and government performance.[43] Cooperation is often required—between legislature and executive, between workers and managers, among political parties, between the government and private groups, among small firms, and so on. Yet explicit "contracting" and "monitoring" in such

cases is often costly or impossible, and third-party enforcement is impractical. Trust lubricates cooperation. The greater the level of trust within a
community, the greater the likelihood of cooperation. And cooperation
itself breeds trust. The steady accumulation of social capital is a crucial
part of the story behind the virtuous circles of civic Italy.

The trust that is required to sustain cooperation is not blind. Trust entails a prediction about the behavior of an independent actor. "You do not
trust a person (or an agency) to do something merely because he says he
will do it. You trust him only because, knowing what you know of his
disposition, his available options and their consequences, his ability and
so forth you expect that he will *choose* to do it."[44] In small, close-knit
communities, this prediction can be based on what Bernard Williams calls
"thick trust," that is, a belief that rests on intimate familiarity with *this*
individual. In larger, more complex settings, however, a more impersonal or indirect form of trust is required.[45] How does personal trust become social trust?

NORMS OF RECIPROCITY AND
NETWORKS OF CIVIC ENGAGEMENT

Social trust in complex modern settings can arise from two related
sources—norms of reciprocity and networks of civic engagement.[46] Social norms, according to James Coleman, transfer the right to control an
action from the actor to others, typically because that action has "externalities," that is, consequences (positive or negative) for others. Sometimes
externalities can be captured through a market exchange, but often they
cannot. Norms arise when "an action has similar externalities for a set of
others, yet markets in the rights of control of the action cannot easily be
established, and no single actor can profitably engage in an exchange to
gain rights of control."[47] Norms are inculcated and sustained by modeling
and socialization (including civic education) and by sanctions.[48]

An example may clarify: Novembers here are windy, and my leaves are
likely to end up on other people's yards. However, it is not feasible for my
neighbors to get together to bribe me to rake. The norm of keeping lawns
leaf-free is powerful in my neighborhood, however, and it constrains my
decision as to whether to spend Saturday afternoon watching TV. This
norm is not actually taught in local schools, but neighbors mention it
when newcomers move in, and they reinforce it in frequent autumnal
chats, as well as by obsessive raking of their own yards. Non-rakers risk
being shunned at neighborhood events, and non-raking is rare. Even
though the norm has no legal force, and even though I prefer watching the
Buckeyes to raking up leaves, I usually comply with the norm.

Norms such as those that undergird social trust evolve because they lower transaction costs and facilitate cooperation.[49] The most important of these norms is reciprocity. Reciprocity is of two sorts, sometimes called "balanced" (or "specific") and "generalized" (or "diffuse").[50] Balanced reciprocity refers to a simultaneous exchange of items of equivalent value, as when office-mates exchange holiday gifts or legislators log-roll. Generalized reciprocity refers to a continuing relationship of exchange that is at any given time unrequited or imbalanced, but that involves mutual expectations that a benefit granted now should be repaid in the future. Friendship, for example, almost always involves generalized reciprocity. Cicero (a native, by the way, of central Italy) stated the norm of generalized reciprocity with admirable clarity: "There is no duty more indispensable than that of returning a kindness. All men distrust one forgetful of a benefit."[51]

The norm of generalized reciprocity is a highly productive component of social capital. Communities in which this norm is followed can more efficiently restrain opportunism and resolve problems of collective action.[52] Reciprocity was at the core of the "tower societies" and other self-help associations that eased the security dilemma for citizens in the northern communal republics of medieval Italy, as well as the mutual aid societies that arose to address the economic insecurities of the nineteenth century. The norm of generalized reciprocity serves to reconcile self-interest and solidarity:

> Each individual act in a system of reciprocity is *usually* characterized by a combination of what one might call short-term altruism and long-term self-interest: I help you out now in the (possibly vague, uncertain and uncalculating) expectation that you will help me out in the future. Reciprocity is made up of a series of acts each of which is short-run altruistic (benefiting others at a cost to the altruist) but which together *typically* make every participant better off.[53]

An effective norm of generalized reciprocity is likely to be associated with dense networks of social exchange. In communities where people can be confident that trusting will be requited, not exploited, exchange is more likely to ensue. Conversely, repeated exchange over a period of time tends to encourage the development of a norm of generalized reciprocity.[54] In addition, certain sorts of social networks themselves facilitate the resolution of dilemmas of collective action. Mark Granovetter has stressed that trust is generated and malfeasance discouraged when agreements are "embedded" within a larger structure of personal relations and social networks.[55]

Personal interaction generates information about the trustworthiness of other actors that is relatively inexpensive and reliable. As the folk theorem from game theory reminds us, ongoing social relations can generate incentives for trustworthiness. In addition, continuing relations "often become overlaid with social content that carries strong expectations of trust and abstention from opportunism. . . . Prisoner's Dilemmas are . . . often obviated by the strength of personal relations."[56] The embeddedness approach predicts that the mix of order and disorder, of cooperation and opportunism, in a society will depend on the pre-existing social networks.

Any society—modern or traditional, authoritarian or democratic, feudal or capitalist—is characterized by networks of interpersonal communication and exchange, both formal and informal. Some of these networks are primarily "horizontal," bringing together agents of equivalent status and power. Others are primarily "vertical," linking unequal agents in asymmetric relations of hierarchy and dependence. In the real world, of course, almost all networks are mixes of the horizontal and the vertical: Even bowling teams have captains, while prison guards occasionally fraternize with inmates. The actual networks that characterize an organization may be inconsistent with the ideology that inspires it.[57] Nominally similar groups may have different types of networks. For example, all religious groups blend hierarchy and equality, but networks within Protestant congregations are traditionally thought to be more horizontal than networks in the Catholic Church.[58] Nonetheless, the basic contrast between horizontal and vertical linkages, between "web-like" and "maypole-like" networks, is reasonably clear.

Networks of civic engagement, like the neighborhood associations, choral societies, cooperatives, sports clubs, mass-based parties, and the like examined in Chapters 4 and 5, represent intense horizontal interaction. Networks of civic engagement are an essential form of social capital: The denser such networks in a community, the more likely that its citizens will be able to cooperate for mutual benefit. Why, exactly, do networks of civic engagement have this powerfully beneficial side-effect?

· Networks of civic engagement increase the potential costs to a defector in any individual transaction. Opportunism puts at risk the benefits he expects to receive from all the other transactions in which he is currently engaged, as well as the benefits from future transactions. Networks of civic engagement, in the language of game theory, increase the iteration and interconnectedness of games.[59]
· Networks of civic engagement foster robust norms of reciprocity. Compatriots who interact in many social contexts "are apt to develop strong norms of acceptable behavior and to convey their mutual expectations to one another in many reinforcing encounters." These norms are reinforced by "the network of relationships that depend on the establishment of a reputation for keeping promises and accepting the norms of the local community regarding behavior."[60]

- Networks of civic engagement facilitate communication and improve the flow of information about the trustworthiness of individuals. Networks of civic engagement allow reputations to be transmitted and refined.[61] As we have seen, trust and cooperation depend on reliable information about the past behavior and present interests of potential partners, while uncertainty reinforces dilemmas of collective action. Thus, other things being equal, the greater the communication (both direct and indirect) among participants, the greater their mutual trust and the easier they will find it to cooperate.[62]

- Networks of civic engagement embody past success at collaboration, which can serve as a culturally-defined template for future collaboration. "The cultural filter provides continuity so that the informal solution to exchange problems in the past carries over into the present and makes those informal constraints important sources of continuity in long-run social change."[63]

As we observed in Chapter 5, the civic traditions of northern Italy provide a historical repertoire of forms of collaboration that, having proved their worth in the past, are available to citizens for addressing new problems of collective action. Mutual aid societies were built on the razed foundations of the old guilds, and cooperatives and mass political parties then drew on the experience of the mutual aid societies. The contemporary Italian environmental movement draws on these earlier precedents. Conversely, where no prior example of successful civic collaboration exists, it is more difficult to overcome barriers of suspicion and shirking. Faced with new problems requiring collective resolution, men and women everywhere look to their past for solutions. Citizens of civic communities find examples of successful horizontal relationships in their history, whereas those in less civic regions find, at best, examples of vertical supplication.

A vertical network, no matter how dense and no matter how important to its participants, cannot sustain social trust and cooperation. Vertical flows of information are often less reliable than horizontal flows, in part because the subordinate husbands information as a hedge against exploitation. More important, sanctions that support norms of reciprocity against the threat of opportunism are less likely to be imposed upwards and less likely to be acceded to, if imposed.[64] Only a bold or foolhardy subordinate, lacking ties of solidarity with peers, would seek to punish a superior.

Patron-client relations, for example, involve interpersonal exchange and reciprocal obligations, but the exchange is vertical and the obligations asymmetric. Pitt-Rivers calls clientelism "lopsided friendship."[65] Furthermore, the vertical bonds of clientelism "seem to undermine the horizontal group organisation and solidarity of clients and patrons alike—but especially of the clients."[66] Two clients of the same patron, lacking direct ties, hold nothing hostage to one another. They have nothing to stake against mutual defection and nothing to fear from mutual alienation. They have no occasion to develop a norm of generalized reciprocity and no history of mutual collaboration to draw on. In the vertical patron-client relationship, characterized by dependence instead of mutuality, opportunism is more likely on the part of both patron (exploitation) and client (shirking). The fact that vertical networks are less helpful than horizontal networks in solving dilemmas of collective action may be one reason why capitalism turned out to be more efficient than feudalism in the eighteenth century, and why democracy has proven more effective than autocracy in the twentieth century.

Kinship ties have a special role in the resolution of dilemmas of collective action. In some respects bonds of blood are comparable to horizontal ties of civic engagement, but family is more nearly universal. It is no accident that family firms and close-knit ethnic minorities (Jews in Europe, overseas Chinese in Asia, and so on) have been important in the early stages of the commercial revolution. However, networks of civic engagement are more likely to encompass broad segments of society and thus undergird collaboration at the community level. Ironically, as Granovetter has pointed out, "strong" interpersonal ties (like kinship and intimate friendship) are less important than "weak ties" (like acquaintanceship and shared membership in secondary associations) in sustaining community cohesion and collective action. "Weak ties are more likely to link members of *different* small groups than are strong ones, which tend to be concentrated within particular groups."[67] Dense but segregated horizontal networks sustain cooperation *within* each group, but networks of civic engagement that cut across social cleavages nourish wider cooperation. This is another reason why networks of civic engagement are such an important part of a community's stock of social capital.

If horizontal networks of civic engagement help participants solve dilemmas of collective action, then the more horizontally structured an organization, the more it should foster institutional success in the broader community. Membership in horizontally ordered groups (like sports clubs, cooperatives, mutual aid societies, cultural associations, and voluntary unions) should be positively associated with good government. Since the organizational realities of political parties vary from party to party and region to region (vertical in some places, horizontal in others), we should expect party membership as such to be unrelated to good government. Membership rates in hierarchically ordered organizations (like the Mafia or the institutional Catholic Church) should be negatively associated with good government; in Italy, at least, the most devout churchgoers are the least civic-minded.[68] All these expectations are consistent with the evidence of this study, as we saw in Chapters 4 and 5.[69] Good government in Italy is a by-product of singing groups and soccer clubs, not prayer.

This interpretation of the beneficial effects of civic networks is in some respects contrary to other theories of political and economic development. In *The Rise and Decline of Nations*, Mancur Olson, building on his own seminal explication of the logic of collective action, argues that small interest groups have no incentive to work toward the common good of society and every incentive to engage in costly and inefficient "rent-seeking"—lobbying for tax breaks, colluding to restrain competition, and so on.[70] Worse yet, in the absence of invasion or revolutionary change, the thicket of special interest groups in any society grows ever denser, choking off innovation and dampening economic growth. More and stronger groups mean less growth. Strong society, weak economy.

Just as Olson laments the economic effects of associationism, some students of political development argue that a strong, well organized, and exuberant society impedes the effectiveness of government. Joel Migdal, for example, has recently argued:

> social structure, particularly the existence of numerous other social organizations that exercise effective social control, has a decisive [negative] effect on the likelihood of the state's greatly expanding its capabilities. . . . The major struggles in many societies, especially those with fairly new states . . . are over whether the state will be able to displace other organizations in society that make rules against the wishes and goals of state leaders.[71]

In short, more and stronger groups mean feeble government. Strong society, weak state.

The evidence and the theory of our study contradict both these theses. Historically, we argued in Chapter 5, norms and networks of civic engagement have fostered economic growth, not inhibited it. This effect continues today. Over the two decades since the birth of the regional governments, civic regions have grown faster than regions with fewer associations and more hierarchy, *controlling for their level of development in 1970*. Of two regions equally advanced economically in 1970, the one with a denser network of civic engagement grew significantly faster in the ensuing years.[72] Similarly, as we saw in Chapter 4, civic associations are powerfully associated with effective public institutions. The theory sketched in this chapter helps explain why social capital, as embodied in horizontal networks of civic engagement, bolsters the performance of the polity and the economy, rather than the reverse: Strong society, strong economy; strong society, strong state.

HISTORY AND INSTITUTIONAL PERFORMANCE:
TWO SOCIAL EQUILIBRIA

In all societies, to summarize our argument so far, dilemmas of collective action hamper attempts to cooperate for mutual benefit, whether in politics or in economics. Third-party enforcement is an inadequate solution to this problem. Voluntary cooperation (like rotating credit associations) depends on social capital. Norms of generalized reciprocity and networks of civic engagement encourage social trust and cooperation because they reduce incentives to defect, reduce uncertainty, and provide models for future cooperation. Trust itself is an emergent property of the social system, as much as a personal attribute. Individuals are able to be trusting (and not merely gullible) because of the social norms and networks within which their actions are embedded.[73]

Stocks of social capital, such as trust, norms, and networks, tend to be self-reinforcing and cumulative. Virtuous circles result in social equilibria with high levels of cooperation, trust, reciprocity, civic engagement, and collective well-being. These traits define the civic community. Conversely, the absence of these traits in the *un*civic community is also self-reinforcing. Defection, distrust, shirking, exploitation, isolation, disorder, and stagnation intensify one another in a suffocating miasma of vicious circles. This argument suggests that there may be at least *two* broad equilibria toward which all societies that face problems of collective action (that is, *all* societies) tend to evolve and which, once attained, tend to be self-reinforcing.

The strategy of "never cooperate" is a stable equilibrium, for reasons that are well explicated in standard accounts of the prisoner's dilemma.[74] Once trapped in this situation, no matter how exploitative and backward, it is irrational for any individual to seek a more collaborative alternative, except perhaps within the immediate family. The "amoral familism" that Banfield observed in the Mezzogiorno is, in fact, not irrational, but the only rational strategy for survival in this social context.[75] Actors in this social equilibrium may well realize that they are worse off than they would be in a more cooperative equilibrium, but getting to that happier equilibrium is beyond the power of any individual.

In this setting, we should expect the Hobbesian, hierarchical solution to dilemmas of collective action—coercion, exploitation, and dependence—to predominate. This oppressive state of affairs is clearly inferior to a cooperative outcome, for it dooms the society to self-perpetuating backwardness. Nevertheless, it is preferable to a purely anarchic "state of nature," as has also been clear to southern Italians from medieval to modern times. This Hobbesian outcome has at least the virtue that it is attainable by individuals who are unable to trust their neighbors. Minimal security, no matter how exploitative and inefficient, is not a contemptible objective for the powerless.

The difficulty of solving dilemmas of collective action in this Hobbesian equilibrium means that society is worse off than in a cooperative outcome. This shortfall is probably even greater in a complex industrial or postindustrial context, where impersonal cooperation is essential, than a simple agricultural society. As Douglass North, an astute theorist of economic history, has observed, "the returns on opportunism, cheating, and shirking rise in complex societies."[76] Thus, the importance of social capital (to inhibit opportunism, cheating, and shirking) increases as economic development proceeds. This may help explain why the gap between the civic North and the uncivic South has widened over the last century.

Authoritarian government, patron-clientelism, extralegal "enforcers," and the like represent a second-best, "default" solution: Through them, individuals can find some refuge from the war of all against all, without pursuing the impossible dream of cooperation. Force and family provide a primitive substitute for the civic community. This equilibrium has been the tragic fate of southern Italy for a millennium.

Given an adequate stock of social capital, however, a happier equilibrium is also attainable. Assuming that prisoner's dilemmas are iterated or interconnected (as they are in a civic community), "brave reciprocity" is also a stable equilibrium strategy, as the game theorist Robert Sugden has recently shown: "Cooperate with people who cooperate with you (or who cooperate with people like you), and don't be the first to defect." Sugden shows, specifically, that in what he calls "the mutual-aid game" (a formalization of the implicit bargaining that underlies mutual aid societies, cooperatives, rotating credit associations, Hume's game of the two farmers, and so on) cooperation can be sustained indefinitely. To be sure, even in an indefinitely repeated mutual-aid game, "always defect" is *also* a stable equilibrium, but if a society can somehow move toward the cooperative solution, it will be self-reinforcing.[77] In a society characterized by dense networks of civic engagement, where most people abide by civic norms, it is easier to spot and punish the occasional "bad apple," so that defection is riskier and less tempting.

Sugden's analysis leads to the conclusion that both "always defect" and "reciprocate help" are contingent conventions—that is, rules that have evolved in particular communities and, having so evolved, are stable, but that might have evolved otherwise. In other words, reciprocity/trust and dependence/exploitation can each hold society together, though at quite different levels of efficiency and institutional performance. Once in either of these two settings, rational actors have an incentive to act consistently with its rules. History determines which of these two stable outcomes characterizes any given society.

Historical turning points thus can have extremely long-lived consequences. As the "new institutionalists" have emphasized, institutions— and we would add, the social settings that condition their operation— evolve through history, but they do not reliably reach unique and efficient equilibria.[78] History is not always efficient, in the sense of weeding out social practices that impede progress and encourage collective irrationality. Nor is this inertia somehow attributable to individual irrationality. On the contrary, individuals responding rationally to the social context bequeathed to them by history reinforce the social pathologies.

Recent theorists of economic history have dubbed this feature of social systems "path dependence": where you can get to depends on where you're coming from, and some destinations you simply cannot get to from here.[79] Path dependence can produce durable differences in performance between two societies, even when the formal institutions, resources, relative prices, and individual preferences in the two are similar. The implications of this point for economic (and political) development are profound: "If the process by which we arrive at today's institutions is relevant and constrains future choices, then not only does history matter but persistent poor performance and long-run divergent patterns of development stem from a common source."[80]

Douglass North has illustrated this point by tracing the post-colonial experiences of North and South America to their respective colonial legacies.[81] After independence, both the United States and the Latin republics shared constitutional forms, abundant resources, and similar international opportunities; but North Americans benefited from their decentralized, parliamentary English patrimony, whereas Latin Americans were cursed with centralized authoritarianism, familism, and clientelism that they inherited from late medieval Spain. In our language, the North Americans inherited civic traditions, whereas the Latin Americans were bequeathed traditions of vertical dependence and exploitation. The point is not that the preferences or predilections of individual North and South Americans differed, but that historically derived social contexts presented them with a different set of opportunities and incentives. The parallel between this North-South contrast and our Italian case is striking.[82]

Using the term "institution" in a broad sense to mean "the rules of the game in a society," North points out that institutional patterns are self-reinforcing, even when they are socially inefficient.[83] First, it is almost always easier for an individual agent to adapt to the existing rules of the game than to seek to change them. Indeed, those rules tend to induce the rise of organizations and groups with a stake in their inefficiencies. Second, once development has been set on a particular course, organizational learning, cultural habits, and mental models of the social world reinforce that trajectory. Cooperation or shirking and exploitation become ingrained. Informal norms and culture change more slowly than formal rules, and tend to remold those formal rules, so that the external imposition of a common set of formal rules will lead to widely divergent outcomes. All of these hypotheses are consistent with the deep continuities traced in Chapter 5.

Each chapter in this book has begun with one question and ended with another. Chapter 2 began with "How did the new regional institutions affect the practice of politics?" and ended with "How successful was each institution at governing?" Chapter 3 answered that question, leading us naturally to ask "Why were some so much more successful than others?" Chapter 4 traced differences in performance to differences in civic engagement, which in turn raised the question, "Where did those differences in civic-ness come from?" Chapter 5 traced those differences to distinctive traditions that have endured for nearly a thousand years, posing the puzzle, "How could such differences have proved so stable?" Chapter 6 has explicated the vicious and virtuous circles that have led to contrasting, path-dependent social equilibria.

This explanation, however persuasive, poses starkly yet another question: "Why did the North and South get started on such divergent paths in the eleventh century?" The hierarchical Norman regime in the South is perhaps readily explained as the consequence of conquest by an unusually effective force of foreign mercenaries. More problematical and potentially more interesting are the origins of the communal republics. How did the inhabitants of north-central Italy first come to seek collaborative solutions to their Hobbesian dilemmas? The response to that question must await further research, not least because historians report that the answer seems lost in the mists of the Dark Ages.[84] Our interpretation, however, highlights the unique importance of trying to pierce those mists.

Social scientists have long debated what causes what—culture or structure. In the context of our argument this debate concerns the complicated causal nexus among the cultural norms and attitudes and the social structures and behavioral patterns that make up the civic community. Quite apart from the ambiguity of "culture" and "structure," however, this debate is somewhat misplaced. Most dispassionate commentators recognize that attitudes and practices constitute a mutually reinforcing equilibrium.[85] Social trust, norms of reciprocity, networks of civic engagement, and successful cooperation are mutually reinforcing. Effective collaborative institutions require interpersonal skills and trust, but those skills and that trust are also inculcated and reinforced by organized collaboration. Norms and networks of civic engagement contribute to economic prosperity and are in turn reinforced by that prosperity.

Linear causal questions must not crowd out equilibrium analysis. In this context, the culture-vs.-structure, chicken-and-egg debate is ultimately fruitless. More important is to understand how history smooths some paths and closes others off. Douglass North summarizes the challenges ahead:

> Path dependence means that history matters. We cannot understand today's choices (and define them in the modeling of economic performance) without tracing the incremental evolution of institutions. But we are just beginning the serious task of exploring the implications of path dependence. . . . Informal constraints matter. We need to know much more about culturally derived norms of behavior and how they interact with formal rules to get better answers to such issues. We are just beginning the serious study of institutions.[86]

LESSONS FROM THE ITALIAN REGIONAL EXPERIMENT

The twentieth century is ending, as it began, with high aspirations for extending the benefits of democratic self-government to ever larger numbers of men and women.[87] What factors will affect whether these hopes will be realized? Our study has explored both the power of institutional reform as a strategy for political change and the constraints on institutional performance posed by the social context. Twenty years after the establishment of regional government in Italy, what have we learned from this experiment in building new institutions of democracy?

For at least ten centuries, the North and the South have followed contrasting approaches to the dilemmas of collective action that afflict all societies. In the North, norms of reciprocity and networks of civic engagement have been embodied in tower societies, guilds, mutual aid societies, cooperatives, unions, and even soccer clubs and literary societies. These horizontal civic bonds have undergirded levels of economic and institutional performance generally much higher than in the South, where social and political relations have been vertically structured. Although we are accustomed to thinking of the state and the market as alternative mechanisms for solving social problems, this history suggests that *both* states *and* markets operate more efficiently in civic settings.

This civic equilibrium has shown remarkable stability, as we saw in Chapter 5, although its effects have been disrupted from time to time by exogenous forces like pestilence, war, and world trade shifts. The contrasting, Hobbesian equilibrium in the South has been even more stable, though less fruitful. Mutual distrust and defection, vertical dependence and exploitation, isolation and disorder, criminality and backwardness have reinforced one another in the interminable vicious circles traced in this chapter and the previous one. People in Bologna and Bari, in Florence and Palermo, have followed contrasting logics of communal life for a millennium or more.

When the regional reform was introduced in 1970, therefore, the new institutions were implanted in very different social contexts. As we learned in Chapter 4, civic regions were characterized by a dense network of local associations, by active engagement in community affairs, by egalitarian patterns of politics, by trust and law-abidingness. In less civic regions, political and social participation was organized vertically, not horizontally. Mutual suspicion and corruption were regarded as normal. Involvement in civic associations was scanty. Lawlessness was expected. People in these communities felt powerless and exploited. They were right.

These contrasting social contexts plainly affected how the new institutions worked. As we saw in Chapter 3, objective measures of effectiveness and subjective measures of citizen satisfaction concur in ranking some regional governments consistently more successful than others. Virtually without exception, the more civic the context, the better the government. In the late twentieth century, as in the early twelfth century, collective institutions work better in the civic community. By the 1980s, the North has also attained great advantages in physical and human capital, but those advantages are accentuated and in part explained by its long-standing edge in social capital.

This is one lesson gleaned from our research: *Social context and history profoundly condition the effectiveness of institutions.* Where the regional soil is fertile, the regions draw sustenance from regional traditions, but where the soil is poor, the new institutions are stunted. Effective and responsive institutions depend, in the language of civic humanism, on republican virtues and practices. Tocqueville was right: Democratic government is strengthened, not weakened, when it faces a vigorous civil society.

On the demand side, citizens in civic communities expect better government and (in part through their own efforts), they get it. They demand more effective public service, and they are prepared to act collectively to achieve their shared goals. Their counterparts in less civic regions more commonly assume the role of alienated and cynical supplicants.

On the supply side, the performance of representative government is facilitated by the social infrastructure of civic communities and by the democratic values of both officials and citizens. Most fundamental to the civic community is the social ability to collaborate for shared interests. Generalized reciprocity (not "I'll do this for you, because you are more powerful than I," nor even "I'll do this for you now, if you do that for me now," but "I'll do this for you now, knowing that somewhere down the road you'll do something for me") generates high social capital and underpins collaboration.

The harmonies of a choral society illustrate how voluntary collaboration can create value that no individual, no matter how wealthy, no matter how wily, could produce alone. In the civic community associations proliferate, memberships overlap, and participation spills into multiple arenas of community life. The social contract that sustains such collaboration in the civic community is not legal but moral. The sanction for violating it is not penal, but exclusion from the network of solidarity and cooperation. Norms and expectations play an important role. As Thompson, Ellis, and Wildavsky put it, "Ways of life are made viable by classifying certain behaviors as worthy of praise and others as undesirable, or even unthinkable."[88] A conception of one's role and obligations as a citizen, coupled with a commitment to political equality, is the cultural cement of the civic community.

Where norms and networks of civic engagement are lacking, the outlook for collective action appears bleak. The fate of the Mezzogiorno is an object lesson for the Third World today and the former Communist lands of Eurasia tomorrow, moving uncertainly toward self-government. The "always defect" social equilibrium may represent the future of much of the world where social capital is limited or nonexistent. For political stability, for government effectiveness, and even for economic progress social capital may be even more important than physical or human capital. Many of the formerly Communist societies had weak civic traditions before the advent of Communism, and totalitarian rule abused even that limited stock of social capital. Without norms of reciprocity and networks of civic engagement, the Hobbesian outcome of the Mezzogiorno—amoral familism, clientelism, lawlessness, ineffective government, and economic stagnation—seems likelier than successful democratization and economic development. Palermo may represent the future of Moscow.

The civic community has deep historical roots. This is a depressing observation for those who view institutional reform as a strategy for political change. The president of Basilicata cannot move his government to Emilia, and the prime minister of Azerbaijan cannot move his country to the Baltic. "A theory of change that gives priority to ethos can have unfortunate consequences. . . . It may lead to minimizing efforts at change because people are believed to be hopelessly enmeshed in an ethos."[89] More than one Italian regionalist told us privately that publicity about our results might unintentionally undermine the regional reform movement. One able reformist regional president in an uncivic region exclaimed when he heard our conclusions: "This is a counsel of despair! You're telling me that nothing I can do will improve our prospects for success. The fate of the reform was sealed centuries ago."[90]

The full results of the regional reform, however, are far from an invitation to quietism. On the contrary, a second lesson of the regional experiment is (as Chapter 2 demonstrates) that *changing formal institutions can change political practice*. The reform had measurable and mostly beneficial consequences for regional political life. As institutionalists would predict, institutional changes were (gradually) reflected in changing identities, changing values, changing power, and changing strategies. These trends transpired in the South no less than the North. In both South and North, the new institution nurtured a more moderate, pragmatic, tolerant elite political culture. In both South and North, the reform altered old patterns of power and produced more genuine subnational autonomy than unified Italy had ever known. In both South and North, the reform itself generated pressures, both inside and outside the government, in support of further decentralization. In both South and North, the regional government is generally regarded by community leaders and ordinary voters as an improvement over the institutions it replaced—certainly more accessible and probably more effective. The regional reform allowed social learning, "learning by doing."[91] Formal change induced informal change and became self-sustaining.

The new institution has not yet lived up to the highest expectations of its optimistic advocates. Factionalism and gridlock, inefficiency and simple incompetence, still plague many regions. This is especially so in the South, which was much less well positioned than the North to take advantage of the new powers. Both North and South have made progress in the last twenty years, but compared to the North, the southern regions are no better off today than they were in 1970. Compared to where the South would be today without the regional reform, however, the South is much better off. That is the view of most southerners.

Has the reform also begun to reverse the vicious uncivic circles that have trapped the Mezzogiorno in backwardness for a millennium? We cannot say, for the final lesson from this research is that *most institutional history moves slowly*. Where institution building (and not mere constitution writing) is concerned, time is measured in decades. This was true of the German Länder, it has been true of the Italian regions and of the communal republics before them, and it will be true of the ex-Communist states of Eurasia, even in the most optimistic scenarios.

History probably moves even more slowly when erecting norms of reciprocity and networks of civic engagement, although we lack the benchmarks to be sure. For convenience's sake, we might date the founding of the communal republics and the Norman kingdom, and thus the start of Italy's civic split between North and South, in (say) the year 1100. But it seems highly unlikely that surveys of nobles, peasants, and townspeople in 1120 would have detected the initial stages of the North-South division.

Two decades are time enough to detect the impact of institutional reform on political behavior, but not to trace its effects on deeper patterns of culture and social structure.

Those concerned with democracy and development in the South should be building a more civic community, but they should lift their sights beyond instant results. We agree with the prescription of the Italian economic historian Vera Zamagni, who urges local transformation of local structures rather than reliance upon national initiatives:

> It is a dangerous illusion to believe that the Mezzogiorno can be changed from outside *despite* its existing political-economic-social structure. . . . Beyond any doubt, the temporal perspective required for such a political and cultural revolution is long. But it does not seem to us that the path taken so far, with the results it has produced, has been any shorter.[92]

Building social capital will not be easy, but it is the key to making democracy work.

Research Methods

IN ADDITION to the statistical indicators of institutional performance reported in Chapter 3, this project drew broadly from the diverse methodological tool-kit of modern social science.

Surveys of Regional Councilors

Extensive interviews were conducted with regional councilors in 1970, 1976, 1981–82, and 1989 in a sample of regions selected to represent the diverse socioeconomic and political patterns of Italy's regions. The foundations of our study were laid in 1970, as we interviewed 112 newly elected regional councilors, roughly a one-in-two sample of the councils in Lombardia, Emilia-Romagna, Lazio, Puglia, and Basilicata. "Tell us about the most important problems facing this region," we asked. "What are the goals of the regional reform, and how do the regional council and the regional government actually work? Who has influence and over what? What about relations with the central authorities? What is the job of the regional councilor? How do the parties operate here?"

Since the regions still existed mostly on paper, our questions were mostly aimed at what the councilors expected to happen in the coming months and years after the transfer of powers from the central government. In addition to this open-ended, ninety-minute interview, we also posed several written questionnaires, tapping attitudes to national and regional issues and more basic features of elite political culture, as well as information on the councilor's personal and political background.

Six years later, in June-July 1976, we returned to interview a second wave of councilors. (At this time we added Veneto to our sample of selected regions, in order to include a region in which there was a dominant Catholic subculture.) This second wave included 194 interviews with two different types of regional councilors. The first group was composed of those councilors who had already been interviewed in 1970, regardless of whether or not they had been re-elected in 1975. Of the original 112 interviewed in 1970, we were able to reinterview 95, or 85 percent. (Sixty-nine of those interviewed in the first wave were still on the council in 1976; 26 had not been re-elected.) To this "panel" survey, we added interviews with 99 new respondents, selected so that our sample as a whole also accurately represented the incumbent councils in the six regions.[1]

In 1981–82 we conducted a third wave of interviews with 234 regional councilors, including 135 of the councilors interviewed in 1976 (75 of whom were still in the council), as well as 99 newly elected councilors. Finally, in 1989 we completed a fourth round of 178 interviews with councilors in each of our six selected regions, this time forgoing any attempt to reinterview previous respondents, and focusing only on incumbents.[2]

Surveys of Community Leaders

In 1976 in our six selected regions we interviewed a sample of 115 community leaders, including journalists from independent newspapers of different political tendencies; mayors of a large city (not the regional capital) and a small city, each from a diverse political orientation; interest-group leaders representing trade unions, farmers, industrialists, and bankers; provincial presidents; regional civil servants; and political leaders. These observers were asked to assess regional politics and government and to provide detailed accounts of their own involvement in regional affairs.

In 1981–82 we interviewed a second sample of 118 community leaders, adopting a sampling procedure similar to the one used in 1976, except that the political leaders were replaced by more interest-group representatives. Finally, in 1989 we returned to interview a comparable third wave of 198 community leaders.[3] All together, we interviewed more than four hundred community leaders in the three waves. Transcripts of the interviews and questionnaires were analyzed in the same manner as those for the councilors.

Nationwide Mail Survey of Community Leaders

In the spring of 1983 we extended our investigation of the views of community leaders beyond our six selected regions, mailing a questionnaire to approximately twenty-five people representing interest groups and local governments in each of the country's twenty regions, for a total sample of more than 500. As in the case of the interviews with community leaders in our six selected regions, the categories sampled included local and provincial leaders; farm leaders; trade union leaders; journalists; bankers; and key representatives of chambers of commerce, large and small industry, artisanry, and cooperatives. Respondents returned 308 (more than 60 percent) of the questionnaires, an unusually high response rate for a mail survey; detailed analysis confirmed that the replies provided an unusually good representation of informed opinion about regional issues. Our earlier face-to-face interviews with community leaders had shown them to be a well informed group, so our mail survey was able to probe for detailed assessments of the operations of the regional government, as well as to replicate other questions posed in our other surveys of elite and mass opinion. The disadvantage of having only a limited number of respondents within each region was more than offset by the nationwide scope of the sample.

Mass Surveys

Nationwide mass surveys were carried out on our behalf by the DOXA polling organization in 1977, 1981, 1982, and 1988; in addition, comparable surveys conducted by DOXA for other purposes in 1979 and 1987 were also made available to us. In each of these surveys, DOXA interviewed a national sample of approximately 2000 citizens, asking their views on the regions and the evolution of the regional reform. The questions in the mass surveys were similar to those used in the elite interviews because we wanted to compare elite and mass attitudes on the regional reform. We were particularly interested in gauging knowledge and satisfaction or dissatisfaction about the regions among the general public. Many of these surveys also included questions on broader political and social issues, enabling us to assess the political climate and culture in the various regions and to track changes in voters' attitudes across more than a decade.

In addition to these specially commissioned surveys, we found much valuable evidence in twenty-nine Eurobarometer surveys conducted for the European Commission between 1975 and 1989.[4] Virtually every semiannual Eurobarometer survey has included standard questions on political outlook and involvement, as well as on social background characteristics. In addition, questions have been posed with some regularity about media consumption, religiosity, alienation, and membership in secondary associations. Each Eurobarometer survey includes a representative sample of more than one thousand Italians. Thus, for standard questions, our aggregate sample totals more than 30,000, while for more occasional questions, such as those on associational membership, our aggregate sample generally totals between four thousand and ten thousand.[5] Since our analysis aggregates responses from different years, we have routinely confirmed that temporal differences have not influenced our findings.

Finally, we were able to exploit two important national surveys of the Italian electorate directed by Professor Samuel H. Barnes in 1968 and by Professor Barnes and Professor Giacomo Sani in 1972. These wide-ranging surveys were especially helpful in establishing a benchmark of political attitudes and civic behavior around the time of the launching of the regional experiment.[6]

Institutional/Political Case Studies

Between 1976 and 1989 we conducted case studies on the internal politics of the regional institutions and on political developments within each of our six selected regions. We made regular visits to the six regions to meet with political leaders, party representatives, top civil servants, interest group leaders, and others. We became personally acquainted with key participants in the political and economic life of the region, from whom we gained an intimate knowledge of the internal political maneuvering and personalities that have animated regional politics over the last two decades.

Another important source of information on regional political developments was the local press. Similarly, transcripts of regional council debates proved to be a rich source of detail on the political maneuvers discussed in the interviews. As our study continued, we expanded the number of ordinary regions in which we collected this type of information to include Toscana, Umbria, and Marche, and as indicated below, we completed a fuller study of one of the special regions, Friuli-Venezia Giulia.

Analysis of Legislation

We examined all regional legislation from 1970 to 1984, with special emphasis on our six selected regions, seeking to evaluate the regional legislative performance. The role of the region as a primary legislative body at the subnational level justifies a special emphasis on the character of legislative outputs. (These legislative analyses are described in more detail in Chapter 3.)

Case Studies of Regional Planning

In 1976 we initiated comprehensive case studies in the six selected regions of regional social and economic planning, broadly defined—case studies that were to cover more than a decade. Our objective was to recreate the policy process from the demand side, follow it through the "black box" of government, and trace its progress into the stage of administrative implementation and its final impact on society. Information for these studies of regional planning and policy making was collected through periodic and extended visits to the six selected regions to talk to regional and local civil servants and representatives of the sectors affected, as well as leaders in cultural and academic circles, and to collect a rich array of documentary and statistical information. Later, this process was also extended to three other regions—Toscana, Umbria, and Marche.

Citizen Contact Experiment

In order to assess the twenty regional governments from the point of view of the ordinary citizen, in January-February 1983 through the POLIS network of correspondent-researchers of the Carlo Cattaneo Institute we carried out a "citizen contact" study, monitoring how each regional bureaucracy handled typical requests for information from anonymous citizens in the region. (This study is described in more detail in Chapter 3.)

Special Study of Friuli-Venezia Giulia

In 1983 we were invited by the government of Friuli-Venezia Giulia (one of the five "special" regions) to carry out a study there comparable to our detailed studies in the six selected regions, including surveys of councilors and community leaders, case studies of regional planning and legislation, and general political analysis. Although our evidence from Friuli-Venezia Giulia lacks the temporal depth of our selected regional studies, it extended the scope of our research beyond the "ordinary" regions to encompass the particular challenges facing the five special regions.

NOTES

1. For an initial report on this panel survey, see Robert D. Putnam, Robert Leonardi, and Raffaella Y. Nanetti, "Attitude Stability among Italian Elites," *American Journal of Political Science* 23 (1979): 463–494.

2. In the case of Basilicata, this fourth wave of interviews was actually carried out three years earlier, in 1986.

3. The 1989 surveys with community leaders included all but Basilicata among our six selected regions, and added Toscana, Abruzzi, and Sicilia.

4. These data were made available through the Inter-university Consortium for Political and Social Research. The Eurobarometer data were originally collected by Jacques-Rene Rabier, Helene Riffault, and Ronald Inglehart. Neither the col-

lectors of the original data nor the Consortium bear any responsibility for the analyses or interpretations reported here.

5. Questions on alienation were posed only in 1986 and 1988, so our aggregate sample on that topic totals more than two thousand.

6. These data were made available through the Inter-university Consortium for Political and Social Research. Neither the collectors of the original data nor the Consortium bear any responsibility for the analyses or interpretations reported here.

Statistical Evidence on Attitude Change
among Regional Councilors

THE FOLLOWING tables provide statistical support for the conclusions in Chapter 2 regarding alternative explanations for growing moderation in successive regional councils.

Replacement effects can be assessed by comparing the attitudes of councilors leaving and arriving in any given year. For example, Table B.1.a shows that 37 percent of the councilors first elected in 1975 expressed extremist views on the *Left-Right Issues Index* in our 1976 interviews, as compared to 28 percent of the ex-councilors whom we reinterviewed in 1976. Table B.3.a shows that 44 percent of the councilors newly elected in 1975 stressed irreconcilable social conflict, as compared to only 31 percent of those they replaced. In both cases, those leaving the council were more moderate than their replacements.

Individual change among incumbent councilors can be directly assessed from our panel data. For example, Table B.1.a shows that of the councilors reelected in 1975, 45 percent had expressed extremist views in 1970, but only 28 percent did so in our second wave of interviews six years later. Analogous comparisons in each of the subtables in Tables B.1, B.2, and B.3 show consistent individual-level change in a moderating direction between 1970 and 1976, and again between 1976 and 1981–82, more substantial in most cases than the aggregate changes in the council as a whole. Table B.1.a, for example, shows that between 1970 and 1976 the fraction of Left-Right extremists fell by 11 percent among all incumbents, but by 17 percent among the holdovers. In other words, the aggregate changes were concentrated among holdovers.

Comparison of the top and bottom half of each table shows that institutional socialization was particularly strong in 1970–75, that is, during the first legislative period of the new governments. Moreover, individual conversion was more marked among reelected councilors than among those who had left the council by the time of our follow-up interviews. In Table B.1.a, for example, those who left the council in 1975 only moved from 35 percent extremist in 1970 to 28 percent extremist in 1976, whereas extremism among those who stayed on after 1975 dropped from 45 percent in 1970 to 28 percent in 1976.

National political trends can be assessed, in part, by considering newly elected councilors as a kind of control group. (Keep in mind that in the broader national electorate—a control group of a different sort—there was no evidence at all of depolarization during these years.) *If* we assume that councilors newly elected in 1975 had had views in 1970 comparable to those held by the then-newly elected councilors—*but* that these not-yet-elected politicos were not subject to institutional socialization—then most of the individual change we observe in our panels is attributable to institutional socialization, although national trends probably had some effect. For example, in Table B.1.a extremism was evinced by 37 percent of the newcomers in 1975, as compared to 42 percent of their counterparts five years earlier, for a "gain" of 5 points, as compared to a "gain" of 17 points among the holdover councilors, at least 12 points of which are thus allocable to institutional effects. On the stated assumptions, institutional socialization accounts for nearly two-thirds of the individual conversion between 1970 and 1976 and for nearly half of the individual conversion between 1976 and 1981–82, with the balance in each case attributable to national trends. Of course, a more direct and precise estimate of national trends would have required comparable panel surveys with politicians outside the regional government.

TABLE B.1

Declining Ideological Extremism, 1970–1975 and 1975–1980:
Replacement, National Politics, or Conversion?

	Of Councilors Who in 1975 Elections:			Of All Incumbents in Year Shown
	Left	Stayed	Arrived	
Percentage who were Left-Right extremists as of:				
1970	35%	45%		42%
1976	28%	28%	37%	31%

	Of Councilors Who in 1980 Elections:			Of All Incumbents in Year Shown
	Left	Stayed	Arrived	
Percentage who were Left-Right extremists as of:				
1976	32%	29%		31%
1981–1982	24%	22%	20%	21%

Note: Extremism as used here is based on the *Left-Right Issues Index*, as defined in Tables 2.2 and 2.3 and Figure 2.1. Underlined categories represent incumbent councilors in the indicated years.

TABLE B.2

Increasing Cross-Party Sympathy, 1970–1975 and 1975–1980:
Replacement, National Politics, or Conversion?

	Of Councilors Who in 1975 Elections:			Of All Incumbents in Year Shown
	Left	*Stayed*	*Arrived*	
Mean Cross-Party Sympathy as of:				
1970	27.4	26.6		26.9
1976	26.8	33.3	29.5	31.0

	Of Councilors Who in 1980 Elections:			Of All Incumbents in Year Shown
	Left	*Stayed*	*Arrived*	
Mean Cross-Party Sympathy as of:				
1976	30.4	31.4		31.0
1981–1982	34.8	35.6	35.2	35.4

Note: Cross-party sympathy is mean sympathy (on scale from 0 to 100) expressed by respondents toward *all parties other than their own*, as displayed in Figure 2.2. Underlined categories represent incumbent councilors in the indicated years.

TABLE B.3

Declining Salience of Conflict, 1970–1975 and 1975–1980:
Replacement, National Politics, or Conversion?

	Of Councilors Who in 1975 Elections:			Of All Incumbents in Year Shown
	Left	*Stayed*	*Arrived*	
Percentage who stressed irreconcilable conflict as of:				
1970	47%	54%		52%
1976	31%	32%	44%	36%

	Of Councilors Who in 1980 Elections:			Of All Incumbents in Year Shown
	Left	*Stayed*	*Arrived*	
Percentage who stressed irreconcilable conflict as of:				
1976	34%	39%		36%
1981–1982	29%	25%	32%	29%

Note: Stress on irreconcilable conflict is measured by question in Figure 2.3.a. Underlined categories represent incumbent councilors in the indicated years.

Institutional Performance (1978–1985)

COMPONENTS OF INDEX OF INSTITUTIONAL
PERFORMANCE, 1978–1985

Variable 1   Reform legislation, 1978–1984
Variable 2   Day care centers, 1983
Variable 3   Housing and urban development, 1979–1987
Variable 4   Statistical and information services, 1981
Variable 5   Legislative innovation, 1978–1984[a]
Variable 6   Cabinet stability, 1975–1985[b]
Variable 7   Family clinics, 1978
Variable 8   Bureaucratic responsiveness, 1983
Variable 9   Industrial policy instruments, 1984
Variable 10 Budget promptness, 1979–1985[b]
Variable 11 Local health unit spending, 1983
Variable 12 Agricultural spending capacity, 1978–1980

[a] Data for Variable 5 are unavailable for the five "Special Regions" (Valle d'Aosta, Trentino-Alto Adige, Friuli-Venezia Giulia, Sicilia, and Sardegna).

[b] Scoring for Variables 6 and 10 has been reversed from that described in the text, so that a high absolute score corresponds to high performance.

TABLE C.1

Intercorrelations (r) among Components of Index of Institutional Performance, 1978–1985

	Index	Var 1	Var 2	Var 3	Var 4	Var 5	Var 6	Var 7	Var 8	Var 9	Var 10	Var 11	Var 12
Index	1.0000	0.8742*	0.8506*	0.8067*	0.7970*	0.7787*	0.6813*	0.6400*	0.6246*	0.5803*	0.5772*	0.5449*	0.4682
Var 1	0.8742*	1.0000	0.7721*	0.5982*	0.7293*	0.7611*	0.4925	0.5943*	0.5030	0.3936	0.4425	0.4603	0.4424
Var 2	0.8506*	0.7721*	1.0000	0.8687*	0.5889*	0.8113*	0.4997	0.6895*	0.3561	0.3251	0.1588	0.5191*	0.3843
Var 3	0.8067*	0.5982*	0.8687*	1.0000	0.5732*	0.8272*	0.5526*	0.5626*	0.2813	0.4807	0.2546	0.5391*	0.1210
Var 4	0.7970*	0.7293*	0.5889*	0.5732*	1.0000	0.6065*	0.2790	0.5321*	0.4194	0.5406*	0.4414	0.3515	0.4548
Var 5	0.7787*	0.7611*	0.8113*	0.8272*	0.6065*	1.0000	0.4874	0.4684	0.4568	0.5677	0.4669	0.1799	0.4294
Var 6	0.6813*	0.4925	0.4997	0.5526*	0.2790	0.4874	1.0000	0.3330	0.5758*	0.2469	0.5488*	0.3150	0.3188
Var 7	0.6400*	0.5943*	0.6895*	0.5626*	0.5321*	0.4684	0.3330	1.0000	0.1873	0.2625	0.0117	0.2255	0.1997
Var 8	0.6246*	0.5030	0.3561	0.2813	0.4194	0.4568	0.5758*	0.1873	1.0000	0.2406	0.6098*	0.3282	0.3240
Var 9	0.5803*	0.3936	0.3251	0.4807	0.5406*	0.5677	0.2469	0.2625	0.2406	1.0000	0.6149*	0.2225	0.1045
Var 10	0.5772*	0.4425	0.1588	0.2546	0.4414	0.4669	0.5488*	0.0117	0.6098*	0.6149*	1.0000	0.1171	0.3757
Var 11	0.5449*	0.4603	0.5191*	0.5391*	0.3515	0.1799	0.3150	0.2255	0.3282	0.2225	0.1171	1.0000	-0.0386
Var 12	0.4682	0.4424	0.3843	0.1210	0.4548	0.4294	0.3188	0.1997	0.3240	0.1045	0.3757	-0.0386	1.0000

* Significance (one-tailed) < .01.

Regional Abbreviations Used in Scattergrams

Abbreviation	Region
Ab	Abruzzi
Ba	Basilicata
Cl	Calabria
Cm	Campania
Em	Emilia-Romagna
Fr	Friuli-Venezia Giulia
La	Lazio
Li	Liguria
Lo	Lombardia
Ma	Marche
Mo	Molise
Pi	Piemonte
Pu	Puglia
Sa	Sardegna
Si	Sicilia
To	Toscana
Tr	Trentino-Alto Adige
Um	Umbria
Va	Valle d'Aosta
Ve	Veneto

Local Government Performance (1982–1986) and Regional Government Performance (1978–1985)

THE FOCUS of this study is the performance of regional government. One might wonder, however, how the quality of government at the regional level is related (if at all) to the quality of local governments in the same region. If the performance of a regional government is determined primarily by "endogenous" factors, such as the strategies and choices of particular incumbents, then there is little reason to expect it to be correlated with the performance of local governments in the same area. But if "ecological" factors, such as the social or economic structure of a region or its civic traditions are more important determinants, then those same factors should influence the quality of adjacent local governments, too.

A thorough evaluation of the quality of Italian local governments is, of course, beyond our scope. However, some relevant evidence comes from several nationwide studies of local government performance conducted on behalf of the Italian *Corte dei Conti*, a national administrative tribunal. These studies examined levels of local government activity within each region, evaluating a wide variety of programs and services, from personnel training to sports facilities and school cafeterias, from urban planning offices to trash and sewer services, from libraries to municipal water systems. This information can be aggregated into a rough-and-ready, region-by-region assessment of local government activity. A complete list of the relevant measures is given in Table E.1.[1]

In partial confirmation of the *Corte dei Conti* studies, this summary measure of local government performance is highly correlated with citizen satisfaction with local government, aggregated at the regional level.[2] In other words, the *Corte dei Conti* and Italian voters generally agree on the quality of local government in each of the various regions, although the available data do not allow us to link the performance of a particular local government with citizen evaluations of that government. Figure E.1 shows that local government performance, as measured by services rendered, is in turn very highly correlated with the quality of regional government. Similarly, our mass surveys tell us that voters' evaluations of their own regional and local governments are strongly correlated. Figure

TABLE E.1
Components of Index of Local Government Performance
(1982–1986)

Content	Factor Loading
Communal sports facilities implementation	0.939
Communal sewer system implementation	0.930
Communal libraries implementation	0.919
Communal trash collection implementation	0.917
Communal technical services implementation	0.912
Communal day care center implementation	0.883
Communal water system implementation	0.850
Communal school transport implementation	0.806
Communal administrative training	0.673
Communal personnel mobility	0.640
Communal meeting rooms implementation	0.546
Communal administration reorganization	0.528
Communal school cafeteria implementation	0.499
Communes with urban planning office	0.375
Communes with technical office	0.342

FIGURE E.1
Regional and Local Government Performance

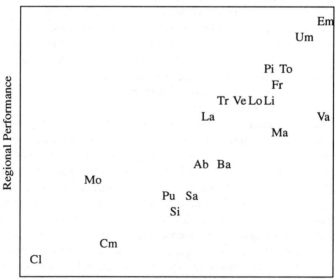

Local Government Performance
Correlation: $r = .89$

FIGURE E.2
Regional and Local Government Satisfaction

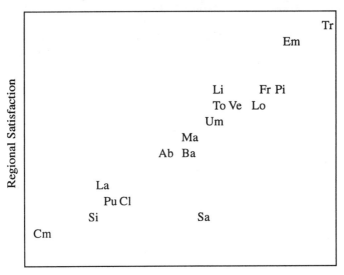

Local Government Satisfaction
Correlation: $r = .90$

E.2 shows that aggregate satisfaction with local government is very highly correlated with aggregate satisfaction with regional government.[3] (On the other hand, aggregate satisfaction with *national* government is uncorrelated with satisfaction with either regional or local government; in other words, higher satisfaction with regional and local governments does not simply reflect more lenient standards of evaluation in the high-performance regions.) In short, we and Italian voters agree that the better the performance of the regional government in a given region, the better the quality of local government there. Good government regionally and good governments locally go together, precisely as we should expect if government performance is determined by civic traditions and social capital.

NOTES

1. Our sources for this information are *Primo rapporto sullo stato dei poteri locali/ 1984* (Rome: Sistema Permanente di Servizi, 1984), pp. 91, 118, 121; *XIII rapporto/1979 sulla situazione sociale del paese*, Censis Ricerca (Roma: Fondazione Censis, 1979), p. 519; and *Quarto rapporto sullo stato dei poteri locali/ 1987* (Rome: Sistema Permanente di Servizi, 1987), pp. 48–51. Fifteen separate service indicators have been combined into a single factor score, based on a principal components analysis.

2. The crude correlation between mean satisfaction with local government and our index of local government performance, aggregated regionally, is $r = .72$; when weighted by sample size, to adjust for sampling error in the smallest regions, $r = .83$.

3. Across our four surveys of the 1980s, the mean correlation at the *individual* level of analysis between evaluations of regional and local governments is $r = .62$.

Traditions of Civic Involvement (1860–1920)

COMPONENTS OF INDEX OF TRADITIONS OF CIVIC INVOLVEMENT, 1860–1920

Variable 1   Strength of Socialist and Popular parties, 1919–1921
Variable 2   Incidence of cooperatives per capita, 1889–1915
Variable 3   Membership in mutual aid societies, 1873–1904
Variable 4   Electoral turnout, 1919–1921
Variable 5   Local associations founded before 1860

TABLE F.1
Intercorrelations (r) among Components of Index of Traditions of Civic Involvement, 1860–1920

	Index	Var 1	Var 2	Var 3	Var 4	Var 5
Index	1.000	0.973*	0.931*	0.906*	0.782*	0.563*
Var 1	0.973*	1.000	0.901*	0.877*	0.707*	0.539
Var 2	0.931*	0.901*	1.000	0.764*	0.676*	0.494
Var 3	0.906*	0.877*	0.764*	1.000	0.609*	0.464
Var 4	0.782*	0.707*	0.676*	0.609*	1.000	0.131
Var 5	0.563*	0.539	0.494	0.464	0.131	1.000

* Significance (one-tailed) < .01.

Notes

Preface

1. See Robert D. Putnam, Robert Leonardi, and Raffaella Y. Nanetti, "Attitude Stability among Italian Elites," *American Journal of Political Science* 23 (August 1979): 463–494; Robert D. Putnam, Robert Leonardi, and Raffaella Y. Nanetti, "Le regioni 'misurate,'" *Il Mulino* 24 (March-April 1980): 217–243; Robert Leonardi, Raffaella Y. Nanetti, and Robert D. Putnam, "Devolution as a Political Process: The Case of Italy," *Publius* 11 (Winter 1981): 95–117; Robert D. Putnam, Robert Leonardi, Raffaella Y. Nanetti, and Franco Pavoncello, "Sul rendimento delle istituzioni: il caso dei governi regionali italiani," *Rivista Trimestrale del Diritto Pubblico* 2 (1981): 438–479; Robert D. Putnam, Robert Leonardi, Raffaella Y. Nanetti, and Franco Pavoncello, "L'evaluation de l'activitè regionale: le cas italien," *Pouvoirs* 19 (1981): 39–58; Robert D. Putnam, Robert Leonardi, and Raffaella Y. Nanetti, "L'istituzionalizzazione delle Regioni in Italia," *Le Regioni* 10 (November-December 1982): 1078–1107; Robert D. Putnam, Robert Leonardi, Raffaella Y. Nanetti, and Franco Pavoncello, "Explaining Institutional Success: The Case of Italian Regional Government," *American Political Science Review* 77 (1983): 55–74; Robert D. Putnam, Robert Leonardi, and Raffaella Y. Nanetti, *La Pianta e le Radici: Il Radicamento dell'Istituto Regionale nel Sistema Politico Italiano* (Bologna: Il Mulino, 1985); Robert Leonardi, Robert D. Putnam, and Raffaella Y. Nanetti, *Il Caso Basilicata: L'effetto Regione dal 1970 al 1986* (Bologna: Il Mulino, 1987); Raffaella Y. Nanetti, Robert Leonardi, and Robert D. Putnam, "The Management of Regional Policies: Endogenous Explanations of Performance," in *Subnational Politics in the 1980s: Organization, Reorganization and Economic Development*, Louis A. Picard and Raphael Zariski, eds. (New York: Praeger, 1987), pp. 103–118; Robert D. Putnam, Robert Leonardi, and Raffaella Y. Nanetti, "Indagini sul governo regionale del Friuli-Venezia Giulia," in Arduino Agnelli and Sergio Bartole, eds., *La Regione Friuli-Venezia Giulia* (Bologna: Il Mulino, 1987), pp. 499–563; and Robert Leonardi, Raffaella Y. Nanetti, and Robert D. Putnam, "Italy—Territorial Politics in the Post-War Years: The Case of Regional Reform," in R.A.W. Rhodes and Vincent Wright, eds., *Tensions in Territorial Politics of Western Europe* (London: Frank Cass, 1987), pp. 88–107.

2. See, in particular, Raffaella Y. Nanetti, *Growth and Territorial Policies: The Italian Model of Social Capitalism* (New York: Pinter, 1988); Robert Leonardi and Douglas A. Wertman, *Italian Christian Democracy: The Politics of Dominance* (London: Macmillan, 1989); Robert Leonardi and Raffaella Y. Nanetti, eds., *The Regions and European Integration: The Case of Emilia-Romagna* (New York: Pinter, 1990); and Robert Leonardi, *Regions and the European Community: The Regional Response to the Single Market in the Underdeveloped Parts of the EC* (London: Frank Cass, 1992).

Chapter 1
Introdution: Studying Institutional Performance

1. See the Frontispiece for a map of this journey.

2. For a comprehensive account of the Seveso disaster and its aftermath, see Michael R. Reich, *Toxic Politics: Responding to Chemical Disasters* (Ithaca: Cornell University Press, 1991), pp. 98–139.

3. See Terry M. Moe, "The New Economics of Organization," *American Journal of Political Science* 78 (November 1984): 739–777; Geoffrey Brennan and James M. Buchanan, *The Reason of Rules: Constitutional Political Economy* (New York: Cambridge University Press, 1985); Kenneth A. Shepsle, "Institutional Equilibria and Equilibrium Institutions," in *Political Science: The Science of Politics*, Herbert F. Weisberg, ed. (New York: Agathon Press, 1986), pp. 51–81; Elinor Ostrom, "An Agenda for the Study of Institutions," *Public Choice* 48 (1986): 3–25; Kenneth A. Shepsle, "Studying Institutions: Some Lessons from the Rational Choice Approach," *Journal of Theoretical Politics* 1 (1989): 131–137; Terry M. Moe, "Political Institutions: The Neglected Side of the Story," *Journal of Law, Economics, and Organization* 6 (1990): 213–253; and Douglass C. North, "Institutions and a Transaction Costs Theory of Exchange," in *Perspectives on Positive Political Economy*, eds. James E. Alt and Kenneth Shepsle (New York: Cambridge University Press, 1990), Chapter 7.

4. See James G. March and Johan P. Olsen, *Rediscovering Institutions: The Organizational Basis of Politics* (New York: The Free Press, 1989) and *The New Institutionalism in Organizational Analysis*, eds. Walter W. Powell and Paul J. Dimaggio (Chicago: University of Chicago Press, 1991).

5. See Stephen Skowronek, *Building a New American State* (New York: Cambridge University Press, 1982); *Bringing the State Back In*, eds. Peter B. Evans, Dietrich Rueschemeyer, and Theda Skocpol (New York: Cambridge University Press, 1985); and Peter Hall, *Governing the Economy: The Politics of State Intervention in Britain and France* (New York: Oxford University Press, 1986).

6. For a clear, persuasive illustration of this interpretation, see Shepsle, "Studying Institutions."

7. For further discussion of evaluating institutional performance, see Chapter 3.

8. For a discussion of the evolution of formal legal studies and institutionalism as modes of political analysis, see *Comparative Politics: A Reader*, eds. Harry Eckstein and David Apter (London: The Free Press of Glencoe, 1963), pp. 10–11.

9. Ibid., p. 100.

10. See in particular Mill's discussion of proportional representation, modes of voting, and the role and composition of parliamentary governments in "Considerations on Representative Government."

11. Eckstein and Apter, *Comparative Politics*, p. 98. Other examples of this genre include James Bryce, *Modern Democracies* (New York: The MacMillan Co., 1921) and Harold Laski, *A Grammar of Politics*, 4th ed. (London: George Allen and Unwin, 1938). Among the generation of scholars influenced by the

events surrounding World War II, a particular version of institutional studies became popular, which emphasized the crucial role the electoral system played in determining political outcomes. See, for instance, F. A. Hermens, *Democracy or Anarchy? A Study of Proportional Representation* (Notre Dame, Indiana: The Review of Politics, 1941) and Maurice Duverger, *Political Parties: Their Organization and Activity in the Modern State* (New York: John Wiley, 1954).

12. Arturo Israel, *Institutional Development: Incentives to Performance* (Baltimore: Johns Hopkins University Press, 1987).

13. Elinor Ostrom, *Governing the Commons: The Evolution of Institutions for Collective Action* (New York: Cambridge University Press, 1990). For a fuller discussion of dilemmas of collective action, see Chapter 6.

14. Robert A. Dahl, *Polyarchy: Participation and Opposition* (New Haven: Yale University Press, 1971); Seymour Martin Lipset, *Political Man* (New York: Doubleday, 1960).

15. Israel, *Institutional Performance*, p. 112.

16. Gabriel A. Almond and Sidney Verba, *The Civic Culture: Political Attitudes and Democracy in Five Nations* (Princeton: Princeton University Press, 1963). Among other efforts at broad-ranging comparative political analysis based upon sociocultural variables, see Harry Eckstein and Ted Robert Gurr, *Patterns of Authority: A Structural Basis for Political Inquiry* (New York: John Wiley and Sons, 1975); Samuel Beer, *British Politics in the Collectivist Age* (New York: Norton, 1982); Anthony King, "Ideas, Institutions and the Policies of Government," *British Journal of Political Science* 3 (1973): 291–313; Ronald Inglehart, *Culture Shift in Advanced Industrial Society* (Princeton, N.J.: Princeton University Press, 1990); Michael Thompson, Richard Ellis, and Aaron Wildavsky, *Cultural Theory* (San Francisco: Westview Press, 1990) and Harry Eckstein, *Regarding Politics: Essays on Political Theory, Stability, and Change* (Berkeley: University of California Press, 1992), Chapters 7–8.

17. Alexis de Tocqueville, *Democracy in America*, ed. J. P. Mayer, trans. George Lawrence (Garden City, N.Y.: Anchor Books, 1969).

18. Philip Selznick, *TVA and the Grass Roots: A Study in the Sociology of Formal Organization* (Berkeley, California: University of California Press, 1953), p. 250. See also Stein Rokkan, "The Structuring of Mass Politics in the Small European Democracies," *Comparative Studies in Society and History* 10 (1968): 173, for a discussion of the dilemma the social scientist faces between "[the] obligation to reduce the welter of empirical facts to a body of parsimoniously organized general propositions . . . [and the] pressure to treat each case *sui generis* as a unique configuration worthy of an understanding all on its own."

19. Findings pass this test when they hit the researcher between the eyes.

Chapter 2
Changing the Rules: Two Decades of Institutional Development

1. Sidney Tarrow, "Local Constraints on Regional Reform: A Comparison of Italy and France," *Comparative Politics* 7 (October 1974): 36.

2. For the classic discussion of institutionalization and political development,

see Samuel P. Huntington, *Political Order in Changing Societies* (New Haven: Yale University Press, 1968).

3. James G. March and Johan P. Olsen, *Rediscovering Institutions: The Organizational Basis of Politics* (New York: Free Press, 1989), p. 159, p. 164.

4. Cited in Harry Eckstein, "Political Culture and Change," *American Political Science Review* 84 (1990): 254. For a review of the consequences of attempts to create new subnational institutions in France from 1870 to 1990, see Vivien A. Schmidt, *Democratizing France: The Political and Administrative History of Decentralization* (New York: Cambridge University Press, 1990).

5. Percy A. Allum and G. Amyot, "Regionalism in Italy: Old Wine in New Bottles?" *Parliamentary Affairs* 24 (Winter 1970/71): 53–78.

6. Emiliana Noether in *Regionalismo e centralizzazione nella storia di Italia e Stati Uniti*, Luigi De Rosa and Ennio Di Nolfo, eds. (Florence: Olschki, 1986), p. 34.

7. Giulio Lepschy, "How Popular is Italian?" in *Culture and Conflict in Postwar Italy: Essays on Mass and Popular Culture*, Zygmunt G. Barański and Robert Lumley, eds. (London: Macmillan, 1990), p. 66.

8. See Carlo Ghisalberti, "Accentramento e decentramento in Italia," in *Regionalismo e centralizzazione*, edited by De Rosa and Di Nolfo. The decision of Italy's unifiers to reject regionalism in place of centralism continues to be debated by Italian historians. For a thoughtful argument that the sociocultural backwardness of the South made it unprepared for local autonomy, see Carlo Tullio-Altan, *La nostra Italia: Arretratezza socioculturale, clientelismo, trasformismo e rebellismo dall' Unità ad oggi* (Milan: Feltrinelli, 1986), pp. 50–52.

9. Martin Clark, *Modern Italy 1871–1982* (New York: Longman, 1984), p. 58; Robert C. Fried, *Planning the Eternal City: Roman Politics and Planning since World War II* (New Haven: Yale University Press, 1973), pp. 168–69; Raphael Zariski, *Italy: The Politics of Uneven Development* (Hinsdale, Illinois: Dryden Press, 1972), pp. 121–122.

10. Percy A. Allum, *Italy: Republic without Government?* (New York: Norton, 1973), pp. 221–223; Robert C. Fried, *The Italian Prefects* (New Haven: Yale University Press, 1963).

11. Clark, *Modern Italy*, pp. 58–61.

12. For a similar analysis of center-periphery relations in Italy at the beginning of the 1970s, as the regional reform was getting underway, see Sidney Tarrow, *Between Center and Periphery: Grassroots Politicians in Italy and France* (New Haven: Yale University Press, 1977).

13. Clark, *Modern Italy*, pp. 238–240.

14. For more detailed accounts of the regional reform movement, see Robert Leonardi, Raffaella Y. Nanetti, and Robert D. Putnam, "Devolution as a Political Process: The Case of Italy," 11 *Publius* (Winter 1981): 95–117; Robert Leonardi, Raffaella Y. Nanetti, and Robert D. Putnam, "Italy—Territorial Politics in the Post-War Years: The Case of Regional Reform," in *Tensions in the Territorial Politics of Western Europe*, edited by R. A. W. Rhodes and Vincent Wright (London: Frank Cass & Company, 1987), pp. 88–107; Peter Gourevitch, "Reforming the Napoleonic State: The Creation of Regional Governments in France and Italy,"

in *Territorial Politics in Industrial Nations*, edited by Sidney Tarrow, Peter J. Katzenstein and Luigi Graziano (New York: Praeger, 1978), pp. 28–63; and Tarrow, "Local Constraints on Regional Reform," pp. 1–36.

15. Regional governments were established by 1949 in Sicily, Sardinia, Valle d'Aosta, and Trentino-Alto Adige. Creation of the fifth special region, Friuli-Venezia Giulia, complicated by the Trieste dispute with Yugoslavia, was postponed until 1964.

16. More than 7 percent of the entire population of southern Italy moved to the North in just five years, 1958–1963. See Paul Ginsborg, "Family, Culture and Politics in Contemporary Italy," in *Culture and Conflict in Postwar Italy: Essays on Mass and Popular Culture*, edited by Zygmunt G. Barański and Robert Lumley (London: Macmillan, 1990), p. 33; and Paul Ginsborg, *A History of Contemporary Italy: Society and Politics 1943–1988* (London: Penguin Books, 1990), pp. 218–220.

17. Allum, *Italy: Republic without Government?* p. 236.

18. Clark, *Modern Italy*, pp. 391–392.

19. *XV rapporto/1981 sulla situazione social del paese*, Censis Ricerca (Rome: Franco Angeli, 1981), p. 503. By 1991 the total number of regional bureaucrats had reached 90,000; *Il Messaggero* (Rome), August 10, 1991, p. 12.

20. *Ottavo rapporto sullo stato dei poteri locali/1991* (Rome: Sistema Permanente di Servizi, 1991), pp. 231–240. Despite demands from regions for greater taxing authority, income raised directly by the regions (as distinct from funds devolved by the state) fell from 4.3 percent in 1980 to 1.8 percent in 1989. This inconsistency between centralized taxing authority and decentralized spending authority remains a serious obstacle to regional autonomy and accountability. As Table 2.7 shows, most Italians support regional demands for greater financial autonomy, and by 1991 further reform proposals of this sort were under active consideration. See *Il Messaggero* (Rome), August 10, 1991, p. 12.

21. Max Weber, "Politics as a Vocation," in *From Max Weber: Essays in Sociology*, eds. and trans. H.H. Gerth and C. Wright Mills (New York: Oxford University Press, 1958), p. 128.

22. This chapter's description of the changing regional political elite is based on our surveys of regional councilors in six diverse regions in 1970, 1976, 1981–82, and 1989.

23. Marcello Fedele, *Autonomia Politica Regionale e Sistema dei Partiti* (Milan: Giuffrè, 1988), p. 18, p. 42. Fedele's sample of regions is identical to ours, except that he includes Toscana instead of Basilicata, and his sample of parties includes only the DC, the PCI, and the PSI, whereas our sample also includes the minor parties.

24. The significant exception is Lazio (the region centered on Rome), roughly half of whose councilors have been raised in other regions, mainly in the South. This incidence of newcomers on the Lazio council reflects the rapid and sustained influx of Southern immigrants into Rome over the last four decades.

25. Declining turnover is sometimes taken to be an indicator of legislative institutionalization, but it does not fit the Italian regional case so neatly. Turnover was relatively low for the founding generation of councilors; two-thirds of those

elected in 1970 were reelected in 1975, a rather high level of stability compared to subnational legislatures elsewhere. Turnover modestly increased to roughly 50 percent in subsequent legislatures, however, so that average tenure on the regional council has stabilized at slightly less than two five-year terms.

26. For a discussion of institutionalization in the American Congress that touches on many of the issues raised here see, Nelson W. Polsby, "The Institutionalization of the U.S. House of Representatives," *American Political Science Review* 62 (March 1968): 144–168.

27. Much of this change occurred even before the advent of Thatcher and Reagan, and it was completed before the collapse of Communism in Eastern Europe.

28. These results are fully confirmed by questions that invited councilors to place each political party on a 100-point left-right scale. Between 1970 and 1989, the average placements of left-wing parties shifted rightwards, and the average placement of right-wing parties shifted leftward, while centrist parties oscillated in a narrow range around the middle of the scale, so that altogether the parties steadily converged toward the center of the political spectrum.

29. Comparative research has uncovered contrasting patterns of elite and mass consensus, including a "competitive elite" model (where partisan distances are greatest at the elite level), a "consensual elite" model (where partisan distances are greatest at the mass level), and a "coalescent elite" model (where partisan distances are greatest at the intermediate level of party activists and smallest at the elite level). It is generally argued that a unified elite governs more effectively and more stably than a disunited elite, although perhaps also more oligarchically. For a theoretical discussion of this issue, as well as citations to the relevant literature, see Robert D. Putnam, *The Comparative Study of Political Elites* (Englewood Cliffs, N.J.: Prentice-Hall, 1976), pp. 115–132.

30. The analysis summarized in this paragraph is based on quantitative coding of "political style" like that described in Robert D. Putnam, *The Beliefs of Politicians: Ideology, Conflict, and Democracy in Britain and Italy* (New Haven: Yale University Press, 1973), pp. 34–41. The 1989 surveys were restricted to closed-ended questions that did not allow for extended discussions of policy issues.

31. Giovanni Sartori, "European Political Parties: The Case of Polarized Pluralism," *Political Parties and Political Development*, edited by Joseph LaPalombara and Myron Weiner (Princeton: Princeton University Press, 1966), pp. 137–176.

32. For a discussion of this "problem" in conjunction with postwar changes in West European party systems see Otto Kirchheimer, "The Transformation of the Western European Party Systems" in *Political Parties and Political Development*, edited by LaPalombara and Weiner, pp. 177–200.

33. An exhaustive list of possible explanations would distinguish various subtypes and hybrids, such as life cycle change combined with selective retirement. (Attributing moderation simply to aging politicos, for example, would not do the trick since the average age of successive councils did not change.) To distinguish among these complex alternatives would require more elaborate analyses and more robust data than ours. The three theories discussed in the text are the most plausible and parsimonious.

34. Since our 1989 survey was not a panel—that is, we did not reinterview

respondents from our 1981–82 survey—we cannot carry this detailed analysis of change through the 1980s.

35. Statistical analysis of social change is notoriously labyrinthine; the relevant evidence appears in Appendix B.

36. See Joseph LaPalombara, "Italy: Fragmentation, Isolation, and Aliena-tion," in *Political Culture and Political Development*, edited by Lucian W. Pye and Sidney Verba (Princeton: Princeton University Press, 1965), pp. 282–329, and Putnam, *Beliefs of Politicians*, pp. 56–58, pp. 82–90.

37. Samuel P. Huntington, *Political Order in Changing Societies*, p. 20.

38. Even in Calabria, by all accounts the least successful of all the regions, James Walston, *The Mafia and Clientelism: Roads to Rome in Post-War Calabria* (New York: Routledge, 1988), p. 79, p. 127, argues that the advent of the regional government has meant a significant decline in the importance of deputies, minis-ters, and the prefect, and a rise in the power of regional officials.

39. The fraction of regional government coalitions that dissolved within six months of a national political crisis declined from 37 percent in 1970–1975 to 8 percent in 1985–1990. Marcello Fedele, "I processi politico-istituzionali nei sis-temi regionali," a research report to the Parliamentary Committee for Regional Questions, Dossier n. 416, 10th Legislature (Rome: Camera dei Deputati, 1990). We are grateful to Nando Tasciotti for bringing this report to our attention.

40. In 1970 the average councilor met more often with local party leaders than with regional cabinet members, but that pattern too had been reversed by 1989.

41. Councilors attributed minimal importance in voters' decisions to national, regional, and local party leaders and to regional and local party platforms.

42. The research center of the Conference of Regional Presidents (*Cinsedo*) has estimated that 82 percent of the resources available to the "ordinary" regions (though only 36 percent of the resources of the "special" regions) are bound by decisions taken by Rome. See *Il Messaggero* (Rome), August 10, 1991, p. 12.

43. Raphael Zariski, "Approaches to the Problem of Local Autonomy: The Lessons of Italian Regional Devolution," *West European Politics* 8 (July 1985): 64–81; Bruno Dente, "Intergovernmental Relations as Central Control Policies: The Case of Italian Local Finance," *Government and Policy* 3 (1985): 383–402.

44. Morton Grodzins, *The American System: A New View of Government in the United States*, edited by Daniel Elazar (Chicago: Rand McNally and Co., 1966), pp. 8–9, p. 14, introduced this metaphor to describe intergovernmental relations in the United States.

45. See Zariski, "Approaches to the Problem of Local Autonomy," and Nicola Bellini, "The Management of the Economy in Emilia-Romagna: The PCI and the Regional Experience," in *The Regions and European Integration: The Case of Emilia-Romagna*, edited by Robert Leonardi and Raffaella Y. Nanetti (New York: Pinter, 1990), p. 121.

46. The recent literature on decentralization and center-periphery relations in Western states is vast. For useful compendia of comparative studies, see *Territo-rial Politics in Industrial Nations*, edited by Tarrow, Katzenstein and Graziano; *Decentralist Trends in Western Democracies*, edited by L. J. Sharpe (Beverly Hills: Sage Publications, 1979); *Centre-Periphery Relations in Western Europe*, edited by Yves Mény and Vincent Wright (London: Allen & Unwin, 1985); *Ten-*

sions in the Territorial Politics of Western Europe, edited by Rhodes and Wright; and *Central and Local Government Relations: A Comparative Analysis of West European Unitary States*, edited by Edward C. Page and Michael J. Goldsmith (Beverly Hills: Sage Publications, 1987).

47. Intriguingly, ordinary voters are somewhat less critical of the regions on this score; only 40–45 percent of them agreed with this proposition in our surveys of 1982, 1987, and 1988.

48. Table 2.5 is based on our 1982 nationwide survey of community leaders. Virtually identical results were obtained in our 1989 survey of community leaders in selected regions.

49. Damningly, these criticisms are voiced most strongly by just those sectors (industry, labor, agriculture, and commerce) most often in contact with the regional administration; local government officials are somewhat more tolerant of the region's administrative failings, probably because they appreciate the frustrations of public management in Italy.

50. Detailed analysis shows that in nearly every sector, spokesmen for smaller groups—smaller towns, smaller farmers, smaller businesses, and so on—are more favorable to the regional reform than spokesmen for larger groups. The smaller interest groups seem to be particularly sensitive to the advantages of dealing with the region, as compared with distant Roman bureaucracies.

51. Robert D. Putnam, "The Political Attitudes of Senior Civil Servants in Western Europe: A Preliminary Report," *British Journal of Political Science* 3 (1973): 278.

52. Ironically, awareness of the regional government was most scant in the two "special" southern regions, the oldest of all the regions; in 1982 fully half the citizens of Sicily and Sardinia claimed to have heard nothing at all about their own regional governments, by then more than thirty-five years old.

53. M. Kent Jennings and Harmon Zeigler, "The Salience of American State Politics," *American Political Science Review* 64 (1970): 523–535.

54. Responses to the questions presented in Table 2.7 were quite stable throughout our surveys in the 1980s.

55. Since we shall later present much evidence of justified southern unhappiness over the current failings of their regional governments, it is important to emphasize that support for greater regional autonomy on the questions represented in Table 2.7 is almost as strong among southerners as among northerners.

56. Throughout all data analyses in this book, "North" refers to all regions from Toscana, Umbria, and Marche northwards and "South" to all regions from Lazio and Abruzzi southwards.

57. This generalization refers to respondents who declared themselves "very" or "rather" satisfied. Two of the twenty regions, Valle d'Aosta and Molise, are too small to appear in national mass samples and are thus necessarily excluded from this analysis.

58. Figure 2.9 is based on our 1988 survey, but the same pattern appears in all of our surveys.

59. We began posing these questions to community leaders in 1976, but we did not ask them of the mass public until 1981.

60. Throughout our mass surveys, youth is never correlated with evaluations of the practical operations of the regional government, but is always a strong predictor of support for the principle of regional reform. In other words, younger Italians are more likely to be "sympathetic critics."

61. See Fedele, "I processi politico-istituzionali nei sistemi regionali," and the data presented at p. 41 above.

62. We are grateful to the DOXA survey organization for their collaboration with our research, including putting at our disposal data from their previous studies.

63. To ensure comparability over time, the data on community leaders in Table 2.9 are limited to our six selected regions, but in 1982 and 1989, when we sampled other regions as well, the distribution of opinion in those six regions accurately reflected nationwide opinion.

64. In 1987 southern voters said, by a ratio of 37 percent to 24 percent, that more good than bad had come from the regional reform; the equivalent ratio for northern voters was 45 percent to 11 percent. In 1989 southern community leaders, by a ratio of 54 percent to 15 percent, saw more good than bad in the regional reform; the equivalent ratio for northern community leaders was 68 percent to 3 percent. See also note 55 above.

65. Elisabeth Noelle and Erich Peter Neumann, *Jahrbuch der Öffentlichen Meinung* (Allensbach: Institut für Demoskopie, 1967), p. 458; Elisabeth Noelle-Neumann, *The Germans: Public Opinion Polls, 1967–1980* (Westport, Connecticut: Greenwood Press, 1981), p. 175; and unpublished German polling results supplied to us by DOXA (Milan). Arnold Brecht, *Federalism and Regionalism in Germany* (New York: Oxford University Press, 1945) examines German federalism and regionalism from the era preceding German unification in the 1870s. For a comprehensive overview of German intergovernmental relations, see Joachim Jens Hesse, "The Federal Republic of Germany: From Co-operative Federalism to Joint Policy-Making," in *Tensions in the Territorial Politics of Western Europe*, edited by Rhodes and Wright, pp. 70–87.

66. See *Il Messaggero* (Rome), August 10, 1991, p. 12; *La Repubblica* (Rome), November 20, 1991, p. 17; and *Ottavo rapporto sullo stato dei poteri locali/1991*, pp. 18–19.

Chapter 3
Measuring institutional Performance

1. Robert A. Dahl, "The Evaluation of Political Systems," in *Contemporary Political Science: Toward Empirical Theory*, edited by Ithiel de Sola Pool (New York: McGraw-Hill, 1967), p. 179.

2. Kenneth Shepsle, "Responsiveness and Governance," *Political Science Quarterly* 103 (Fall 1988): 461–484.

3. Robert Dahl, *Polyarchy: Participation and Opposition* (New Haven: Yale University Press, 1971), p. 1. See also John Stuart Mill, "Of the Proper Functions of Representative Bodies," in *"On Liberty" and "Considerations on Representative Government"*, ed. R. B. MacCallum (Oxford: Basil Blackwell, 1948).

4. In the language of statistical methodology, these four tests correspond to *face validity* (do the indicators seem on their face to measure significant features of institutional success?), *internal validity* (are the indicators intelligibly intercorrelated, so that we can reasonably combine them into a single index?), *test-retest reliability* (are scores on the index relatively stable over time?), and *external validity* (are scores on the index strongly correlated with independent measures of institutional performance?).

5. Harry Eckstein, "The Evaluation of Political Performance: Problems and Dimensions," *Sage Professional Papers in Comparative Politics* 2, no. 1–17 (1971); and Ted Robert Gurr and M. McClelland, "Political Performance: A Twelve-Nation Study," *Sage Professional Papers in Comparative Politics* 2, no. 1–18 (1971).

6. J. Roland Pennock, "Political Development, Political Systems, and Political Goods," *World Politics* 18 (1966): 421.

7. Eckstein, "Evaluation of Political Performance," p. 8.

8. The electoral cycles for the five "special regions" follow a slightly different calendar, and we have used data for the legislative periods corresponding most closely to the 1975–1985 period. We are grateful to Professor Marcello Fedele for generously sharing data on cabinet stability from the project reported in his "I processi politico-istituzionali nei sistemi regionali."

9. The data are drawn from *Secondo rapporto sullo stato dei poteri locali/ 1985* (Rome: Sistema Permanente di Servizi, 1985), p. 163, supplemented by data gathered directly from the regional governments.

10. *XV rapporto/1981 sulla situazione sociale del paese*, Censis Ricerca (Rome: Franco Angeli, 1981), p. 509.

11. See footnote 30 below. For a detailed description of our evaluative procedures, together with an explanation of the specific scores for each region in each policy sector, see our *La Pianta e le Radici: Il radicamento dell'istituto regionale nel sistema politico italiano* (Bologna: Il Mulino, 1985), pp. 203–278. For an account of relevant policy initiatives in the most effective of the twenty regions, see Raffaella Y. Nanetti, "Social, Planning, and Environmental Policies in a Post-Industrial Society," in *The Regions and European Integration: The Case of Emilia-Romagna*, edited by Robert Leonardi and Raffaella Y. Nanetti (New York: Pinter, 1990), pp. 145–170. Professor Nanetti carried out this portion of our project.

12. See Jack L. Walker, "The Diffusion of Innovations among the American States," *American Political Science Review* 63 (1969): 880–899.

13. "Factor loading" in Table 3.1 refers to the correlation between any single indicator and the composite index, which is a factor score based on a principal-components analysis of the twelve subscores. This method provides the most reliable and valid means of combining multiple indicators of a theoretical variable into a single index; see R. A. Zeller and E. G. Carmines, *Measurement in the Social Sciences* (New York: Cambridge University Press, 1980). *All indices in this book are based on this technique.*

14. Strictly speaking, our scoring is based on the percentage of months that a given model law was in force between the date of first passage of that law in any

region and December 1984, when we closed the books on this part of our project. As of December 1984 the average model law had been adopted by slightly more than half of the regions. Data are unavailable for this variable for the five Special Regions.

15. These data on day care centers are drawn from an unpublished presentation by Pierluigi Bersani to an international seminar on "Participation and Management in Child-Care Services," Bologna, October 17–19, 1984.

16. *XIII rapporto/1979 sulla situazione sociale del paese*, Censis Ricerca (Rome: Fondazione Censis, 1979), p. 410.

17. For a detailed account of one region's industrial policy initiatives, see Nicola Bellini, Maria Grazia Giordani, and Francesca Pasquini, "The Industrial Policy of Emilia-Romagna: The Business Service Centres," in *Regions and European Integration*, edited by Leonardi and Nanetti, pp. 171–186.

18. Both Friuli-Venezia Giulia and Calabria were at the time controlled by centrist governments, suggesting that this indicator does not simply reflect the ideological predisposition of the incumbent cabinet. The data are drawn from *Primo rapporto sullo stato dei poteri locali/ 1984* (Rome: Sistema Permanente di Servizi, 1984), p. 54.

19. *Primo rapporto sullo stato dei poteri locali/ 1984*, pp. 50–51.

20. Ibid., p. 220.

21. Our precise measure is a factor score index of the various annual measures, which are themselves highly intercorrelated; that is, the regions that were most effective at disbursing funds for housing in 1979 were also the most effective in 1981, 1985, and 1987. Sources for these data include *XIII rapporto/1979 sulla situazione sociale del paese*, Censis Ricerca (Rome: Fondazione Censis, 1979), p. 476, p. 481; *XV rapporto/1981 sulla situazione sociale del paese*, Censis Ricerca (Rome: Franco Angeli, 1981), p. 417; *Annuario 1985 delle autonomie locali*, ed. Sabino Cassese (Rome: Edizioni delle Autonomie, 1984), p. 103; *XXI rapporto/ 1987 sulla situazione sociale del paese*, Censis Ricerca (Rome: Franco Angeli, 1987), p. 794.

22. Robert Leonardi conceived and directed this project.

23. These three sectors—agriculture, health, and vocational education—together account for two-thirds of all regional expenditures. Of all requests, 33 percent were satisfied at the letter stage, 57 percent needed telephone calls, and 10 percent required a personal visit.

24. The sixty-six bivariate correlations among the twelve measures average $r = .43$. All but one of the sixty-six are in the correct direction, and two-thirds are statistically significant at the .05 level, despite the modest number of cases. The first factor to emerge from a principal components factor analysis—on which the Index of Institutional Performance is based—accounts for more than half the total common variance among the twelve indicators.

25. For a detailed account of this earlier research, see Robert D. Putnam, Robert Leonardi, Raffaella Y. Nanetti, and Franco Pavoncello, "Explaining Institutional Success: The Case of Italian Regional Government," *American Political Science Review* 77 (March 1983): 55–74.

26. There is a wide-ranging debate in the public policy literature on the useful-

ness of citizens' assessments in the evaluation of municipal services. For a good overview of this debate see Jeffrey L. Brudney and Robert E. England, "Urban Policy Making and Subjective Service Evaluations: Are They Compatible?" *Public Administration Review* 42 (March-April 1982): 127–135. For a positive evaluation of the usefulness of citizen assessments, see Roger Parks, "Complementary Measures of Police Performance," in *Public Policy Evaluation*, Sage Yearbook in Politics and Public Policy, ed. Kenneth M. Dolbeare (Beverly Hills, California: Sage Publications, 1975), pp. 185–215; Peter Rossi and Richard A. Berk, "Local Roots of Black Alienation," *Social Science Quarterly* 54 (March 1974): 741–758; and H. Schuman and B. Gruenberg, "Dissatisfaction with City Services: Is Race an Important Factor?" in *People and Politics in Urban Society*, ed. Harlan Hahn (Beverly Hills, California: Sage, 1972), pp. 369–392. For a negative evaluation of the usefulness of citizen assessments, see Brian Stipak, "Citizen Satisfaction with Urban Services: Potential Misuse as a Performance Indicator," *Public Administration Review* 39 (January-February 1979): 46–52.

27. Stipak, "Citizen Satisfaction with Urban Services."

28. These national surveys were conducted on our behalf by the DOXA polling institute in 1977, 1979, 1981, 1982, 1987, and 1988. Regional scores from one survey to the next were highly correlated ($r = .7 - .8$, figures that are significantly attenuated by sampling error). Our index of citizen satisfaction is a factor score based on a principal components analysis of mean regional satisfaction in each of the six national surveys; the mean loading on this index is .87. Two regions, Valle d'Aosta and Molise, are so small that they are excluded from all DOXA surveys and thus from this analysis.

29. We do not entirely understand why the citizens of Trentino-Alto Adige are happier about their regional government than seems warranted by its performance. However, this Alpine region includes a large, ethnically conscious German-speaking minority, for whom the regional government represents a significant measure of ethnic autonomy and a recognition of their special status. These *Südtiroler* may feel particular satisfaction with the symbolism of this "special" region, quite apart from its performance in terms of public policy. If this region is excluded from the calculation, the correlation between citizen satisfaction and our Index of Institutional Performance rises to $r = .90$.

30. Citizen satisfaction is significantly correlated with virtually every one of our performance indicators, taken individually. The strongest individual correlates are (r in parentheses) Legislative Innovation (.89), Cabinet Stability (.80), Reform Legislation (.74), and Bureaucratic Responsiveness (.73).

31. This generalization is true both *across* all regions and *within* each region. The only partial exception to this generalization is that in many regions during the late 1980s, satisfaction with *all* levels of government—national, local, and regional—increased somewhat more rapidly in smaller towns than in larger cities. We have no explanation for this intriguing finding, but it does not seriously impair our argument.

32. To avoid ambiguities about government and opposition roles, only avowed PCI and DC supporters are included in this figure.

33. See Table 2.5.

34. Methodologically, the effect of small samples and sampling error is to de-

press ("attenuate") correlations artificially; correcting for that attenuation would strengthen the correlation between the leaders' views and our Index. In other words, the data in Figure 3.4 understate the true correlation.

35. Separate analyses of the "special" and "ordinary" regions in Figure 3.4 suggest slightly different patterns in the two groups, although the samples are too small to be certain. The impact of a given difference in performance on satisfaction appears to be somewhat greater in the special regions than in the ordinary regions, perhaps because community leaders in the special regions have had longer to become confirmed critics or confirmed advocates of the regional government. Nevertheless, within each group of regions, satisfaction and performance are closely correlated.

36. The performance of regional government and the satisfaction of citizens with their regional government are also closely correlated with the performance and satisfaction ratings of *local* governments within those regions, as demonstrated in Appendix E. This suggests that the basic determinants of government performance have less to do with the policies and personalities of particular incumbents and more to do with the surrounding social environment. By contrast, aggregate satisfaction with *national* government is uncorrelated with any of these other evaluations; regions where people are relatively satisfied with regional and local government are not simply populated by "easy graders." These facts are wholly consistent with the contextual interpretation of government performance offered in Chapters 4–6.

Chapter 4
Explaining Institutional Performance

1. Robert A. Dahl, *Democracy and its Critics* (New Haven: Yale University Press, 1989), pp. 251–254. See also Dahl, *Polyarchy*, pp. 62–80. Seymour Martin Lipset, *Political Man* (New York: Doubleday, 1960), Chapter 2, is the fount of contemporary empirical work on this issue. C. F. Cnudde and D. Neubauer, *Empirical Democratic Theory* (Chicago: Markham, 1969) is a convenient collection of the 1960s' work on modernization and democracy. For a recent sophisticated analysis that confirms the correlation between economic development and democracy, see John Helliwell, "Empirical Linkages between Democracy and Economic Growth," NBER Working Paper 4066 (Cambridge, Massachussetts: National Bureau of Economic Research, 1992).

2. Kenneth A. Bollen and Robert W. Jackman, "Economic and Noneconomic Determinants of Political Democracy in the 1960s," *Research in Political Sociology* (1985), pp. 38–39, as cited in Samuel H. Huntington, *The Third Wave: Democratization in the Late Twentieth Century* (Norman, Oklahoma: University of Oklahoma Press, 1991), p. 60.

3. Robert C. Fried and Francine F. Rabinovitz, *Comparative Urban Politics: A Performance Approach* (Englewood Cliffs, N.J.: Prentice Hall, 1980), p. 66.

4. Economic modernity is here measured by a factor score based on per capita income and gross regional product, the agricultural and industrial shares of the workforce, and the agricultural and industrial share of value added, all in the period 1970–1977. These components are very highly intercorrelated (mean load-

ing = .90). Any one of these measures, as well as many other indicators of affluence and socioeconomic modernization—from automobiles to indoor plumbing—tells essentially the same story.

5. Size is another factor that differentiates Lombardia from Basilicata, but considering all twenty regions, population size and institutional performance are absolutely uncorrelated.

6. The correlation between economic modernity and institutional performance is $r = -.03$ *among* the more developed regions in the upper right quadrant of Figure 4.2, and $r = .05$ *among* the less developed regions in the lower left quadrant.

7. See J. G. A. Pocock, *The Machiavellian Moment: Florentine Political Thought and the Atlantic Republican Tradition* (Princeton: Princeton University Press, 1975).

8. Of course, neither "republican" nor "liberal" has the same meaning in this historical dialogue as in contemporary American partisan politics. For the classic liberal interpretation of Anglo-American political thought, see Louis Hartz, *The Liberal Tradition in America* (New York: Harcourt, Brace, 1955).

9. Don Herzog, "Some Questions for Republicans," *Political Theory* 14 (1986): 473.

10. In this wide-ranging debate, see (among many others) Robert N. Bellah, Richard Madsen, William M. Sullivan, Ann Swidler, and Steven M. Tipton, *Habits of the Heart: Individualism and Commitment in American Life* (New York: Harper and Row, 1986); Isaac Kramnick, "Republican Revisionism Revisited," *American Historical Review* 87, no. 3 (June 1982): 629–664; Alasdair MacIntyre, *After Virtue* (Notre Dame: Notre Dame University Press, 1981); Pocock, *The Machiavellian Moment*; Dorothy Ross, "The Liberal Tradition Revisited and the Republican Tradition Addressed," in John Higham and Paul Conkin, eds., *New Directions in American Intellectual History* (Baltimore: Johns Hopkins University Press, 1979); Michael Sandel, "The Procedural Republic and the Unencumbered Self," *Political Theory* 12 (1984): 81–96; Quentin Skinner, "The Idea of Negative Liberty: Philosophical and Historical Perspectives," in *Philosophy in History*, eds. Richard Rorty, J. B. Schneewind, and Quentin Skinner (New York: Cambridge University Press, 1984); Michael Walzer, "Civility and Civic Virtue in Contemporary America," in his *Radical Principles* (New York: Basic Books, 1980); and Gordon Wood, *The Creation of the American Republic: 1776–1787* (Chapel Hill: University of North Carolina Press, 1969).

11. Cited in Bellah et al., *Habits of the Heart*, p. 28.

12. Harry N. Hirsch, "The Threnody of Liberalism: Constitutional Liberty and the Renewal of Community," *Political Theory* 14 (1986): 441.

13. William A. Galston, "Liberal Virtues," *American Political Science Review* 82 (1988): 1281.

14. Within empirical political science, much of the inspiration for this approach to understanding differences in democratic performance is traceable to the landmark study by Gabriel A. Almond and Sidney Verba, *The Civic Culture: Political Attitudes and Democracy in Five Nations* (Princeton: Princeton University Press, 1963).

15. Walzer, "Civility and Civic Virtue," p. 64.

16. Skinner, "The Idea of Negative Liberty," p. 218.

17. Alexis de Tocqueville, *Democracy in America*, ed. J. P. Mayer, trans. George Lawrence (Garden City, N.Y.: Anchor Books, 1969), pp. 525–528.

18. Edward C. Banfield, *The Moral Basis of a Backward Society* (Chicago: The Free Press, 1958), p. 85.

19. Here, and throughout our discussion of civic virtue, we draw on the insights of Jeff W. Weintraub, *Freedom and Community: The Republican Virtue Tradition and the Sociology of Liberty* (Berkeley: University of California Press, 1992).

20. Walzer, "Civility and Civic Virtue," p. 62.

21. Gianfranco Poggi, *Images of Society: Essays on the Sociological Theories of Tocqueville, Marx, and Durkheim* (Stanford: Stanford University Press, 1972), p. 59.

22. Mark Granovetter, "Economic Action and Social Structure: the Problem of Embeddedness," *American Journal of Sociology* 91 (November 1985): 481–510.

23. Albert O. Hirschman, *Getting Ahead Collectively: Grassroots Experiences in Latin America* (New York: Pergamon Press, 1984), p. 57 *et passim*.

24. Tocqueville, *Democracy in America*, pp. 513–514.

25. Ibid., p. 515.

26. Almond and Verba, *The Civic Culture*, chapter 11.

27. Arend Lijphart, *Democracy in Plural Societies* (New Haven: Yale University Press, 1977), pp. 10–11; Lipset, *Political Man*; David Truman, *The Governmental Process: Political Interests and Public Opinion* (New York: Knopf, 1951).

28. "Nothing, in my view, more deserves attention than the intellectual and moral associations in America. American political and industrial associations easily catch our eyes, but the others tend not to be noticed." Tocqueville, *Democracy in America*, p. 517.

29. Tocqueville, *Democracy in America*, p. 190.

30. Not all associations of the like-minded are committed to democratic goals nor organized in an egalitarian fashion; consider, for example, the Ku Klux Klan or the Nazi party. In weighing the consequences of any particular organization for democratic governance, one must also consider other civic virtues, such as tolerance and equality.

31. Milton J. Esman and Norman T. Uphoff, *Local Organizations: Intermediaries in Rural Development* (Ithaca: Cornell University Press, 1984), p. 40.

32. Esman and Uphoff, *Local Organizations*, pp. 99–180, and David C. Korten, "Community Organization and Rural Development: A Learning Process Approach," *Public Administration Review* 40 (September-October 1980): 480–511. Esman and Uphoff find that such factors as natural resources, physical infrastructure, economic resources, income distribution, literacy, and partisan polarization are apparently unrelated to the developmental effectiveness of local organizations. For further evidence of the effectiveness of local participation in Third World development, see John D. Montgomery, *Bureaucrats and People: Grassroots Participation in Third World Development* (Baltimore: Johns Hopkins University Press, 1988), pp. 42–57 and the works cited there.

33. Banfield, *Moral Basis of a Backward Society*, p. 10.

34. See Alessandro Pizzorno, "Amoral Familism and Historical Marginality," *International Review of Community Development* 15 (1966): 55–66, and Sydel F. Silverman, "Agricultural Organization, Social Structure, and Values in Italy: Amoral Familism Reconsidered," *American Anthropologist* 70, no. 1 (February 1968): 1–19. The debate triggered by Banfield's book has been part of a broader scholarly controversy about the causal priority to be assigned "culture" and "structure." We return to this issue in Chapter 6.

35. *Le Associazioni Italiane*, ed. Alberto Mortara (Milan: Franco Angeli, 1985). The data are as of 1982. Our analysis excludes for-profit commercial organizations, tourist bureaus, and local branches of national organizations; the latter are excluded on the assumption that "imported" organizations may be a flawed indicator of local associational propensities. Labor unions and Catholic organizations, excluded by this proviso, are discussed later in this chapter, at pp. 106–107 and pp. 107–109, respectively.

36. The incidence of sports clubs and other associations is reasonably closely associated across Italy's regions ($r = .59$). To avoid having a single sector of activity dominate our measure of associational membership, we have constructed a factor score which weights each of these two categories (sports and other) equally. However, none of the statistical results reported in this book depends on the precise weight assigned to sports clubs.

37. Tocqueville, *Democracy in America*, pp. 517–518.

38. Our data on newspaper readership come from the *Annuario Statistico Italiano* (Rome: Istituto Centrale di Statistica, 1975), p. 135. These data are highly consistent with evidence from aggregated Eurobarometer surveys in 1976, 1980, 1983, 1986, and 1989 ($r = .91$). The Eurobarometer data also illustrate the strength of the connection between associational membership and newspaper readership at the *individual* level: 53 percent of group members read a newspaper more than once a week, as compared to 33 percent of nonmembers. This is specifically true of membership in virtually all types of associations, including sports clubs, *but not* of membership in religious groups.

39. Roberto Cartocci, "Differenze territoriali e tipi di voto: le consultazioni del maggio-giugno 1985," *Rivista Italiana di Scienza Politica* 15 (December 1985): 441. See also PierVincenzo Uleri, "The 1987 Referendum," in *Italian Politics: A Review*, vol. 3, eds. Robert Leonardi and Piergiorgio Corbetta (New York: Pinter Publishers, 1989), pp. 155–177.

40. Like all indices in this volume, the Index of Referenda Turnout, 1974–1987, is a factor score, based on the only factor to emerge from a principal components analysis of turnout in the five referenda. All correlations involving referenda voting reported in this chapter apply to turnout in *each* referendum, taken separately. In other words, the patterns are wholly unaffected by the content of the issues in each referendum.

41. See, for example, Richard S. Katz and Luciano Bardi, "Preference Voting and Turnover in Italian Parliamentary Elections," *American Journal of Political Science* 17 (1980): 97–114; and Roberto Cartocci, "Otto risposte a un problema: La divisione dell'Italia in zone politicamente omogenee," *Polis* 1 (December 1987): 481–514. Because of its tiny size, Valle d'Aosta is a single-member dis-

trict and thus does not use the preference vote system, so it is excluded from this analysis.

42. Once again, the Index of Preference Voting, 1953–1979, is a factor score based on the only factor to emerge from a principal components analysis of preference voting in the six elections.

43. These data come from secondary analysis of a 1968 national survey conducted by Samuel H. Barnes; we are grateful to Professor Barnes for enabling us to use these data. Region-by-region comparisons of survey and electoral data suggest that respondents in less civic regions slightly over-report their use of the preference vote, but this mild exaggeration, whatever its cause, does not vitiate the basic comparison.

44. These data come from aggregated Eurobarometer surveys in 1975, 1977, 1983, and 1987. These surveys, supplemented by the 1968 Barnes survey, suggest that somewhat more than one-third of Italian adults are members of one or more secondary associations, *including trade unions*, which account for slightly more than 40 percent of all associational memberships. (Experienced researchers believe that the inevitably limited number of probes in these surveys probably means that the results understate group membership, but this possible bias is constant across all regions.) At the individual level of analysis, group membership in Italy is best predicted by education, gender (unions and sports clubs are the most commonly reported affiliations), and residence in a civic community. Considering all types of groups, including unions, civic-ness increases the membership rate by roughly 10–15 percentage points, maleness increases it by roughly 15–20 percentage points, and education beyond primary school increases it by roughly 20–25 percentage points. Among less educated women in the least civic regions, only 15 percent claim group membership; among university educated men in the most civic regions, 66 percent report group membership.

45. The correlation between institutional performance and our measure of the civic community is $r = .53$ *among* the twelve regions in the upper right quadrant of Figure 4.5, and $r = .68$ *among* the eight regions in the lower left quadrant. Both are statistically significant (p < .04).

46. The partial correlation between economic development and institutional performance, controlling for the Civic Community Index, is $r = -.34$, which is statistically insignificant and in the wrong direction, whereas the correlation between the Civic Community Index and institutional performance remains highly significant (p < .0001). The bivariate correlation between the Civic Community Index and our measure of economic development is $r = .77$. Statistical mavens will recognize the potential problem of multicollinearity here, but in Chapter 5 we shall present additional evidence that distinguishes the effects of economic development and the civic community. It is worth recalling the redistributive formula according to which the central authorities provide special funding to the poorer regions. These transfers are intended to shield the poorer regions from the effects of their poverty, and this external aid may help account for the fact that regional wealth itself appears not to favor institutional performance, once we have controlled for the civic community.

47. In the 1968 Barnes national survey, 39 percent of the respondents in the

less civic regions claimed to know a member of parliament personally, as contrasted with 23 percent in the more civic regions. In our 1977 survey, more than twice as many citizens in less civic regions said that they had contacted a regional official as in more civic regions.

48. Compare Sidney Verba, Norman H. Nie, and N.-O. Kim, *The Modes of Democratic Participation: A Cross-National Comparison* (Beverly Hills, Calif.: Sage, 1971).

49. Harry Eckstein and Ted Robert Gurr, *Patterns of Authority: A Structural Basis for Political Inquiry* (New York: John Wiley and Sons, 1975).

50. This comparison is consistent with Giovanni Sartori's report in *Il Parlamento Italiano* (Naples: Edizioni Scientifiche Italiane, 1963) that among deputies in the national parliament between 1946 and 1958, 61 percent of all southerners were from upper class backgrounds, as compared to 39 percent of deputies from the Center-North, that is, the more civic section of the country. We should not exaggerate the social origins of the regional councilors anywhere. As discussed in Chapter 2, even in the South the councilors are drawn mostly from middle class backgrounds.

51. In 1970 and 1976 we asked all councilors, "With regard to this region, there is a lot of discussion of the desirability of increasing popular participation. In your opinion, what practical role can the citizens of the community have in regional affairs?" Responses were coded along a number of dimensions, including support for greater popular participation.

52. Income distribution as reconstructed from the aggregated 1975–1989 Eurobarometer surveys (the within-region coefficient of variation in reported family income) is more egalitarian in civic regions ($r = .81$). Controlling for civic-ness, income inequality and performance are uncorrelated, although multicollinearity shadows the results.

53. Robert D. Putnam, "Studying Elite Political Culture: The Case of Ideology," *American Political Science Review* 65 (September 1971): 651–681, found that among Italian (and British) politicians strong attachment to a set of values and beliefs is not incompatible with willingness to compromise.

54. See Carol A. Mershon, "Relationships Among Union Actors after the Hot Autumn," *Labour* 4 (1990): 46–52, and I. Regalia, "Democracy and Unions: Towards a Critical Appraisal," *Economic and Industrial Democracy* 9 (1988): 345–371.

55. Salvatore Coi, "Sindacati in Italia: iscritti, apparato, finanziamento," *Il Mulino* 28 (1979): 201–242, quotation at p. 206. Coi points out that unionization is actually greater in the public sector and in agriculture than in industry.

56. Among male manual workers the unionization rate is 39 percent in more civic regions, compared to 21 percent in less civic regions. Among male executives and professionals, the rate of union membership is 15 percent in more civic regions, as contrasted with 8 percent in less civic regions. Twelve percent of male farmers in more civic regions are union members, four times the rate in less civic regions. All in all, roughly 15 percent of all Italian adults are union members, and 25 percent are members of union households. All these data are drawn from aggregated Eurobarometer surveys in 1976, 1985, 1988, and 1989.

57. See Chapter 5, pp. 157–158, for historical confirmation of this point.

58. See Percy Allum, "Uniformity Undone: Aspects of Catholic Culture in Postwar Italy," in *Culture and Conflict in Postwar Italy: Essays on Mass and Popular Culture*, edited by Zygmunt G. Barański and Robert Lumley (London: Macmillan, 1990).

59. Church attendance is far higher among women and the older generation, but these differences in civic involvement persist when we control for gender and age. All findings reported in this paragraph are based on aggregated Eurobarometer surveys between 1975 and 1989.

60. Gianfranco Poggi, *Italian Catholic Action* (Stanford: Stanford University Press, 1967); Allum, "Uniformity Undone," esp. p. 85, p. 91; and Paul Ginsborg, *A History of Contemporary Italy: Society and Politics 1943–1988* (London: Penguin Books, 1990), pp. 169–170, p. 348.

61. A partial, but understandable exception to this generalization is that citizens in civic communities express greater interest in *local* affairs than do their counterparts in less civic areas.

62. The generalizations in this paragraph are based on aggregated Eurobarometer surveys between 1975 and 1989.

63. Sidney G. Tarrow, *Peasant Communism in Southern Italy* (New Haven: Yale University Press, 1967), esp. pp. 80–81, pp. 198–246; quotations at p. 7 and p. 75 (emphasis in original).

64. These data are drawn from Eurobarometer surveys in 1986 and 1988. "Low" education refers to the 62 percent of the adult population who left school before age 15; "high" refers to all others. This sense of powerlessness is closely linked to dissatisfaction with the state of Italian democracy. The Index of Powerlessness is correlated $r = -.19$ with education, $r = -.15$ with the Civic Community Index, and $r = -.26$ with the respondent's satisfaction "with the way democracy works in Italy."

65. Benjamin Barber, *Strong Democracy: Participatory Politics for a New Age* (Berkeley: University of California Press, 1984), p. 179.

66. See Chapter 5 (pp. 146–148) for a more detailed discussion of organized criminality in the less civic regions.

67. Even in civic regions only one-third of the respondents picked the "trusting" alternative, but this is only a few percentage points less than for identical questions posed to Americans in the same period. See Eric M. Uslaner, "Comity in Context: Confrontation in Historical Perspective," *British Journal of Political Science* 21 (1991): 61.

68. The "law-and-order" items are drawn from a 1972 national survey directed by Samuel H. Barnes and Giacomo Sani, to whom we are grateful for making these data available. Ronald Inglehart in *The Silent Revolution: Changing Values and Political Styles among Western Publics* (Princeton: Princeton University Press, 1977) and *Culture Shift in Advanced Industrial Society* (Princeton: Princeton University Press, 1990) argues that the balance between "materialist" and "post-materialist" values has important consequences for political behavior. Drawing on the aggregated 1976–1989 Eurobarometer surveys, we find that, controlling for age, education, family income, church attendance, gender, and regional affluence, people in more civic regions are significantly more likely to emphasize "more say in government" and "protect free speech," and significantly less

likely to emphasize "maintain order in the nation." Differences on Inglehart's fourth value ("fighting rising prices") are not significant. These contrasts, though modest in absolute size, are consistent with our account of the civic community: As between two equally educated, equally affluent, equally religious men or women of the same age, one in a civic region and one not, the citizen of the civic community is more concerned about democracy and less about authority. Like Inglehart, we believe such cultural differences are important, although our interpretation of their origins (Chapters 5 and 6) is somewhat different from his.

69. These data are drawn from aggregated Eurobarometer surveys between 1975 and 1989. The results summarized in Figure 4.14 combine "very satisfied" and "fairly satisfied." Given the massive sample, the region-by-region results are quite reliable. In a multiple regression predicting life satisfaction from income, church attendance, the civic community, age, education, sex, and date of interview (to test for possible trends over time), only the first three are significant. The *betas* are .16 for religious observance, .15 for income, and .14 for the civic community.

70. See, for example, Richard Dagger, "Metropolis, Memory, and Citizenship," *American Journal of Political Science* 25 (1981): 715–737; Alasdair MacIntyre, *After Virtue* (Notre Dame: Notre Dame University Press, 1981); and Michael Taylor, *Community, Anarchy and Liberty* (New York: Cambridge University Press, 1982). To be sure, not all advocates of the ideals of the civic community have lauded traditional village life; Tocqueville, for example, feared that the power of kith and kin in rural France would inhibit civic engagement. On diversity among peasant villages, concerning the degree to which they display voluntary collaboration for collective goods, see Robert Wade, *Village Republics: Economic Conditions for Collective Action in South India* (New York: Cambridge University Press, 1988).

71. James Watson, *The Mafia and Clientelism: Roads to Rome in Post-War Calabria* (New York: Routledge, 1988), pp. 98–99. As indicated by its title, even the occasional *Circolo dei Nobili* (Nobles' Club) is hardly a force for egalitarian social solidarity.

72. Our story here intersects with a longstanding debate about the effectiveness of patronage-based political machines in urban America. The white-gloved advocates of "good government" (sometimes termed "goo-goos" by their adversaries) were contemptuous of "bossism," while the gnarled-hand defenders of patronage argued that the machines integrated immigrant groups into political life and ensured prompt street sweeping and responsive welfare officers. Government by patronage works, the party regulars claimed. What both sides overlooked, our Italian contrast makes clear, is the fundamental social egalitarianism and the dense horizontal networks of civic solidarity that traditionally formed the American social fabric, even in large cities. Loosely speaking, American cities had patronage, but not clientelism. Whether the urban machines were actually as efficient as their defenders claim, and whether, on the other hand, that social fabric has become dangerously frayed in recent years, are two important questions that deserve further inquiry. For an analysis of American urban politics parallel in some respects to our Italian research, see Terry Nichols Clark and Lorna Crowley

Ferguson, *City Money: Political Processes, Fiscal Strain, and Retrenchment* (New York: Columbia University Press, 1983).

73. Defined by the *Oxford English Dictionary* as "want of good citizenship."

74. Cicero, *Republic*, I, 25, as quoted in George H. Sabine, *A History of Political Theory*, 3rd ed. (New York: Holt, Rinehart, and Winston, 1961), p. 166.

75. Edmund Burke, *Reflections on the Revolution in France* (1790, reprint ed., New York: Liberal Arts Press, 1955), p. 110.

76. Gabriel Almond, "Comparative Political Systems," *Journal of Politics* 18 (1956): 391–409. See also Gabriel Almond and G. Bingham Powell, *Comparative Politics: A Developmental Approach* (Boston: Little Brown, 1966); James Bryce, *Modern Democracies* (New York: The Macmillan Co., 1921), chapter 15; and Robert A. Dahl, *Polyarchy: Participation and Opposition* (New Haven: Yale University Press, 1971), pp. 110–111.

77. Giovanni Sartori, *Parties and Party Systems: A Framework for Analysis* (New York: Cambridge University Press, 1976), esp. chapters 6 and 10.

78. G. Bingham Powell, *Contemporary Democracies: Participation, Stability, and Violence* (Cambridge: Harvard University Press, 1982), p. 41.

79. Michael Walzer, "Civility and Civic Virtue in Contemporary America," p. 69.

80. Barber, *Strong Democracy*, p. 117.

81. Robert D. Putnam, Robert Leonardi, Raffaella Y. Nanetti, and Franco Pavoncello, "Explaining Institutional Success: The Case of Italian Regional Government," *American Political Science Review* 77 (March 1983): 56, 67.

82. These data are drawn from the aggregated 1975–1989 Eurobarometer surveys. According to these data, 54 percent of northerners left school by age 15, compared to 57 percent of southerners. The 1981 census found illiteracy reduced to trivial proportions and concentrated in the oldest age cohorts, although it remained slightly higher in the South (4.6 percent) than in the North (0.9 percent).

83. It is often assumed that the Mezzogiorno is less urban than northern Italy, but this is simply untrue. In 1986, 51 percent of northerners lived in towns of 20,000 or fewer inhabitants, as compared to 42 percent of southerners, and 15 percent of northerners lived in cities of more than 250,000, compared to 22 percent of southerners. Even excluding Lazio (dominated by Rome), the comparable figures for the Mezzogiorno were 46 percent and 14 percent. In short, the South is somewhat more urban than the North.

84. Samuel P. Huntington, *Political Order in Changing Societies* (New Haven: Yale University Press, 1968); Nelson W. Polsby, "The Institutionalization of the U.S. House of Representatives," *American Political Science Review* 62 (1968): 144–168; John R. Hibbing, "Legislative Institutionalization with Illustrations from the British House of Commons," *American Journal of Political Science* 32 (August 1988): 681–712.

85. Putnam, Leonardi, Nanetti, and Pavoncello, "Explaining Institutional Success," p. 72.

86. Of the four most successful regional governments between 1978 and 1985, three had PCI-led governments for the entire 1970–1985 period and the fourth had a PCI-led government during the 1975–1985 period, when its performance visibly

improved. But all four regions have civic traditions that (as we shall see in Chapter 5) predate the Communist party by centuries. (If there is a causal link between civic-ness and Communist strength, it must run from the former to the latter.) In a multiple regression framework, both the Civic Community Index (*beta* = .76, T = 9.19, p < .0000) and the number of years of PCI government (*beta* = .31, T = 3.73, p < .002) are significant predictors of our Index of Institutional Performance. On the other hand, controlling for civic-ness, PCI involvement in government is unrelated to citizens' satisfaction with their regional government.

87. In 1985 the PCI entered the government of Calabria, the least civic of the twenty regions, and between 1984 and 1989 the PCI participated in the regional government of Sardinia, also relatively uncivic, but our evaluations of performance did not encompass this period.

Chapter 5
Tracing the Roots of the Civic Community

1. The historical overview of Italian civic life in this chapter cannot pretend to be a comprehensive account of eight rich centuries of Italian history. Our story begins in the eleventh century primarily because the character of social and political life in the Dark Ages between the fall of Rome and 1000 remains in many respects obscure. Most unfortunate from the point of view of the theoretical argument we pursue here, the origins and prehistory of the northern communes are still shrouded in mist. J. K. Hyde, *Society and Politics in Medieval Italy: The Evolution of the Civil Life, 1000–1350* (London: Macmillan, 1973) observes that "significantly, no historian has succeeded in proving the continuance of civic institutions from late Roman to medieval times for any city north of Rome. . . . To try to catch a glimpse of an emergent Italian commune is a frustrating experience; so often the evidence seems to come just too soon or just too late" (p. 14, p. 49). See also Daniel Waley, *The Italian City-Republics*, 2nd ed. (New York: Longman, 1978), pp. 1–8. We are grateful to the distinguished Italian medievalist Richard Goldthwaite for encouraging our historical inquiries and for cautioning us about missteps along the way, although he bears no responsibility for mistakes that remain.

2. J. K. Hyde, *Society and Politics in Medieval Italy*, p. 38. The division between the Norman kingdom in the South and the communal republics in the North corresponds in many respects to the boundary between the Byzantine and Roman Catholic domains in the preceding epoch. Whether this parallelism reflects real and enduring regional traditions even deeper than those discussed in this chapter is an important question for future research.

3. *The Times Atlas of World History*, 3rd edition, eds. Geoffrey Barraclough and Norman Stone (London: Times Books, 1989), p. 124.

4. Harry Hearder, *Italy: A Short History* (New York: Cambridge University Press, 1990), p. 69.

5. John Larner, *Italy in the Age of Dante and Petrarch: 1216–1380* (New York: Longman, 1980), pp. 27–28.

6. Hyde, *Society and Politics in Medieval Italy*, p. 119.

7. Larner, *Italy*, pp. 16–37.

8. *Times Atlas of World History*, p. 124.

9. Denis Mack Smith, *A History of Sicily: Medieval Sicily: 800–1713* (New York: Viking Press, 1968), p. 54; Larner, *Italy*, pp. 28–29.

10. Larner, *Italy*, p. 31.

11. Denis Mack Smith, *History of Sicily*, pp. 55–56. See also Giovanni Tobacco, *The Struggle for Power in Medieval Italy: Structures of Political Rule* (New York: Cambridge University Press, 1989), p. 191 and pp. 237–244.

12. Pietr Kropotkin, *Mutual Aid: A Factor of Evolution* (London: Heinemann, 1902), p. 166.

13. Frederic C. Lane, *Venice and History* (Baltimore: Johns Hopkins University Press, 1966), chapter 32, "At the Roots of Republicanism," p. 535.

14. Hyde, *Society and Politics in Medieval Italy*, p. 57. See also Larner, *Italy*, p. 86, and Tobacco, *Struggle for Power in Medieval Italy*, esp. p. 188 and pp. 203–204.

15. Lauro Martines, *Power and Imagination: City-States in Renaissance Italy* (Baltimore: Johns Hopkins University Press, 1988), p. 148, estimates that between 2 and 12 percent of communal inhabitants were enfranchised, but Larner, *Italy*, p. 122, reports that one in five males had political rights in Florence, and Waley, *Italian City-Republics*, pp. 51–54, implies even higher participation rates.

16. Waley, *Italian City-Republics*, pp. 29–31, 51–52.

17. Lane, *Venice and History*, p. 524.

18. For a useful overview of the governmental institutions of the republics, see Waley, *Italian City-Republics*, pp. 25–54.

19. Marvin B. Becker, *Medieval Italy: Constraints and Creativity* (Bloomington: Indiana University Press, 1981), p. 60.

20. At least since the eighteenth century, *laissez faire* economists and politicians have been deeply skeptical about the social and economic effects of guilds. Recently, Mancur Olson has restated this argument in his stimulating book, *The Rise and Decline of Nations: Economic Growth, Stagflation, and Social Rigidities* (New Haven: Yale University Press, 1982): "Although they provided insurance and social benefits for their members, the guilds were, above all, distributional coalitions that used monopoly power and often political power to serve their interests. . . . [T]hey also reduced economic efficiency and delayed technological innovation." (p. 125) Although this is not the place for a comprehensive evaluation of the social consequences of the medieval guilds, our argument in this book suggests that whatever their other, more deleterious effects, the guilds marked an important stage in the development of horizontal social networks that contribute favorably both to governmental and to economic performance. For a related argument on the positive functions served by guilds, see Charles R. Hickson and Earl A. Thompson, "A New Theory of Guilds and European Economic Development," *Explorations in Economic History* 28 (1991): 127–168, and Avner Greif, Paul Milgrom, and Barry Weingast, "The Merchant Gild as a Nexus of Contracts," unpublished manuscript (Stanford, California: Hoover Institute, 1992).

21. Kropotkin, *Mutual Aid*, p. 174.

22. Larner, *Italy*, p. 196.

23. Ibid., p. 113.

24. Hyde, *Society and Politics in Medieval Italy*, p. 80.

25. Hearder, *Italy: A Short History*, p. 76.

26. Becker, *Medieval Italy*, p. 36, footnote 32.

27. Larner, *Italy*, p. 114. Tobacco, *The Struggle for Power in Medieval Italy*, p. 222, reports that by the beginning of the thirteenth century, Florence boasted 150 private defensive towers.

28. Waley, *Italian City-Republics*, pp. 97, 114.

29. Hyde, *Society and Politics in Medieval Italy*, p. 83.

30. Ibid., p. 95.

31. Waley, *Italian City-Republics*, pp. 32–36.

32. Ibid., p. 13.

33. William J. Bouwsma, "Italy in the late Middle Ages and the Renaissance," in *The New Encyclopedia Britannica: Macropaedia* (Chicago: Encyclopedia Britannica, 1978), vol. 9, p. 1134.

34. Martines, *Power and Imagination*, p. 111.

35. Larner, *Italy*, p. 189.

36. John Hicks, *A Theory of Economic History* (New York: Oxford University Press, 1969), Chapters 3–4.

37. Hicks, *Theory of Economic History*, p. 40.

38. Ibid., Chapter 5.

39. Becker, *Medieval Italy*, p. 19.

40. Crafts and small manufactories were also important to the economies of the communal republics. The wool industry, for example, sustained a third of the Florentine population. However, these activities were not unique to the Italian city-states, whereas Italians had more nearly a monopoly in long-distance commerce and finance. By the 1290s, for instance, London hosted no fewer than 14 Italian bank branches and Paris 20. See Larner, *Italy*, pp. 187, 189.

41. Becker, *Medieval Italy*, pp. 85, 177 (emphasis in original). See also Janet Coleman, "The Civic Culture of Contracts and Credit: A Review Article," *Comparative Studies in Society and History* 28 (1986): 778–784.

42. Carlo M. Cipolla, *Before the Industrial Revolution: European Society and Economy, 1000–1700*, 2nd edition (London: Metheun, 1980), pp. 198–199. See also Hyde, *Society and Politics in Medieval Italy*, p. 71.

43. Larner, *Italy*, p. 198.

44. Ibid., p. 115.

45. Hyde, *Society and Politics in Medieval Italy*, p. 94.

46. Bouwsma, "Italy in the late Middle Ages and the Renaissance," p. 1134. Larner, *Italy*, p. 183, and Hyde, *Society and Politics in Medieval Italy*, p. 153, give a slightly different list of the largest Italian cities, moving Milan and Genoa ahead of Palermo, but all agree on Italy's pre-eminence in Europe.

47. Larner, *Italy*, p. 29.

48. Bouwsma, "Italy in the Late Middle Ages and the Renaissance," p. 1136.

49. Larner, *Italy*, p. 160, reports that "by the middle of the sixteenth century the Church in the north and centre of the peninsula owned only 10–15 percent of the land, whereas in the south it still retained 65–75 percent."

50. Cipolla, *Before the Industrial Revolution*, p. 148. Cipolla in this passage is describing the difference between feudal and communal patterns across Europe,

but he makes clear that this distinction applies specifically to the contrast between northern and southern Italy.

51. Philip Ziegler, *The Black Death* (London: Penguin, 1970), pp. 40–62; Hearder, *Italy: A Short History*, pp. 98–99.

52. Hyde, *Society and Politics in Medieval Italy*, p. 107.

53. Ibid., p. 142.

54. Larner, *Italy*, p. 146, notes that "the very need felt for the ratification of the *signore*'s more important acts of state in general councils suggests a mentality which held fast to the principle that 'what touches all, should be approved by all'." See also Perry Anderson, *Lineages of the Absolutist State* (London: Verso, 1974), p. 162.

55. See the useful map in *The Times Atlas of World History*, p. 124, on which Figure 5.1 is in part based. See also Hyde, *Society and Politics in Medieval Italy*, Map 4, and Larner, *Italy*, pp. 137–150.

56. Nicolò Machiavelli, *The Discourses* (London: Penguin Books, 1970), ed. Bernard Crick, trans. Leslie J. Walker, Book I, Chapter 55, p. 243, p. 246.

57. Bouwsma, "Italy in the Late Middle Ages and the Renaissance," p. 1142.

58. Hyde, *Society and Politics in Medieval Italy*, p. 8, citing Matteo Palmieri's *Della Vita Civile*, published in the 1430s. On Italian political thought in this period, see especially J. G. A. Pocock, *The Machiavellian Moment: Florentine Political Thought and the Atlantic Republican Tradition* (Princeton: Princeton University Press, 1975).

59. Larner, *Italy*, p. 51.

60. Bouwsma, "Italy in the Late Middle Ages and the Renaissance," p. 1139.

61. Strictly speaking, the Sicilian and continental portions of the southern kingdom had been split between the Aragon and Angevin dynasties in 1282, but they would later be reunited as the Kingdom of the Two Sicilies. Excluded from the map are some peripheral areas—Sardinia, western Piedmont, and Trentino— that in this epoch looked more closely toward Spain, France, and Germany, respectively.

62. Hearder, *Italy: A Short History*, pp. 131–132, p. 136; Waley, *Italian City-Republics*, p. 17, and Cipolla, *Before the Industrial Revolution*, p. 162, p. 262.

63. Carlo Tullio-Altan, in *La nostra Italia: Arretratezza socioculturale, clientelismo, trasformismo e rebellismo dall' Unità ad oggi* (Milan: Feltrinelli, 1986), pp. 31–35. Following Max Weber, Tullio-Altan, a distinguished Italian sociologist, attributes the eclipse of communal republicanism, and the socioeconomic progress it had spawned, to the Counter-Reformation, which shielded Italy from the influence of the Protestant ethic that linked individual salvation and social responsibility. A fuller historical account would obviously also have to take account of the shift of trade routes from the Mediterranean to the Atlantic, among many other factors.

64. Sydel F. Silverman, *Three Bells of Civilization: The Life of an Italian Hill Town* (New York: Columbia University Press, 1975), pp. 93–95; Silverman, "Agricultural Organization, Social Structure, and Values in Italy: Amoral Familism Reconsidered," *American Anthropologist* 70 (February 1968): 9.

65. Maurice Vaussard, *Daily Life in Eighteenth Century Italy*, trans. Michael Heron (New York: Macmillan, 1963), p. 17.

66. During the heyday of the communal republics, the North was more urban than the South, but this has not been the case throughout history. Leaving aside the historic southern metropolises of Naples, Palermo, and Rome, a large fraction of southern peasants traditionally lived in "agro-towns," commuting daily to the fields. As we noted in Chapter 4, note 83, in contemporary Italy, the South is more urban than the North.

67. Harry Hearder, *Italy in the Age of the Risorgimento: 1790–1870* (New York: Longman, 1983), p. 126.

68. Bouwsma, "Italy in the Late Middle Ages and the Renaissance," p. 1139.

69. Gianni Toniolo, *An Economic History of Liberal Italy: 1850–1918*, trans. Maria Rees (New York: Routledge, 1990), p. 38, quoting P. Villani, *Mezzogiorno tra riforme e rivoluzione* (Bari: Laterza, 1973), p. 155.

70. Anthony Pagden, "The Destruction of Trust and its Economic Consequences in the Case of Eighteenth-century Naples," in *Trust: Making and Breaking Cooperative Relations*, ed. Diego Gambetta (Oxford: Blackwell, 1988), pp. 127–141.

71. Maurice Agulhon, *The Republic in the Village: The People of the Var from the French Revolution to the Second Republic*, trans. Janet Lloyd (New York: Cambridge University Press, 1982), esp. pp. 124–149.

72. Ibid., pp. 131–132.

73. Ibid., p. 128.

74. Ibid., pp. 157, 302.

75. Ibid., p. 150.

76. In 1859–60 the Piedmontese monarchy, after a complicated diplomatic chess game, annexed most of the Italian peninsula, and Victor Emmanuel II was proclaimed king of united Italy in 1861. Venetia was added in 1866 and finally Rome in 1870, the date generally treated as marking the achievement of Unification. Later, Triestino and Trentino-Alto Adige were won in the 1919 Treaty of Versailles. For more details, see Hearder, *Italy in the Age of the Risorgimento: 1790–1870*.

77. See Kent Roberts Greenfield, *Economics and Liberalism in the Risorgimento: A Study of Nationalism in Lombardia, 1814–48* (Baltimore: Johns Hopkins University Press, 1965) for a treatment of Lombard liberals in this respect, as well as Raymond Grew, *A Sterner Plan for Italian Unity: The Italian National Society in the Risorgimento* (Princeton: Princeton University Press, 1963).

78. Carlo Trigilia, "Sviluppo economico e transformazioni sociopolitiche dei sistemi territoriali a economia diffusa," *Quaderni della Fondazione Giangiacomo Feltrinelli* (Milan) 16 (1981): 57.

79. See Martin Clark, *Modern Italy 1871–1982* (New York: Longman, 1984), pp. 76–77, and Maurice F. Neufeld, *Italy: School for Awakening Countries: The Italian Labor Movement in Its Political, Social, and Economic Setting from 1800 to 1960* (Ithaca, New York: New York State School of Industrial and Labor Relations, Cornell University, 1961), pp. 60, 175–176. Fraternal ethnic associations that sprang up among American immigrant groups in the nineteenth century also often served as mutual aid societies. See Michael Hechter, *Principles of Group Solidarity* (Berkeley: University of California Press, 1987), pp. 112–120.

80. Neufeld, *Italy: School for Awakening Countries*, pp. 176–177.

81. Ibid., p. 177.

82. Clark, *Modern Italy*, p. 76.

83. Denis Mack Smith, *Italy: A Modern History* (Ann Arbor: University of Michigan Press, 1959), p. 243.

84. Neufeld, *Italy: School for Awakening Countries*, p. 185.

85. Ibid., p. 64.

86. Clark, *Modern Italy*, p. 87, p. 107; see also Paul Ginsborg, "Family, Culture and Politics in Contemporary Italy," in *Culture and Conflict in Postwar Italy: Essays on Mass and Popular Culture*, eds. Zygmunt G. Barański and Robert Lumley (London: Macmillan, 1990), p. 29.

87. Compare Chapter 4, pp. 107–109.

88. Clark, *Modern Italy*, p. 142.

89. Donald H. Bell, "Worker Culture and Worker Politics," *Social History* 3 (January 1978): 1–21.

90. Samuel H. Barnes, *Representation in Italy: Institutionalized Tradition and Electoral Choice* (Chicago: University of Chicago Press, 1977) presents systematic evidence supporting this interpretation.

91. See Sidney G. Tarrow, *Peasant Communism in Southern Italy* (New Haven: Yale University Press, 1967), esp. pp. 239–241 and pp. 300–342, and Luigi Graziano, "Patron-Client Relationships in Southern Italy," *European Journal of Political Research* 1 (1973): 3–34. After the Fascist parenthesis, former *popolari* activists, such as Alcide de Gasperi, founded the Christian Democratic (DC) party, which became the dominant political force in Republican Italy. Unlike the *Partito popolare*, however, the DC drew much of its electoral support from patron-clientelist networks in the Mezzogiorno.

92. Sydel F. Silverman, "Agricultural Organization, Social Structure, and Values in Italy," p. 9.

93. Ginsborg, "Family, Culture and Politics," pp. 28–29.

94. As quoted in Piero Bevilacqua, "Uomini, terre, economie," in *La Calabria*, eds. Piero Bevilacqua and Augusto Placanica (Turin: Einaudi, 1985), pp. 295–296.

95. Denis Mack Smith, *Italy: A Modern History*, p. 35.

96. Some scholars emphasize agricultural landholding patterns as the crucial variable that explains mores, politics, social relations, and economics in Italy. See, for example, Silverman, "Agricultural Organization, Social Structure, and Values in Italy" and (more generally) William Brustein, *The Social Origins of Political Regionalism: France, 1849–1981* (Berkeley: University of California Press, 1988). While not denying all significance to this factor, we doubt that it can account for the civic continuities we describe, in part because traditional landholding patterns in Italy vary in complex ways that are at best imperfectly correlated with those continuities (see Clark, *Modern Italy*, pp. 12–18), in part because of the unique role that Italian cities have played in establishing and maintaining those continuities, and in part because the postwar land reforms in the Mezzogiorno seem to have had little impact on its political culture as described here. See Michael A. Korovkin, "Exploitation, Cooperation, Collusion: An Enquiry into Patronage," *European Journal of Sociology* 29 (1988): 105–126.

97. Paul Ginsborg, *A History of Contemporary Italy: Society and Politics*

1943–1988 (London: Penguin Books, 1990), pp. 33–34; the cited passage is from Piero Bevilacqua, "Quadri mentali, cultura e rapporti simbolici nella società rurale del Mezzogiorno," *Italia Contemporanea* 36 (1984): 69.

98. For these and many other examples, see Tullio-Altan, *La nostra Italia*, p. 27.

99. Cited in Tullio-Altan, *La nostra Italia*, p. 13.

100. Banfield, *Moral Basis of a Backward Society*.

101. Tarrow, *Peasant Communism in Southern Italy*, p. 43.

102. Manlio Rossi-Doria, *Dieci Anni di Politica Agraria nel Mezzogiorno* (Bari: Laterza, 1958), p. 23, as cited in Tarrow, *Peasant Communism*, p. 61.

103. Tarrow, *Peasant Communism*, p. 7, pp. 75–77, *et passim*; Henner Hess, *Mafia and Mafiosi: The Structure of Power*, trans. Ewald Osers (Lexington, Mass.: Lexington Books, 1973).

104. Graziano, "Patron-Client Relationships in Southern Italy," pp. 5, 11; the embedded quotation is from Pasquale Turiello, *Governo e governati in Italia* (Bologna: Zanichelli, 1882), p. 148.

105. A. Caracciolo, *Stato e società civile: Problemi dell'unificazione italiana* (Torino: Einaudi, 1977), p. 86, as cited in Tullio-Altan, *La nostra Italia*, p. 53.

106. Pino Arlacchi, *Mafia, Peasants and Great Estates: Society in Traditional Calabria*, trans. Jonathan Steinberg (New York: Cambridge University Press, 1983); S. N. Eisenstadt and L. Roniger, *Patrons, Clients, and Friends: Interpersonal Relations and the Structure of Trust in Society* (New York: Cambridge University Press, 1984), pp. 65–67; Tarrow, *Peasant Communism in Southern Italy*, p. 68; and Graziano, "Patron-Client Relationships in Southern Italy."

107. Leopoldo Franchetti, *Inchiesta in Sicilia* (Florence: Valecchi, 1974; originally published 1877), as paraphrased in Tullio-Altan, *La nostra Italia*, p. 63. Tullio-Altan (who also cites N. Dalla Chiesa, *Il potere mafioso: Economia e ideologia* [Milan: Mazzotta, 1976], p. 64) argues that clientelism in the South was strongly reinforced after 1876 by the advent of a national ruling alliance between the southern aristocracy and a reactionary part of the northern bourgeoisie.

108. Diomede Ivone, "Moral Economy and Physical Life in a Large Estate of Southern Italy in the 1800s," *Journal of Regional Policy* 11 (January/March 1991): 107–110, summarizing Marta Petrusewicz, *Latifondo: Economia morale e vita materiale in una periferia dell'Ottocento* (Venice: Marsilio, 1989).

109. Graziano, "Patron-Client Relationships in Southern Italy," p. 26.

110. Clark, *Modern Italy*, pp. 69–73.

111. Antonio Gramsci, *Antologia degli Scritti*, eds. Carlo Salinari and Mario Spinella (Rome: Riuniti, 1963) vol. 1, p. 74, as cited in Tarrow, *Peasant Communism*, p. 3.

112. Hess, *Mafia and Mafiosi*, p. 18.

113. Ibid., p. 25. See also Tullio-Altan, *La nostra Italia*, pp. 67–76, and Graziano, "Patron-Client Relationships in Southern Italy," p. 10, who describes the Mafia as "the specific form of traditional Sicilian clientelism."

114. Diego Gambetta, "Mafia: the Price of Distrust," in *Trust*, ed. Gambetta, p. 162.

115. Franchetti, *Inchiesta in Sicilia*, pp. 72–73, as quoted in Tullio-Altan, *La nostra Italia*, pp. 68–69.

116. Ginsborg, *History of Contemporary Italy*, p. 34.

117. Diego Gambetta, "Fragments of an Economic Theory of the Mafia," *European Journal of Sociology* 29 (1988): 127–145, quotation at p. 128.

118. Hess, *Mafia and Mafiosi*, p. 67.

119. Gambetta, "Mafia: the Price of Distrust," p. 173.

120. Eisenstadt and Roniger, *Patrons, Clients, and Friends*, p. 68; Hess, *Mafia and Mafiosi*.

121. Tullio-Altan, *La nostra Italia*, p. 69.

122. Hess, *Mafia and Mafiosi*, pp. 76–77.

123. For a similar analysis of the Mafia and Camorra in today's Italy, see Ginsborg, "Family, Culture and Politics," pp. 41–45.

124. Arlacchi, *Mafia, Peasants and Great Estates*.

125. Our measure of the strength of mutual aid societies is a factor score summarizing the membership in such societies, standardized for regional population, in 1873, 1878, 1885, 1895, and 1904.

126. Our measure of cooperative strength is a factor score summarizing the number of cooperatives, standardized for regional population, in 1889, 1901, 1910, and 1915.

127. Our measure of the strength of the mass-based parties is a factor score summarizing the strength of the socialists and Catholic *popolari* in the national elections of 1919 and 1921, as well as their strength on local councils in this period.

128. Our measure of electoral turnout is a factor score summarizing turnout in the national elections of 1919 and 1921, as well as turnout in the local and provincial elections of 1920; these were the only elections under universal manhood suffrage before the advent of Fascism.

129. Our measure here is the proportion of all local cultural and recreational organizations in the 1982 associational census that had been founded before 1860. This is clearly an indirect and imperfect indicator, since it excludes associations active in the earlier period that did not survive. On the other hand, in the absence of any earlier census of local associations, these data offer the only available nationwide, quantitative index of local nonpolitical and noneconomic associationism in late nineteenth-century Italy.

130. Most of the territories that later became Friuli-Venezia Giulia and Trentino-Alto Adige were annexed to Italy only at the end of World War I and are thus excluded from this historical analysis, as is tiny Valle d'Aosta, which was part of Piedmont in this period.

131. The over-time stability of civic-ness represented in Figure 5.3 rests on somewhat different sets of variables in the two periods. We lack data on any single variable over the entire century-long span. However, the very high decade-to-decade stabilities for such items as mutual aid societies, cooperatives, electoral turnout, and use of the preference vote (uniformly $r > .9$) are consistent with high long-term stability.

132. Samuel H. Barnes and Giacomo Sani, "Mediterranean Political Culture and Italian Politics," *British Journal of Political Science* 4 (July 1974): 289–303, offer evidence that by some measures of political behavior (particularly such indicators of patron-clientelism as preference voting and personal ties to politicians)

southern migrants to the North are more similar to those of native-born northerners than to their erstwhile compatriots in the South, suggesting that "acculturation" to dominant community patterns can occur rather rapidly. Civic behavior, as we contend in the following chapter, is anchored more firmly in social norms and networks than in personal predilections.

133. Our conclusions about the impact of historical traditions on contemporary civic culture and government performance are strikingly parallel to the anthropological findings of Caroline White, *Patrons and Partisans: A Study of Politics in Two Southern Italian comuni* (New York: Cambridge University Press, 1980). White studied two neighboring towns in Abruzzi, one characterized by a century of active civic engagement, egalitarian social relations, "community-mindedness," "open politics," and effective local government, the second by a tradition of patron-clientelism, social hierarchy, personalism, factionalism, and ineffective government. White's explanation for these contrasting syndromes and ours both center on social history. We differ only in the special emphasis she places on landholding patterns.

134. Hyde, *Society and Politics in Medieval Italy*, pp. 17–37, observes that the chief economic contrast within tenth-century Italy was between the backward inland areas and the wealthier coastal cities, found in both the North and the South, but especially the South.

135. Compare Larner, *Italy*, pp. 149–150 and pp. 189–190 and Becker, *Medieval Italy*.

136. Up to the 1970s, industrial employment remained a reasonably good measure of economic modernization in Italy; thereafter, the emergence of a post-industrial, service-based economy meant that industrial employment was no longer so unequivocal an indicator. The Italian censuses of labor force participation in the late nineteenth century are notoriously suspect, so some caution is appropriate in assessing the data on the 1870s and 1880s in Table 5.2. Our analysis is based on official estimates published by the Italian Central Statistical Institute in the 1970s. However, the adjusted data presented in O. Vitali, *Aspetti dello sviluppo economico italiano alla luce della ricostruzione della popolazione attiva* (Rome: Università di Roma, 1970) yield essentially identical results.

137. The national infant mortality rate was 155 per 1000 live births; Emilia-Romagna's rate was 171, and Calabria's 151.

138. In 1977–1985 infant mortality rates per 1000 live births were 15 for Calabria and 11 for Emilia-Romagna.

139. Robert Leonardi, "Peripheral Ascendancy in the European Community: Evidence from a Longitudinal Study," unpub. ms. (Brussels: European Commission, November 1991). Spain, Greece, and Portugal were not members of the Community in 1970 and are thus not included in the analysis.

140. A preliminary version of the following material first appeared in our "Institutional Performance and Political Culture: Some Puzzles about the Power of the Past," *Governance* 1 (July 1988): 221–242.

141. The results reported here draw on historical employment data from 1901 and infant mortality data from 1901–1910, but similar results obtain with data from throughout the period between 1880 and 1920. The contemporary data are

from 1977 (employment) and 1977–1985 (infant mortality), but again the results are robust and do not depend upon the particular dates chosen.

142. The adjusted R^2 for predicting civic-ness in the 1970s is .86, which is entirely attributable to the $r = .93$ correlation with civic traditions in 1860–1920. The *beta* for each of the socioeconomic variables is wholly insignificant.

143. Predicting agricultural employment in 1977, the *beta* for agricultural employment in 1901 is .26 (sig. = .11), while the *beta* for civic traditions is –.73 (sig. = .0003). Predicting industrial employment in 1977, the *beta* for industrial employment in 1901 is .01 (insignificant), while the *beta* for civic traditions is .82 (sig. = .0005). The adjusted R^2 for agricultural employment in 1977 is .69, while the adjusted R^2 for industrial employment in 1977 is .63.

144. In predicting infant morality in 1977–1985, the *beta* for infant mortality in 1901–1910 is .19 (insignificant), while the *beta* for civic traditions is –.75 (sig. = .001). The adjusted R^2 is .56.

145. Good data on regional per capita income are not readily available for the nineteenth century, and by 1911 (when some data become available) income and civics are sufficiently closely correlated ($r = .81$) that this type of statistical analysis is threatened by the technical problem of multicollinearity. However, predicting income in 1987, the *beta* for income in 1911 is .32 (sig. = .003), while the *beta* for civic traditions is .70 (sig. = .0000); the adjusted R^2 is .96. In other words, both civic traditions and income levels in 1911 seem to be independently linked to income in the 1980s, but civics still seems to be a stronger predictor than economics. Meanwhile, controlling for civic traditions (*beta* = .90, sig. = .0003), income in 1911 makes no contribution whatsoever (*beta* = .02, sig. = .91) to explaining civics in the 1970s. All this is broadly consistent with the results reported in the text for employment and infant mortality.

146. Compare Ronald Inglehart, "The Renaissance of Political Culture," *American Political Science Review* 82 (1988): 1203–1230 for a similar argument, although Inglehart's definition of "civic culture" differs somewhat from ours.

147. Union membership was relatively low before World War I, and the available data are not wholly reliable, in part because of the complexities of aggregating evidence from agricultural and industrial unions of different political complexions.

148. From his detailed study of working-class organization in Sesto San Giovanni, Bell reaches a similar conclusion: "Pre-factory cultural traditions significantly conditioned the formation of a modern Italian working class and its political action" ("Worker Culture and Worker Politics," p. 20). See also Donald Howard Bell, *Sesto San Giovanni: Workers, Culture, and Politics in an Italian Town, 1880–1922* (New Brunswick: Rutgers University Press, 1986). Union membership at the regional level in 1921 is correlated $r = .58$ with the fraction of the workforce in industry, and $r = -.49$ with the fraction of the workforce in agriculture, but these correlations are spurious, attributable to the joint dependence of both union membership and economic development on civic traditions.

149. For evidence supporting the assessments in this paragraph, see Vitali, *Aspetti dello sviluppo*, pp. 360–361, pp. 376–389; Toniolo, *Economic History*, esp. pp. 5–8 and pp. 120–123 (though the columns in Toniolo's Table 10.4, p.

122 are unfortunately reversed); Vera Zamagni, *Industrializzazione e squilibri regionali in Italia: Bilancio dell' età giolittiana* (Bologna: Il Mulino, 1978), esp. pp. 198–199; Tullio-Altan, *La nostra Italia*, pp. 38–39; Clark, *Modern Italy*, p. 24, p. 31, p. 132. Toniolo's recent book provides a useful, systematic overview of Italian economic development between 1850 and 1918.

150. See Zamagni, *Industrializzazione*, esp. pp. 205–206; and Istituto Guglielmo Tagliacarne, *I redditi e i consumi in Italia: Un' analisi dei dati provinciali* (Milan: Franco Angeli, 1988), esp. p. 55.

151. For an introduction to the economic literature on regional disparities, see Robert J. Barro and Xavier Sala-i-Martin, "Convergence across States and Regions," *Brookings Papers on Economic Activity*, 1: 1991: 107–182. For brief overviews of the voluminous literature on the "Southern Question," see Toniolo, *Economic History*, esp. pp. 133–150; Clark, *Modern Italy*, esp. pp. 23–28; and Tarrow, *Peasant Communism in Southern Italy*, pp. 17–28.

152. Zamagni, *Industrializzazione*, pp. 199–201.

153. Toniolo, *Economic History*, p. 148.

154. Ibid., p. 52. Literacy was higher in the North than in the South at the time of Unification, and this gap steadily grew between 1871 and 1911. Education was one important latent advantage that helps to explain the North's more rapid progress. North-South educational differences have essentially disappeared in recent decades, however, despite the persisting, even widening economics and civics gaps. See Chapter 4, p. 118.

155. Ibid., p. 121, p. 148.

156. J. R. Siegenthaler, "Sicilian Economic Change since 1860," *Journal of European Economic History* no. 2 (1973): 414, as cited in Zamagni, *Industrializzazione*, p. 215, concludes that "the rigidity of Sicily's social and political structure must be seen as the single most important cause of the island's economic backwardness and its disappearance as virtually the only way towards advancement."

157. Arnaldo Bagnasco, *Tre Italie: La problematica territoriale dello sviluppo italiano* (Bologna: Il Mulino, 1977) and Bagnasco, *La costruzione sociale del mercato: Studi sullo sviluppo di piccola impresa in Italia* (Bologna: Il Mulino, 1988).

158. Michael J. Piore and Charles F. Sabel, *The Second Industrial Divide: Possibilities for Prosperity* (New York: Basic Books, 1984). For a useful compendium of research on industrial districts, "flexible specialization," and their social preconditions, see *Industrial Districts and Inter-firm Co-operation in Italy*, eds. Frank Pyke, Giacomo Becattini, and Werner Sengenberger (Geneva: International Institute for Labor Studies of the International Labor Organisation, 1990), especially Sebastiano Brusco, "The Idea of the Industrial District: Its Genesis," pp. 10–19, and Giacomo Becattini, "The Marshallian Industrial District as a Socioeconomic Notion," pp. 37–51. The "flexible specialization" thesis sometimes includes the hypothesis that such industrial districts represent the "wave of the future" in the world economy, but that is not part of our argument here.

159. Sebastiano Brusco, "The Emilian Model: Productive Decentralisation and Social Integration," *Cambridge Journal of Economics* 6 (1982): 167–184. Patrizio

Bianchi and Giuseppina Gualtieri, "Emilia-Romagna and its Industrial Districts: The Evolution of a Model," *The Regions and European Integration: The Case of Emilia-Romagna*, eds. Robert Leonardi and Raffaella Y. Nanetti (New York: Pinter, 1990), pp. 83–108, note that although the success of small and medium enterprises in the "third Italy" was initially attributed to widespread evasion of tax law and union agreements, subsequent research has generally rejected that interpretation.

160. Mark H. Lazerson, "Organizational Growth of Small Firms: An Outcome of Markets and Hierarchies?" *American Sociological Review* 53 (June 1988): 331.

161. Michael J. Piore and Charles F. Sabel, "Italian Small Business Development: Lessons for U.S. Industrial Policy," in *American Business in International Competition: Government Policies and Corporate Strategies*, eds. John Zysman and Laura Tyson (Ithaca: Cornell University Press, 1983), pp. 401–402.

162. Piore and Sabel, *Second Industrial Divide*, p. 265, p. 275.

163. For evidence of the patterns described in this paragraph, see Brusco, "The Idea of the Industrial District," pp. 15–16; Becattini, "The Marshallian Industrial District," p. 33 and p. 39; Michael J. Piore, "Work, Labour and Action: Work Experience in a System of Flexible Production," p. 55 and pp. 58–59, and Carlo Trigilia, "Work and Politics in the Third Italy's Industrial Districts," pp. 179–182, all in *Industrial Districts and Inter-firm Co-operation in Italy*, eds. Pyke, Becattini, and Sengenberger, as well as Paolo Feltrin, "Regolazione politica e sviluppo economico locale," *Strumenti* 1 (January-April 1988): 51–81. Civic networks appear to foster economic dynamism outside Italy, too. For example, "Silicon Valley's resilience owes as much to its rich networks of social, professional and commercial relations as to the efforts of individual entrepreneurs." AnnaLee Saxenian, "Regional Networks and the Resurgence of Silicon Valley," *California Management Review* 33 (Fall 1990): 89–112.

164. *Atlas of Industrializing Britain, 1780–1914*, eds. John Langton and R.J. Morris (New York: Metheun, 1986), p. xxx.

165. Ginsborg, *History of Contemporary Italy*, p. 219. Though not high by North American standards, these figures are extraordinary on a continent where many families still remain in one location for generations. (Even today, educated Italians, asked "Where do you come from?" often cite the small town from which their parents emigrated decades ago and where they themselves have, in fact, never lived.) In addition, of course, millions of Italians have emigrated to other countries. Indeed, it might be argued that "selective emigration" could account for the backwardness of the South, if civic-minded southerners were disproportionately likely to emigrate. (For some suggestive evidence, see Johan Galtung, *Members of Two Worlds* [New York: Columbia University Press, 1971], pp. 190–191, as cited in Barnes and Sani, "Mediterranean Political Culture and Italian Politics," p. 300.) While we do not discount this argument entirely, it cannot account for the historical continuities traced here, for during most of the nineteenth century the large-scale Italian emigration came largely from the North. Southern emigration did not become substantial until the 1890s. See Clark, *Modern Italy*, p. 32, pp. 165–166.

Chapter 6
Social Capital and Institutional Success

1. If proof were needed, our own surveys found bitter dissatisfaction with public life and private prospects in these regions. The notion sometimes expressed by outsiders that southerners enjoy their backward state—that they prefer the kind of public life they have—is contrary not merely to common sense, but also to empirical evidence.

2. Jeff Frieden, Peter Hall, and Ken Shepsle deserve credit for posing the questions that stimulated this chapter, but bear no responsibility for the results.

3. David Hume, (1740), Book 3, Part 2, Section 5, as quoted in Robert Sugden, *The Economics of Rights, Co-operation and Welfare* (Oxford: Basil Blackwell, 1986), p. 106.

4. Elinor Ostrom, *Governing the Commons: The Evolution of Institutions for Collective Action* (New York: Cambridge University Press, 1990), p. 6. For useful introductions to the burgeoning formal literature on dilemmas of collective action, see Ostrom, as well as Robert H. Bates, "Contra Contractarianism: Some Reflections on the New Institutionalism," *Politics and Society* 16 (1988): 387–401.

5. Diego Gambetta, "Can We Trust Trust?" in *Trust: Making and Breaking Cooperative Relations*, ed. Diego Gambetta (Oxford: Blackwell, 1988), p. 216 (emphasis in original).

6. Pietr Kropotkin, *Mutual Aid: A Factor of Evolution* (London: Heinemann, 1902), p. xv.

7. Douglass C. North, *Institutions, Institutional Change and Economic Performance* (New York: Cambridge University Press, 1990), p. 58.

8. Gambetta, "Can We Trust Trust?" p. 221.

9. North, *Institutions, Institutional Change and Economic Performance*, p. 59.

10. Bates, "Contra Contractarianism," p. 395.

11. Robert Sugden, *Economics of Rights, Co-operation and Welfare*, p. 105 (emphasis in original). Sugden is here discussing an anonymously iterated prisoner's dilemma, but the same point applies to a one-round prisoner's dilemma.

12. Gambetta, "Can We Trust Trust?" p. 217, note 6.

13. D. Fudenberg and E. Maskin, "A folk-theorem in repeated games with discounting and with incomplete information," *Econometrica* 54 (1986): 533–554; strictly speaking, the folk theorem holds that "always defect" is not a unique equilibrium in the repeat-play prisoner's dilemma, as it is in one-round games. See also Robert Axelrod, *The Evolution of Cooperation* (New York: Basic Books, 1984) and Michael Taylor, *Anarchy and Cooperation* (London: Wiley, 1976).

14. North, *Institutions, Institutional Change and Economic Performance*, p. 12.

15. Oliver E. Williamson, *Markets and Hierarchies: Analysis and Antitrust Implications* (New York: Free Press, 1975) and Williamson, *The Economic Institutions of Capitalism* (New York: Free Press, 1985).

16. Ostrom, *Governing the Commons*.

17. Bates, "Contra Contractarianism."

18. Stephen Cornell and Joseph P. Kalt, "Culture and Institutions as Public

Goods: American Indian Economic Development as a Problem of Collective Action," in *Property Rights, Constitutions, and Indian Economics*, ed. Terry L. Anderson (University of Nebraska Press, 1990), p. 33, citing James Buchanan, "Before Public Choice," in *Explorations in the Theory of Anarchy*, ed. Gordon Tullock (Blacksburg, Virginia: Center for the Study of Political Choice, Virginia Polytechnic Institute, 1972); Jack Hirshleifer, "Comment on Peltzman," *Journal of Law and Economics* 19 (1976): 241–244; and Douglass C. North, "Ideology and Political/Economic Institutions," *Cato Journal* 8 (Spring/Summer 1988): 15–28.

19. Bates, "Contra Contractarianism," p. 398. See also Robert H. Bates, "Social Dilemmas and Rational Individuals: An Essay on the New Institutionalism" (Duke University, unpublished manuscript, 1992).

20. On the concept of social capital, see James S. Coleman, *Foundations of Social Theory* (Cambridge, Mass.: Harvard University Press, 1990), pp. 300–321, who credits Glenn Loury with introducing the concept. See Glenn Loury, "A Dynamic Theory of Racial Income Differences," in *Women, Minorities, and Employment Discrimination*, eds. P.A. Wallace and A. Le Mund (Lexington, Mass.: Lexington Books, 1977), and Glenn Loury, "Why Should We Care about Group Inequality?" *Social Philosophy and Policy* 5 (1987): 249–271. For practical applications of the concept of social capital, see also Elinor Ostrom, *Crafting Institutions for Self-Governing Irrigation Systems* (San Francisco: Institute for Contemporary Studies Press, 1992). For a related discussion, see Robert H. Bates, "Institutions as Investments," Duke University Program in Political Economy, Papers in Political Economy, Working Paper 133 (December 1990). The argument that social capital facilitates cooperation in domestic society is parallel in important respects to the thesis of Robert O. Keohane, *After Hegemony: Cooperation and Discord in the World Political Economy* (Princeton: Princeton University Press, 1984), that international regimes facilitate cooperation in the world political economy.

21. Coleman, *Foundations*, p. 302, p. 304, p. 307.

22. Shirley Ardener, "The Comparative Study of Rotating Credit Associations," *Journal of the Royal Anthropological Institute of Great Britain and Ireland* 94 (1964): 201.

23. See Ardener, "Comparative Study of Rotating Credit Associations"; Clifford Geertz, "The Rotating Credit Association: A 'Middle Rung' in Development," *Economic Development and Cultural Change* 10 (April 1962): 241–263; and Carlos G. Vélez-Ibañez, *Bonds of Mutual Trust: The Cultural Systems of Rotating Credit Associations among Urban Mexicans and Chicanos* (New Brunswick, NJ: Rutgers University Press, 1983). Timothy Besley, Stephen Coate, and Glenn Loury, "The Economics of Rotating Savings and Credit Associations," *American Economic Review*, forthcoming 1992, model rotating credit associations formally.

24. Vélez-Ibañez, *Bonds of Trust*, reports a rotating credit association among prisoners in a Mexican jail, to provide marijuana, although we know of no evidence that this is the origin of the term "pot."

25. Geertz, "The Rotating Credit Association," p. 244.

26. Ardener, "Comparative Study of Rotating Credit Associations," p. 216.

27. Ibid. On the importance of reputation in rotating credit associations, see Michael Hechter, *Principles of Group Solidarity* (Berkeley: University of California Press, 1987), pp. 109–111.

28. Vélez-Ibañez, *Bonds of Mutual Trust*, p. 33. On trust, intermediaries, and networks, see Coleman, *Foundations of Social Theory*, Chapter 8.

29. Besley, Coate, and Loury, "Economics of Rotating Savings and Credit Associations."

30. In fact, their lack of feasible alternatives itself may increase their credibility as participants in the rotating credit society. We are indebted to Glenn Loury for this observation.

31. Ostrom, *Governing the Commons*, pp. 183–184.

32. Geertz, "The Rotating Credit Association," p. 243, p. 251.

33. Ostrom, *Governing the Commons*, p. 190

34. A. O. Hirschman, "Against Parsimony: Three Easy Ways of Complicating Some Categories of Economic Discourse," *American Economic Review* Proceedings 74 (1984): 93, as cited in Partha Dasgupta, "Trust as a Commodity," in *Trust*, ed. Gambetta, p. 56.

35. See the account of the "live and let live" norm in trench warfare in Axelrod, *Evolution of Cooperation*, p. 85.

36. Gambetta, "Can We Trust Trust?" p. 234 (emphasis in original).

37. "The more extensively persons call on one another for aid, the greater will be the quantity of social capital generated. . . . Social relationships die out if not maintained; expectations and obligations wither over time; and norms depend on regular communication." Coleman, *Foundations of Social Theory*, p. 321.

38. Coleman, *Foundations of Social Theory*, p. 315. See also Ostrom, *Crafting Institutions*, p. 38: "Social capital is not automatically or spontaneously produced." Robert E. Lucas, Jr., "On the Mechanics of Economic Development," *Journal of Monetary Economics* 22 (1988): 3–42, emphasizes the "external" (or public good) features of human capital. Hechter, *Principles of Group Solidarity*, distinguishes between "public goods" (which are characterized by jointness of supply and nonexcludability) and "collective goods" (which may be to some degree excludable). At least initially, some kinds of social capital may be characterized by excludability; medieval Italian tower societies, for example, did not defend nonmembers. However, as Hechter points out (p. 123 *et passim*), from informal groups that arise initially to produce collective goods may emerge formal groups that produce genuine public goods: Eventually, the civic order fostered by tower societies and the communes they spawned was enjoyed even by nonmembers.

39. See Coleman, *Foundations of Social Theory*, p. 317, and Dasgupta, "Trust as a Commodity," p. 64.

40. Coleman, *Foundations of Social Theory*, pp. 317–318.

41. Kenneth J. Arrow, "Gifts and Exchanges," *Philosophy and Public Affairs* 1 (Summer 1972): 357.

42. Anthony Pagden, "The Destruction of Trust and its Economic Consequences in the Case of Eighteenth-century Naples," in *Trust*, ed. Gambetta, pp. 136–138, citing Antonio Genovesi, *Lezioni di economia civile* (1803).

43. Mark H. Lazerson, "Organizational Growth of Small Firms: An Outcome

of Markets and Hierarchies?" *American Sociological Review* 53 (June 1988): 330–342, reports that personal trust among managers and between workers and management is essential to the high productivity of small firms in Emilia-Romagna.

44. Dasgupta, "Trust as a Commodity," pp. 50–51 (emphasis in original).

45. Bernard Williams, "Formal Structures and Social Reality," in *Trust*, ed. Gambetta, p. 8, p. 12. Glenn Loury has pointed out to us that reliance on personal trust presumes that individuals differ in their trustworthiness, whereas social trust presumes that the structure of the situation is more important than personal character.

46. Compare James G. March and Johan P. Olsen, *Rediscovering Institutions: The Organizational Basis of Politics* (New York: Free Press, 1989), p. 27.

47. Coleman, *Foundations of Social Theory*, p. 251.

48. March and Olsen, *Rediscovering Institutions*, p. 27; Robert Axelrod, "An Evolutionary Approach to Norms," *American Political Science Review* 80 (December 1986): 1095–1111.

49. North, *Institutions, Institutional Change and Economic Performance*, pp. 36–45. See also Kenneth Arrow, *The Limits of Organization* (New York: Norton, 1974), p. 26; and George Akerlof, "Loyalty Filters," *American Economic Review* 73 (1983): 54–63, as cited in Mark Granovetter, "Economic Action and Social Structure: The Problem of Embeddedness," *American Journal of Sociology* 91 (November 1985): 489.

50. Marshall Sahlins, *Stone Age Economics* (Chicago: Aldine-Atherton, 1972) uses "balanced" and "generalized;" Robert O. Keohane, "Reciprocity in International Relations," *International Organization* 40 (1986): 1–27, draws a closely related distinction between "specific" and "generalized" reciprocity. It is important to distinguish the *strategy* of reciprocity (tit-for-tat) from the *norm* of reciprocity, although the two are sometimes empirically related. Our interest here is primarily the norm. See also Axelrod, *Evolution of Cooperation* and "An Evolutionary Approach to Norms."

51. As cited in Alvin W. Gouldner, "The Norm of Reciprocity: A Preliminary Statement," *American Sociological Review* 25 (April 1960): 161.

52. Ostrom, *Governing the Commons*, p. 200, p. 211. Ostrom (p. 38) is skeptical, however, about explanations in which norms are treated as unobservable, "in-the-mind" variables.

53. Michael Taylor, *Community, Anarchy and Liberty* (New York: Cambridge University Press, 1982), pp. 28–29 (emphasis in original). See also Gouldner, "The Norm of Reciprocity," p. 173.

54. Keohane, "Reciprocity in International Relations," p. 21.

55. Granovetter, "Economic Action and Social Structure." He distinguishes his "embeddedness" approach from both an "oversocialized" conception of human action, in which action is wholly determined by roles and norms, and an "undersocialized" conception (more common in simple game theory), in which atomized actors are unconstrained by social relations. On networks and trust as capital assets that undergird social exchange, see also Albert Breton and Ronald Wintrobe, *The Logic of Bureaucratic Conduct*, (New York: Cambridge University Press, 1982), pp. 61–88.

56. Granovetter, "Economic Action and Social Structure," pp. 490–491.

57. See Robert Michels' study of the German Social Democratic party, *Political Parties: A Sociological Study of the Oligarchical Tendencies of Modern Democracy* (New York: Dover, 1959).

58. This distinction and its broader consequences were emphasized, of course, by Max Weber. "To Weber, a religion that is congregational is organized in small, self-managed groups of believers. . . . Congregational forms of organization underscore the equality of believers, drawing all into participation and encouraging equal access to religious knowledge through a common reliance on the Bible." Daniel H. Levine, "Religion, the Poor, and Politics in Latin America Today," in *Religion and Political Conflict in Latin America*, ed. Daniel H. Levine (Chapel Hill: University of North Carolina Press, 1986), p. 15.

59. On interconnectedness—the same players playing several parallel games simultaneously—as distinct from iteration—the same players repeating the same game sequentially—see James K. Sebenius, "Negotiation Arithmetic: Adding and Subtracting Issues and Parties," *International Organization* 37 (Spring 1983): 281–316; and James Alt and Barry Eichengreen, "Parallel and Overlapping Games: Theory and an Application to the European Natural Gas Trade," *Economics and Politics* 1 (1989): 119–144. On the effects of "multiplex" interpersonal relations (ties that encompass more than one sphere of activity) in easing dilemmas of collective action, see the excellent paper by Michael Taylor and Sara Singleton, "The Communal Resource: Transaction Costs and the Solution of Collective Action Problems" (University of Washington, unpub. ms., 1992).

60. Ostrom, *Governing the Commons*, p. 206.

61. On trust, networks, and information, see Coleman, *Foundations of Social Theory*, chapter 8.

62. David Knoke, *Political Networks: The Structural Perspective* (New York: Cambridge University Press, 1990), pp. 68–69.

63. North, *Institutions, Institutional Change and Economic Performance*, p. 37. For an analogous argument that "culture provides a repertoire of capacities from which varying strategies of action may be constructed," see Ann Swidler, "Culture in Action: Symbols and Strategies," *American Sociological Review* 51 (1986): 273–286, quotation at p. 284.

64. Compare Coleman, *Foundations of Social Theory*, pp. 286–287.

65. Julian Pitt-Rivers, *The People of the Sierra* (London: Weidenfeld and Nicolson, 1954), p. 40.

66. S. N. Eisenstadt and L. Roniger, *Patrons, Clients, and Friends: Interpersonal Relations and the Structure of Trust in Society* (New York: Cambridge University Press, 1984), pp. 48–49.

67. Mark S. Granovetter, "The Strength of Weak Ties," *American Journal of Sociology* 78 (1973): 1360–1380, quotation at p. 1376 (emphasis in original).

68. In other historical or social settings, engagement in Catholic groups may have more civic implications, depending on the social and organizational realities in those contexts. On the contrast in Latin America between the hierarchical vision of the "institutional Church" and the communal, egalitarian vision of the "popular Church," see Daniel H. Levine, *Religion and Politics in Latin America: The Catholic Church in Venezuela and Colombia* (Princeton: Princeton University Press, 1981), and the case studies in *Religion and Political Conflict in Latin America*, ed.

Levine. In Italy, our theory suggests, membership in the more egalitarian lay groups within the Church (the *communità di base*) should be *positively* correlated with civic-ness and with institutional performance, but we have found no relevant data to test this hypothesis.

69. Lacking micro-level information on status and power within secondary associations in various parts of Italy, we are forced to assume that across all regions social ties within, say, soccer clubs are equally horizontal and thus equally effective as social capital. In fact, we suspect that soccer clubs and other voluntary associations are socially more hierarchical in the less civic, less successful areas; for evidence on precisely this point, see Caroline White, *Patrons and Partisans: A Study of Politics in Two Southern Italian Comuni* (New York: Cambridge University Press, 1980), pp. 63–67 and pp. 141–145. If this is so, then the actual link between horizontal networks and institutional success is probably *even stronger* than our data show.

70. Mancur Olson, *The Rise and Decline of Nations: Economic Growth, Stagflation, and Social Rigidities* (New Haven: Yale University Press, 1982).

71. Joel S. Migdal, "Strong States, Weak States: Power and Accommodation," in *Understanding Political Development*, eds. Myron Weiner and Samuel P. Huntington (Boston: Little, Brown, 1987), pp. 391–434, quotation at pp. 397–398. Earlier students of political development also argued that social mobilization and mass political participation reduce the stability and effectiveness of governmental institutions. The best-known exposition of this view (though not the most extreme) was Samuel P. Huntington, *Political Order in Changing Societies* (New Haven: Yale University Press, 1968). For a useful overview of recent work, see Joan M. Nelson, "Political Participation," in *Understanding Political Development*, eds. Weiner and Huntington, pp. 103–159, esp. pp. 114–115. Clarifying the difference between this theory and ours will require greater attention to the distinction between horizontal and vertical networks.

72. Regressing gross regional product per capita (GRP) in 1987 jointly on GRP in 1970 and civic community in the 1970s, for 1970 GRP *beta* $= .64$, p $= .0001$, while for civic-ness *beta* $= .35$, p $= .017$ (adj. $R^2 = .92$). The data are too frail to rule out alternative theories, but the facts are clear: Regions that were rich in 1970 were still rich in 1987, but in the interim the richest had grown more slowly, while the most civic had grown more rapidly.

73. The Italian language reflects this intimate connection between trust and gullibility. An honest, decent, well intentioned person is described as *dabbene*, but a credulous fool is labeled derisively *dabbenaggine*. We are indebted to Federico Varese for this reference.

74. "A stable equilibrium is defined for a community of individuals who play some game repeatedly against one another. To say that some strategy *I* is a stable equilibrium in some such game is to say the following: it is in each individual's interest to follow strategy *I* provided that everyone else, or almost everyone else, does the same." Sugden, *Economics of Rights, Co-operation and Welfare*, p. 32; see also pp. 19–31. For a technical specification of the circumstances under which "never cooperate" is a stable equilibrium in an iterated prisoner's dilemma, see Sugden, *Economics of Rights, Co-operation and Welfare*, p. 109.

75. Edward C. Banfield, *The Moral Basis of a Backward Society* (Chicago:

The Free Press, 1958), p. 85. Complete exit from this infernal social setting is one alternative, of course, and once long-distance travel became feasible, emigration became common.

76. North, *Institutions, Institutional Change and Economic Performance*, p. 35.

77. Sugden, *Economics of Rights, Co-operation and Welfare*, pp. 104–127, p. 162. Strictly speaking, Sugden's proof that "always defect" is a *stable* equilibrium in the indefinitely repeated game requires the reasonable assumption that players may very occasionally make "mistakes," that is, defecting when they intended to cooperate or *vice versa*. As Sugden acknowledges, much of his argument rests of the work of Michael Taylor, *Anarchy and Cooperation* (London: Wiley, 1976) and Axelrod, *Evolution of Cooperation*. For a related game (that does not, however, involve a repeated prisoner's dilemma) with two stable equilibria in which "if everyone expects everyone to be honest then everyone will be honest, and if everyone expects everyone to cheat a little then everyone will cheat a little," see Dasgupta, "Trust as a Commodity," pp. 56–59. The theories explored here imply that "always defect" and "reciprocate help" are stable equilibria, but they do not exclude the possibility that other stable equilibria may also exist.

78. March and Olsen, *Rediscovering Institutions*, pp. 55–56 and p. 159.

79. Most work by economic historians so far has focused on technology, rather than institutions, but many of the key issues are parallel. See Paul David, "Clio and the Economics of QWERTY," *American Economic Review* 75 (1985): 332–337; W. Arthur Brian, "Self-Reinforcing Mechanisms in Economics," in *The Economy as an Evolving Complex System*, eds. Philip W. Anderson, Kenneth J. Arrow, and David Pines (Reading, Mass.: Addison-Wesley, 1988); and North, *Institutions, Institutional Change and Economic Performance*, pp. 92–104. North's splendid book is directly relevant to the issues discussed in this chapter and the preceding one.

80. North, *Institutions, Institutional Change and Economic Performance*, p. 93.

81. Ibid., pp. 101–102; pp. 112–117.

82. Not all historians would agree with this interpretation of Latin American history, for there are numerous possible confounding variables, but it is a plausible one. The Italian case is even more powerful analytically because more variables are "controlled" in the intra-Italian comparison, because the North-South divergence in Italy has endured much longer than the inter-American one, and because the Italian divergence has persisted and even grown despite a century under a single national government.

83. North, *Institutions, Institutional Change and Economic Performance*, Chapters 10–12.

84. See Chapter 5, note 1. Another issue worth further detailed investigation, theoretically speaking, is why the damping of cooperation in the aftermath of the Black Death, foreign invasions, and other social and economic disruptions of the fifteenth century did not completely destabilize the civic equilibrium and tip northern society into a series of vicious circles that might have extinguished its civic traditions.

85. See, for example, Michael Thompson, Richard Ellis, and Aaron Wildav-

sky, *Cultural Theory* (San Francisco: Westview Press, 1990), p. 21: "Values and social relations are mutually interdependent and reinforcing: Institutions generate distinctive sets of preferences, and adherence to certain values legitimizes corresponding institutional arrangements. Asking which comes first or which should be given causal priority is a nonstarter." See also Ronald Inglehart, "The Renaissance of Political Culture," *American Political Science Review* 82 (1988): 1203–1230, who emphasizes the reciprocal linkages among political culture, economic development, and stable democracy. An older idiom traced institutional performance to "civic virtue," and our emphasis on civic community echoes that approach. Classically, "the republic made the virtuous individual and the virtuous individual made the republic." (Richard Vetterli and Gary Bryner, *In Search of the Republic: Public Virtue and the Roots of American Government* [Towata, N.J.: Rowman and Littlefield, 1987], p. 20.) In our terms, the civic community is a self-reinforcing equilibrium. For a thought-provoking distinction between political cultures based on "covenant" (voluntary agreement among equals) and hierarchical polities based on conquest, see Daniel J. Elazar, "Federal Models of (Civil) Authority," *Journal of Church and State* 33 (1991): 231–254.

86. North, *Institutions, Institutional Change and Economic Performance*, p. 100, p. 140.

87. Samuel P. Huntington, *The Third Wave: Democratization in the Late Twentieth Century* (Norman, Okla.: University of Oklahoma Press, 1991).

88. Thompson, Ellis, and Wildavsky, *Cultural Theory*, p. 2.

89. Silverman, "Agricultural Organizations, Social Structure and Values in Italy," p. 18. One manifestation of this problem can be seen in the literature on the culture of poverty and the underclass in America. See, for example, E. Banfield, *The Unheavenly City: The Nature and Future of Our Urban Crisis* (Boston: Little, Brown, 1970); Charles Valentine, *Culture and Poverty: Critique and Counter Proposal* (Chicago: University of Chicago Press, 1968); Oscar Lewis, "The Culture of Poverty" in *On Understanding Poverty: Perspectives from the Social Sciences*, ed. Daniel Moynihan (New York: Basic Books, 1968).

90. On the issue of whether trust and cooperative social relations can be "created," or merely "found," see Charles F. Sabel, "Studied Trust: Building New Forms of Cooperation in a Volatile Economy," in *Readings in Economic Sociology*, eds. Frank Romo and Richard Swedberg (New York: Russell Sage, 1992), and Charles F. Sabel, "Flexible Specialisation and the Reemergence of Regional Economies," in *Reversing Industrial Decline? Industrial Structure and Policy in Britain and Her Competitors*, eds. Paul Hirst and Jonathan Zeitlin (New York: Berg, 1989), pp. 17–70.

91. John Friedmann, *Planning in the Public Domain: From Knowledge to Action* (Princeton: Princeton University Press, 1987), pp. 185–223.

92. Vera Zamagni, *Industrializzazione e squilibri regionali in Italia: Bilancio dell'età giolittiana* (Bologna: Il Mulino, 1978), p. 216 (emphasis in original).

abbreviations, in scattergrams, 200
Abruzzi, 68
administrators. *See* national administrators;
  regional administrators
agricultural employment, 153–154, 156
agricultural spending capacity, 71–72,
  198–199
Agulhon, Maurice, 137–138
Almond, Gabriel A., 11, 116
amoral familism, 88, 92, 144, 177,
  222n.34, 245–246n.75
Andreotti, Giulio, 23
aristocracy. *See* nobility
Aristotle, 89
Arlacchi, Pino, 148
Arrow, Kenneth, 170
associations: civic community and, 89–92,
  162, 176; democracy and, 221n.30; effectiveness of, 221n.32; in France, 137–
  138; institutional performance and, 11;
  measuring strength of, 222nn. 35, 36,
  235n.129; in medieval city-states, 125–
  126; membership in, 223n.44; rotating
  credit, 167–171, 241n.24, 242nn. 27,
  30; social capital and, 245n.69; Tocqueville on, 221n.28. *See also* cooperatives;
  labor unions; mutual aid societies; political parties

Bagnasco, Arnaldo, 159–160
Banfield, Edward, 88, 91, 92, 144, 177,
  222n.34
banking, evolution of, 128–129
Barber, Benjamin, 111, 117–118
Bari. *See* Puglia
Basilicata: economic development in, 86;
  local health unit expenditures in, 72
Bassetti, Piero, 24
Bates, Robert, 167
Bollen, Jackson, 84
Bologna. *See* Emilia-Romagna
budget promptness, 67, 198–199
bureaucratic responsiveness, 73, 198–199,
  217n.23, 218n.30. *See also* regional
  administrators
Burke, Edmund, 116

cabinet stability, 67, 198–199, 213n.39,
  218n.30
Calabria: agricultural spending capacity in,
  72; budget promptness in, 67; bureaucratic responsiveness in, 73; civic community in, 114; civic traditions in, 148,
  153–154; economic development in,
  153–154; industrial policy in, 71; infant
  mortality rate in, 236nn. 137, 138; legislative innovation in, 69; political elites
  in, 213n.38; preference voting in, 94; referenda turnout in, 94; reform legislation
  in, 68; statistical and information services in, 68
Campania: bureaucratic responsiveness in,
  73; cabinet stability in, 67; day care centers in, 70; economic development in,
  86; housing and urban development in,
  72; preference voting in, 94; statistical
  and information services in, 68
capital, conventional versus social, 169–
  170
case studies, 12, 14, 190–191
Cassa per il Mezzogiorno, 24
Catholic Church: civic community and,
  107–109, 244–245n.68; history of, 122,
  127, 133, 230n.49
Catholic political movements: Catholic Action, 107–109; and evolution of political
  parties, 141–142; Social Catholicism
  movement, 141
central government. *See* national government
Christian Democratic party (DC): Catholic
  Church and, 107; history of, 233n.91;
  ideological depolarization and, 28, 29;
  regional reform and, 21, 23
Cicero, 116, 172
citizen contact study, 191
citizens. *See* electorate
citizenship. *See* civic community
city-states: early evolution of, 121–122,
  124–130, 152, 228nn. 1, 2, 229n.15,
  230n.27; economic development in,
  127–129, 230n.40, 231n.63; in fifteenth-
  sixteenth centuries, 134–135, 230n.46,

city-states (*cont.*)
246n.84; in fourteenth century, 131–
132, 231; versus Norman kingdom of
Sicily, 130–131; in seventeenth century,
135, 231n.63
civic associations. *See* associations
civic community, 86–116; Catholic Church
and, 107–109; civic associations and,
89–92, 162, 176; civic engagement and,
87–88, 104–105, 148–151, 173–176;
civic humanism and, 86–87, 91–92,
226n.70; civic virtue and, 86–87, 111–
112, 246–247n.85; economic development and, 98–99, 152–162; education
and, 109–111; electoral turnout and, 93,
149, 235n.128; feelings of powerlessness and, 109–111, 225n.64; history of
post-unification, 137–148; history of
pre-modern, 121–137; income distribution and, 224n.52; institutional performance and, 98–99, 115, 223nn. 45, 46;
law enforcement and, 112–113, 225–
226n.68; lessons about, 181–185;
Machiavelli on, 86–87, 132; in medieval
city-states, 126–127; modernity and,
114–115; newspaper readership and, 92–
93, 222n.38; political elites and, 101–
106; political equality and, 88, 102–105;
political parties and, 109; preference
voting and, 94–96, 222–223nn. 41, 42,
43; referenda turnout and, 93–94, 95–
96, 222n.40; satisfaction with life and,
113–114, 226n.69; social capital and,
167, 169–171, 177; social and political
conflict and, 116–118; social trust and,
174–176, 177; socioeconomic modernity
and, 98–99, 153; solidarity, trust, and
tolerance and, 88–89; trust and, 167,
170–171; union membership and, 106–
107, 224n.56. *See also* associations;
collective action; cooperatives; labor
unions; mutual aid societies; political
parties
Civic Community Index, 96–98, 99,
223n.46, 225n.64
Civic Culture, The (Almond and Verba),
11, 90, 220n.14
civic engagement: civic community and,
87–88, 104–105; index of traditions of,
205; networks of, 171, 173–176, 177,
183–184; nineteenth-century traditions
of, 148–149

civic humanism, 86–87, 91–92, 226n.70
civic republicanism. *See* city-states
civic traditions: durability of, 148–150,
151, 235n.131, 246n.84; economic development and, 152–162, 246–247n.85;
institutional performance and, 150–151;
in medieval Italy, 121–137, 246n.84; in
North America, 179; in Northern versus
Southern Italy, 152, 158–159; after
unification, 137–148
civic virtue: civic community and, 111–
112, 246–247n.85; Machiavelli on, 86–
87, 132
clericalism, 108. *See also* Catholic Church
clientelistic politics. *See* patron-clientelist
politics
Coi, Salvatore, 106
Coleman, James, 171, 242n.37
collective action: in city-states, 246n.84;
dilemmas of, 163–167, 177; game theory and, 163–164, 165, 166, 244n.59,
245n.74, 246n.77; networks of civic engagement and, 171, 173–176; Northern
and Southern approaches to, 181–182;
rotating credit associations and, 167–
171. *See also* social capital; trust
commerce, medieval, 127–129, 230n.40,
231n.63
communal republicanism. *See* city-states
Communist Party. *See* Italian Communist
Party
communitarian tradition. *See* civic
humanism
community leaders: national government
and, 52; optimism of about regional governments, 56–57; regional administrators
and, 52; regional autonomy and, 53; satisfaction of with regional governments,
47–50, 58, 76–77, 78–81, 215n.64; surveys of, 188–189
compromise, political elites and, 105–106,
224n.53
"Considerations on Representative Government" (Mill), 9, 208n.10
constituents. *See* electorate
Constitutional Affairs Committee of the
Chamber of Deputies, 61–62
cooperation. *See* collective action
cooperatives: civic community and, 162;
evolution of, 139–141; labor unions
and, 140–141; in Northern versus
Southern Italy, 144; political parties

and, 142, 148; rotating credit associations and, 169. *See also* mutual aid societies

councilors: ideological depolarization of, 28–33, 193–197, 212n.28; local politics and, 39; national government and, 44–47; optimism of about regional governments, 56–57; political culture of, 33–38, 213n.40; political equality and, 224n.51; profile of, 27–28, 211n.24; regional autonomy and, 38–39, 41–44; social origins of, 224n.50; surveys of, 187–188; turnover of, 211n.25. *See also* political elites; tables

credit, invention of, 128

credit associations, rotating, 167–171, 241n.24, 242nn. 27, 30

culture, versus structure, 180–181, 222n.34

Dahl, Robert A., 11, 63

day care centers, 70, 198–199

Democracy in America. See Tocqueville, Alexis de

democratic institutions: associations and, 221n.30; civic community and, 86–87; lessons for, 181–185; in medieval city-states, 124–125, 229n.15; stability of, 245n.71, 246–247n.85; study of, 3, 6–7; success of, 3, 6. *See also* institutional performance; institutions

Democratic Party of the Left. *See* Italian Communist Party

depolarization. *See* ideological depolarization

Deutsch, Karl, 12

Eckstein, Harry, 66

economic development: civic traditions and, 152–162, 175–176, 180, 237nn. 142–145, 246–247n.85; in industrial districts, 160–161, 238–239nn. 158, 159, 163; institutional performance and, 11, 78, 83–86, 154–155, 157, 219–220nn. 4, 6, 220n.6, 223n.46; of medieval city-states, 127–129, 230n.40, 231n.63; of Norman kingdom of Sicily, 122–123; of Northern versus Southern Italy, 158–159, 236n.134; of Sicily, 238n.156. *See also* socioeconomic modernity

education: civic community and, 109–111; institutional performance and, 118; in

Northern versus Southern Italy, 227n.82, 238n.154

electoral turnout, 93, 149, 235n.128

electorate: institutional performance and, 76–81; optimism of about regional governments, 56–57; political parties and, 213n.41; regional autonomy and behavior of, 44; satisfaction with local governments, 201–204; satisfaction with regional governments, 51–60, 76–81, 215n.60, 215n.64

Emilia-Romagna: bureaucratic responsiveness in, 73; civic community in, 114–115; day care centers in, 70; economic development in, 86, 153–154, 243n.43; housing and urban development in, 72; infant mortality rate in, 236nn. 137, 138; legislative innovation in, 69; preference voting in, 94; referenda turnout in, 94; reform legislation in, 68; regional government of, 5–6; statistical and information services in, 68

employment: agricultural versus industrial, 153–154, 156; economic development and, 236n.136, 237n.141

equality. *See* political equality

Esman, Milton, 90–91

factor loading, in indexes, 216n.13

family clinics, 70–71, 198–199

family ties, 175

Fanti, Guido, 24

Fascism: party membership under, 109; regional governance under, 19

Fedele, Marcello, 41

field research, book's, 12

figures: civic community and clericalism, 108; civic community and clientelism, 100; civic community, education, and citizens' feelings of powerlessness, 110; civic community and electoral reformism, 105; civic community in the Italian regions, 97; civic community and leaders' fear of compromise, 106; civic community and leaders' support for equality, 103; civic community and particularized contacting, 100; civic community and republicanism, 104; civic community and satisfaction with life, 113, 226n.69; civic traditions and civic community today, 151; civic traditions in Italian regions, 150; declining support for

figures (*cont.*)
national party discipline, 42; German versus Italian support for subnational government, 59; institutional performance, 76; institutional performance and citizen satisfaction, 77; institutional performance and civic community, 98; institutional performance and civic engagement, 151; institutional performance, civic engagement, and socioeconomic development, 155, 157; institutional performance and community leaders' satisfaction, 81; institutional performance and economic modernity, 85; institutional performance in the Italian regions, 84; left-right depolarization, 30; Northern and Southern satisfaction with national, regional, and local governments, 55; optimism about regional government: councilors, community leaders, and voters, 56; referenda turnout and preference voting, 95, 222–223nn. 40, 41, 42, 43; regional councilors' attitudes toward central government, 45; regional and local contacts of regional councilors, 43; regional and local government performance, 202; regional and local government satisfaction, 203; republican and autocratic traditions, Italy, c. 1300, 134; satisfaction with regional government by performance and party support, 79; sympathy toward political opponents among regional councilors, 32; trends in councilors' views of conflict, 35. *See also* abbreviations; methodology; tables
finances: history of regional, 25–26; national budget and regional, 62; regional autonomy and, 211n.20, 213n.42
Florence, 230nn. 27, 40
folk theorem, 166, 172–173, 240n.13
France, associations in, 137–138
Franchetti, Leopoldo, 145, 146
Frederick II (Sicily), 122–123
Fried, Robert C., 84
Friuli-Venezia Giulia: budget promptness in, 67; historical analysis and, 235n.130; industrial policy in, 71; special study of, 191; statistical and information services in, 68
Fund for the South, 24

Gambetta, Diego, 146
game theory: collective action and, 163–164, 165, 166, 178–179, 244n.59, 245n.74, 246n.77; folk theorem and, 166, 172–173, 240n.13; prisoner's dilemma and, 164, 165, 240nn. 11, 13; study of institutions and, 7
Geertz, Clifford, 168
Gemeinschaft, 114
Genovesi, Antonio, 170
Germany, voter satisfaction in, 58–60
Gesellschaft, 114
GNP. *See* economic development; socioeconomic modernity
governance, book's model of, 9
Gramsci, Antonio, 146
Granovetter, Mark, 172, 175, 243n.55
guilds, 125–126, 162, 229n.20

health services: regional spending for, 72, 198–199; regionalization of, 48–49
Herzog, Don, 87
Hess, Henner, 147
hierarchical politics. *See* vertical politics
Hirschman, Alfred, 169
history: book's study of, 13, 228n.1; effect of on institutions, 8, 17, 177–181, 182, 184, 236n.133; institutional performance and, 121, 133, 177–181, 182. *See also* city-states; Italy; Norman kingdom of Sicily
Hobbes, Thomas, 87, 165
horizontal politics: civic community and, 115; collective action and, 175–176; medieval evolution of, 124, 131; in Northern Italy, 23, 181; political parties and, 142; Protestantism and, 107; social networks and, 173. *See also* patron-clientelist politics; vertical politics
housing, 72–73, 198–199, 217n.21
Hume, David, 163, 164, 165

ideological depolarization, 28–33, 193–197, 212n.28
income distribution, 224n.52
Index: of civic community, 96–98, 99, 223n.46, 225n.64; factor loading in, 216n.13; of institutional performance, 73–76, 77, 80–81, 198–199; of left-right issues, 28–29, 31; of local government performance, 202; of optimism about re-

gional government, 56; of powerlessness, 110, 225n.64; of preference
voting, 95, 222–223nn. 41, 42, 43; of
referenda turnout, 94, 222n.40; of support for national party discipline, 41, 42;
of support for political equality, 102–
103; of support-criticism, 58; of traditions of civic involvement, 205
individualism, liberalism and, 87
industrial districts, 160–161, 238nn. 158,
159, 163
industrial employment, 153–154, 156,
236n.136
industrial policy, 71, 198–199
industrial revolution. *See* economic development; socioeconomic modernity
infant mortality rate, 153–154, 156,
236nn. 137, 138, 237nn. 141, 144
information services, regional, 67–68,
198–199
institutional design, 9–11, 166
institutional performance, 63–82; agricultural spending capacity and, 71–72,
198–199; budget promptness and, 67,
198–199; bureaucratic responsiveness
and, 73, 198–199, 217n.23, 218n.30;
cabinet stability and, 67, 198–199,
213n.39, 218n.30; citizen evaluations
and, 216–217n.26; civic community
and, 98–99, 115, 223nn. 45, 46; civic
traditions and, 150–151, 154–155, 157,
175–176; collective action and, 164,
173–176; day care centers and, 70, 198–
199; defined, 8–9; durability of, 74–76;
economic development and, 11, 78, 83–
86, 154–155, 157, 219–220nn. 4, 6,
220n.6, 223n.46; education and, 118;
explanations of, 9–12, 98–99, 115, 116–
120; family clinics and, 70–71, 198–
199; history and, 121, 133, 177–181,
182; housing and urban development
and, 72–73, 198–199, 217n.21; index
of, 73–76, 77, 80–81, 198–199; indicators of, 66–73, 198–199, 218n.30; industrial policy and, 71, 198–199; institutional design and, 9–11, 166; Italian
Communist Party (PCI) and, 119–120,
227–228nn. 86, 87; legislative innovation and, 69–70, 190, 198–199,
216n.14, 218n.30; lessons about, 181–
185; local governments, of, 201–204;

local health unit expenditures and, 72,
198–199; methodology for measuring,
63–65, 198–199, 216n.4; personal stability and, 118–119; policy analysis and,
65–66; population size and, 220n.5;
reform legislation and, 68, 198–199,
218n.30; social context and, 182; social
and political conflict and, 116–118;
sociocultural factors and, 11–12; spending capacity and, 70, 71–73, 198–199;
statistical and information services and,
67–68; urbanism and, 118. *See also*
civic community
institutional reform, effects of, 17–18
institutions: approaches to study of, 7–10,
208–209n.11; book's study of, 10–11;
civic virtue and, 246–247n.85; effect
of history on, 8, 17, 177–181, 182, 184;
effects of on politics, 7–8, 17, 184; lessons from study of, 181–185; purposes
of, 8–9; social context and, 8, 182; stability of, 245n.71
interocular traumatic test, 13, 209n.19
Israel, Arturo, 10, 11
Italian Communist Party (PCI): ideological
depolarization and, 28, 29; institutional
performance and, 119–120, 227–228nn.
86, 87; Red Belt and, 7; regional reform
and, 19–20, 21, 23
Italian Social Movement, 29
Italy: in eighteenth century, 136; in
fifteenth-sixteenth century, 133–135,
230nn. 46, 49; landholding patterns in,
233n.96, 236n.133; in nineteenth century, 136–148; Norman kingdom of
Sicily, 122–124, 130–131, 133; Northern versus Southern, 130–131, 152,
158–159, 180, 181–185, 211n.16,
214n.55, 227n.83, 228n.2, 231–
232n.66, 236n.134, 246n.82; in seventeenth century, 135–136; unification of,
18–19, 138, 210n.8, 232n.76. *See also*
city-states; Northern Italy; Southern Italy

Jackman, Robert, 84

kinship ties, 175
Kropotkin, Pietr, 165

labor unions: civic community and, 106–
107, 157–158, 224n.56; cooperatives

labor unions (*cont.*)
  and, 140–141; membership in, 223n.44,
  237nn. 147, 148; political parties and,
  142, 148
Lagorio, Lelio, 24
landholding patterns, 233n.96, 236n.133
Lane, Frederick, 124
Langton, John, 161
Larner, John, 130
latifondo, 143–144
Latin America, 179, 246n.82
Law 382, 22
law enforcement, 112–113, 225–226n.68
Lazio: agricultural spending capacity in,
  71; councilors in, 211n.24; statistical
  and information services in, 68
leftist parties. *See* Italian Communist
  Party; Proletarian Democracy; Socialist
  Party
Left-Right Issues Index, 28–29, 31
Lega Lombarda, 61
Lega Veneta, 61
legislative innovation, 69–70, 190, 198–
  199, 216n.14, 218n.30
legislators. *See* councilors
liberalism, 87
Liguria: associations in, 92; economic development in, 86; newspaper readership
  in, 93
Lipset, Seymour Martin, 11
local governments, 46, 201–204, 219n.36
local health unit expenditures, 72, 198–199
Locke, John, 87
Lombardia: economic development in, 86,
  156; institutional performance in, 75;
  preference voting in, 94; statistical and
  information services in, 68
Machiavelli, Nicolò, 86–87, 132
Madison, James, 47, 87
Mafia, 146–148
March, James, 17
Marche, 68
Marshall, Alfred, 160
methodology: for correlating civic community and economic development,
  223n.46, 245n.72; for correlating civic
  traditions and economic development,
  237nn. 142, 143, 144, 145; factor loading in indexes, 216n.13; for measuring
  associationism, 222nn. 35, 36,
  235n.129; for measuring cooperative
  strength, 235n.126; for measuring elec-

toral turnout, 235n.128; for measuring
  institutional performance, 63–65, 198–
  199, 216n.4; for measuring mutual aid
  society strength, 235n.125; for measuring newspaper readership, 222n.38; for
  measuring political party strength,
  235n.127; for measuring socioeconomic
  modernity, 219–220n.4; for performance
  indicators, 217n.24; research, 12–14,
  187–192, 212–213nn. 33, 34, 35,
  214n.57; sample size and, 218–219n.34.
  See also figures; surveys; tables
Metternich, 121
Mezzogiorno. *See* Southern Italy
Migdal, Joel, 176
Milan. *See* Seveso
Mill, John Stuart, 9, 63, 208n.10
model laws. *See* legislative innovation
modernization: civic community and, 114–
  115. *See also* economic development;
  socioeconomic modernity
Molise: agricultural spending capacity in,
  72; economic development in, 86, 156;
  family clinics in, 71; newspaper readership in, 93; reform legislation in, 68; statistical and information services in, 68
Montesquieu, 26
moral resources, 169–170
Morris, R. J., 161
mutual aid societies: civic community and,
  162; evolution of, 139, 140; measuring
  strength of, 235n.125; in Northern versus Southern Italy, 142–143; political
  parties and, 142, 148; rotating credit associations and, 169; in United States,
  232n.79. *See also* cooperatives

Naples, 136
national administrators, 50–51
national government: community leaders
  and, 52; public satisfaction with, 52, 57,
  203, 219n.36; regional autonomy and,
  39–40, 44–47, 213n.39; regional reform
  and, 18–26; social origins of deputies in,
  224n.50
national parties. *See* political parties
networks of civic engagement, 171, 173–
  176, 177, 183–184
"new institutionalism": collective action
  and, 166; institutional theory and, 7, 10,
  17, 179
newspaper readership, 92–93, 222n.38

nobility: in eighteenth century North, 136; in medieval city-states, 124, 129; in Norman kingdom of Sicily, 122, 123–124; after unification, 145

Norman kingdom of Sicily: evolution of, 122–124; versus medieval city-states, 130–131; Papal intervention in, 133

norms of reciprocity, 171–173, 177, 182–183, 184, 243nn. 50, 51, 55

North America, 179

North, Douglass C., 165, 178, 179–180, 181

Northern Italy: civic traditions in, 158–159, 246n.84; community leader satisfaction in, 215n.64; defined, 214n.56; economic development in, 84–86; education in, 227n.82, 238n.154; effects of regionalization on, 61; in eighteenth century, 136; emigration from, 239n.165; in fifteenth-sixteenth centuries, 133–135; horizontal politics in, 23, 181; institutional performance in, 83, 84–1; elites in, 101; regionalist movement in, 62; in seventeenth century, 135–136; Southern immigration to, 211nn. 16, 24, 236n.132; versus Southern Italy, 130–131, 152, 158–159, 180, 181–185, 211n.16, 214n.55, 227n.83, 228n.2, 231–232n.66, 236n.134, 246n.82; voter satisfaction in, 53–56, 214n.55, 215n.64. *See also* city-states; Italy

Olsen, Johan, 17

Olson, Mancur, 176, 229n.20

ordinary regions, 6, 19

organizational theory, 7

organized crime, 146–148

Ostrom, Elinor, 10, 166, 169

Pagden, Anthony, 170

Papal States, 122, 133. *See also* Catholic Church

partisanship. *See* ideological depolarization; political culture

Partito popolare, 141–142, 233n.91

path dependence, 179, 180, 181

patron-clientelist politics: Mafia and, 146–148; political elites and, 102–104; political equality and, 99–101; political parties and, 142; seventeenth century development of, 135; social trust and, 174–175; in Southern Italy, 233n.91,

234n.107; after unification, 144–145; in urban America, 226–227n.72. *See also* vertical politics

peasantry, after unification, 144–146

personal stability, institutional performance and, 118–119

Piedmont: economic development in, 86; institutional performance in, 75

Pietrapertosa, 4–5

Piore, Michael, 160, 161

Pitt-Rivers, Julian, 174

Plato, 11

Poggi, Gianfranco, 89

policy analysis, 65–66

political culture, 33–38, 213n.40, 246–247n.85

political elites, 26–38; civic community and, 101–106; comparative study of, 212n.29; compromise and, 105–106, 224n.53; ideological depolarization of, 28–33, 193–197, 212n.28; political culture of, 33–38, 213n.40; political equality and, 102–105, 224n.51; profile of, 26–28; social origins of, 101, 224n.50. *See also* councilors; national administrators; regional administrators

political equality: civic community and, 88, 102–105; councilors and, 224n.51; political elites and, 102–105, 224n.51

political parties: citizen satisfaction and, 78; civic community and, 109; evolution of, 141–142, 148; measuring strength of, 235n.127; patron-clientelist politics and, 142; regional autonomy and, 39–41, 42, 44, 213n.41; regional personnel and, 50

politics: effects of institutions on, 7–8, 17, 184; effects of regional government on, 60–62; programmatic versus clientelistic, 99

Popular party, 141–142, 233n.91

population size, 220n.5

Potenza. *See* Pietrapertosa

powerlessness, feelings of, 109–111, 225n.64

preference voting, 94–96, 222–223nn. 41, 42, 43

prisoner's dilemma, 164, 165, 240nn. 11, 13

programmatic politics, 99–101

Proletarian Democracy, 29

protest marches, 47

Protestantism, 107, 244n.58
public. *See* electorate
Puglia: associations in, 92; family clinics in, 71; regional government of, 5, 6; statistical and information services in, 68

quantitative techniques. *See* figures; methodology; tables

Rabinovitz, Francine, 84
rational choice modeling, 7
reciprocity, norms of, 171–173, 177, 182–183, 184, 243nn. 50, 51, 55
Red Belt, 7
referenda turnout, 93–94, 95–96, 149, 222n.40
reform legislation, 68, 190, 198–199, 218n.30
regional administrators: community leaders and, 52; versus national administrators, 50–51; numbers of, 211n.19; performance of, 49–51; responsiveness of, 73
regional autonomy, 38–47; councilors' attitudes toward, 38–39, 41–44; electoral behavior and, 44; local governments and, 46; national government and, 44–47, 213n.39; national parties and, 39–41, 42, 44; public attitudes toward, 52–53; regional finances and, 211n.20, 213n.42
regional councilors. *See* councilors
regional governments: autonomy of, 38–47; community leaders' satisfaction with, 47–50, 56–57, 58, 76–77, 78–81, 215n.64; creation of, 4–5, 6–7, 18–26; criticisms of, 48–50, 61, 214nn. 49, 50; effects of, 60–61; future of, 61–62; ideological depolarization of, 28–33, 193–197, 212n.28; Italian unification and, 18–19, 210n.8; lessons from study of, 6–7, 181–185; local governments and, 46, 201–204, 219n.36; personnel problems of, 49–50; political culture of, 33–38; protest marches and, 47; public satisfaction with, 47–60, 77–81, 214n.52, 214n.55, 219nn. 35, 36; in special regions, 211n.15; special versus ordinary, 6, 19. *See also* councilors; political elites; special regions
"regionalist front," 21–26
religiosity, 107–109, 175–176, 225n.59. *See also* Catholic Church
representative institutions. *See* democratic

institutions; institutional performance; institutions
Republic (Plato), 11
republican tradition. *See* city-states; civic humanism
research methods. *See* methodology
rightist parties. *See* Christian Democratic party; Italian Social Movement
The Rise and Decline of Nations (Olson), 176
Roger II (Sicily), 122, 123
rotating credit associations, 167–171, 241n.24, 242nn. 27, 30
Rousseau, Jean-Jacques, 90

Sabel, Charles, 160, 161
Sardinia: associations in, 92; bureaucratic responsiveness in, 73; cabinet stability in, 67
Sartori, Giovanni, 116
satisfaction: of community leaders, 47–50, 58, 76–77, 78–81, 215n.64; of electorate with local governments, 201–204, 219n.36; of electorate with national government, 52, 57, 203, 219n.36; of electorate in Northern Italy, 53–56; of electorate and political parties, 78; of electorate with regional governments, 47–60, 76–81, 214n.52, 214n.55, 219n.36, 219nn. 35, 36; of electorate in Southern Italy, 53–58, 240n.1; of electorate in Trentino-Alto Adige, 77, 218n.29; of German voters, 58–60; with life, 113–114, 226n.69; performance indicators and, 218n.30
scattergrams: abbreviations in, 200. *See also* figures
secularism, 108–109
Selznick, Philip, 11–12
Seveso, 3–5
Sicily: cabinet stability in, 67; economic development of, 238n.156; housing and urban development in, 72; local health unit expenditures in, 72; statistical and information services in, 68. *See also* Norman kingdom of Sicily
Smith, Denis Mack, 123
social capital: associations and, 245n.69; defined, 167, 242n.37; democratic institutions and, 183, 184–185; forms of, 169–171; networks of civic engagement and, 173–176; public versus collective

goods and, 242n.38; rotating credit associations and, 169. *See also* collective action; trust

Social Catholicism movement, 141

social context, 8, 181–182

social trust. *See* trust

Socialist Party (PSI): evolution of, 141–142; ideological depolarization and, 28, 29

sociocultural factors, 11–12, 209n.16

socioeconomic modernity: civic community and, 98–99, 153; institutional performance and, 11, 78, 83–86, 220n.6, 223n.46; measure of, 219–220n.4. *See also* economic development

South America, 179, 246n.82

Southern Italy: *Cassa per il Mezzogiorno* and, 24; Christian Democratic Party and, 233n.91; civic traditions in, 158–159, 236n.133; community leader satisfaction in, 215n.64; defined, 214n.56; economic development in, 84–86; education in, 227n.82, 238n.154; in eighteenth century, 136; emigration from, 211nn. 16, 24, 236n.132, 239n.165, 245–246n.75; in fifteenth-sixteenth centuries, 133–135; institutional performance in, 83, 84–86; Mafia and, 146–148; versus Northern Italy, 130–131, 152, 158–159, 180, 181–185, 211n.16, 214n.55, 227n.83, 228n.2, 231–232n.66, 236n.134, 246n.82; political elites in, 101; public awareness in, 51, 214n.52; regionalization and, 61, 210n.8, 214n.55; in seventeenth century, 135–136; after unification, 143–148; vertical politics in, 23, 177, 181–182, 233n.91, 234n.107, 236n.133; voter satisfaction in, 53–58, 214n.51, 215n.64, 240n.1. *See also* Italy; Norman kingdom of Sicily

special regions: creation of, 6, 19; electoral cycles in, 216n.8; regional governments in, 211n.15; satisfaction and performance in, 219n.35; Trentino-Alto Adige as a, 218n.29

spending capacity, 70, 71–73, 198–199, 217n.21

statistical analysis, 12–13, 193–197. *See also* figures; methodology; tables

statistical and information services, 67–68, 198–199

structure, versus culture, 180–181, 222n.34

Sugden, Robert, 178

Support-criticism Index, 58

surveys: of community leaders, 188–189; of councilors, 187–188; national, 218n.28, 223–224nn.47; regional, 212–213n.34, 214nn. 57, 58, 215n.60. *See also* methodology; tables

tables: assessing legislative innovation, 69; attitudes of Italians toward regional autonomy, 52; civic community, honesty, trust, and law-abidingness, 112; Civic Community Index, 96; civic traditions and socioeconomic development, 153; community leaders' evaluations of regional government, 80; community leaders' views of regional administration, 49; components of Left-Right Issues Index, 31; components of local government performance, 202; declining ideological extremism, 195; declining salience of conflict, 197; democratic attitudes among national and regional administrators, 51; depolarization of regional councilors, 31; evaluations of the regional reform, 58; factor loading in, 216n.13; increasing cross-party sympathy, 196; index of institutional performance, 75; index of preference voting, 95, 222–223nn. 41, 42, 43; index of referenda turnout, 94, 222n.40; influence of party leaders in three areas, 40–41; Italian regional spending, 25; local associations in Italy, 92; public satisfaction with regional government, 54; traditions of civic involvement, 149; trends in elite political culture, 33. *See also* figures; methodology

Tarrow, Sidney, 17, 109, 144

taxation, regions and, 211n.20

Third World, development in, 159, 183

Tocqueville, Alexis de: on associations, 221n.28; civic community and, 88, 89–90, 91, 182, 226n.70; on newspapers, 92; study of institutions and, 11

tolerance. *See* compromise; ideological depolarization

Toniolo, Gianni, 159

Tönnies, Ferdinand, 114

Toscana: local health unit expenditures in, 72; statistical and information services in, 68

trade unions. *See* labor unions

trasformismo, 19, 142

Trentino-Alto Adige: associations in, 92; cabinet stability in, 67; citizen satisfaction in, 77, 218n.29; family clinics in, 71; historical analysis and, 235n.130

trust: Italian language and, 245n.73; networks of civic engagement and, 171, 172–174, 177, 180; norms of reciprocity and, 171–173, 177, 180, 243n.55; origins of, 171–176; personal versus social, 243n.45; productivity and, 243n.43; as social capital, 167, 169–171, 177. *See also* collective action; social capital

Tukey, John, 13

Tullio-Altan, Carlo, 231n.63

TVA and the Grass Roots (Selznick), 11–12

Umbria: cabinet stability in, 67; economic development in, 86; family clinics in, 71

unification, Italian, 18–19, 138, 210n.8, 232n.76

unions. *See* labor unions

United States: civic humanism in, 87, 91–92; evolution of, 179; mutual aid societies in, 232n.79. *See also* Tocqueville, Alexis de

U.S. Constitution, 87

Uphoff, Norman, 90–91

urban development, 72–73, 198–199, 217n.21

urbanism: institutional performance and, 118; in Northern versus Southern Italy, 227n.83, 231–232n.66

Valle d'Aosta: agricultural spending capacity in, 72; associations in, 92; bureaucratic responsiveness in, 73; family clinics in, 71; historical analysis and, 235n.130; preference voting in, 222–223n.41

Vélez-Ibañez, Carlos G., 168, 241n.24

Verba, Sidney, 11

vertical politics: Catholic Church and, 107, 244–245n.68; civic community and, 101–104, 115; medieval evolution of, 124, 131; social networks and, 173; social trust and, 174–175, 177; in South America, 179; in Southern Italy, 23, 177, 181–182, 233n.91, 234n.107, 236n.133. *See also* horizontal politics; patron-clientelist politics

Villari, Pasquale, 144

voters. *See* electorate

Waley, Daniel, 125

Walzer, Michael, 87, 89

Watson, James, 114

Weber, Max, 26, 244n.58

Williams, Bernard, 171

Williamson, Oliver, 166

Winthrop, John, 87

Zamagni, Vera, 185